Summer, 1940

The Battle of Britain

Summer, 1940

The Battle of Britain

ROGER PARKINSON

David McKay Company, Inc.   New York

Contents

List of Illustrations

Note:
All photographs are reproduced by permission of Popperfoto.

Preface

This book combines eye-witness accounts with the official documents of one of the most dramatic periods in Britain's history: the summer months of 1940. Coverage is given to the ending and aftermath of Dunkirk, Hitler's plans for invasion and British plans to counter such an attempt, the Battle of Britain and the start of the mass terror raids on London.

On 1 January 1971 many thousands of previously classified documents were released for public inspection: these included not only the War Cabinet and Chiefs of Staff papers, but also hundreds of files for Air Ministry, Fighter Command and War Office activity. I believe some of these are now used for the first time. The relatively short period covered by the book has allowed me to delve into greater detail than space permitted in the second volume of my trilogy based on the War Cabinet papers, *Blood, Toil, Tears and Sweat*. In addition, I have been able to move further from the War Cabinet conferences into the actual fighting front. The documents, besides reports of top-level conferences, also reveal new information on the fighting itself through the daily signals, reports and pilots' logs.

The conclusion stated in the book differs from many usual versions. But I would like to repeat my words in the text: this conclusion in no way diminishes my admiration for 'The Few' and for those who helped them with their achievement. Indeed my reading of the logs – which some pilots used as very moving diaries – has increased my astonishment at the courage, ability and spirit of mind with which they fought in that 'Spitfire Summer' of 1940.

The amount of eye-witness material already published is enormous;

I have restricted myself to comparatively few sources. I acknowledge my especial debt to the following invaluable works: Arthur Bryant's *The Turn of the Tide*, Churchill's *Their Finest Hour*, Basil Collier's *The Battle of Britain* and the same author's *The Defence of the United Kingdom*, D. M. Crook's *Spitfire Pilot*, Frances Faviell's *A Chelsea Concerto*, Peter Fleming's *Invasion 1940*, Ina Jones' *Tiger Squadron*, and Ronald Wheatley's *Operation Sea Lion*.

I also express thanks to the many people who responded to my request for information. These helpers include Mrs Ruth Bass, Charles C. Butler Esq, Donald Bruce Esq, Lady Betty Cave, Mrs Valerie Cole, Mrs E. Curtis, K. M. Drewery Esq, Mrs Florence Hall, George Jarrett Esq, Mrs H. Jarvis, G. A. Le Good Esq, Charles C. Mackenzie Esq, Mrs B. Obee, Mrs A. M. Peacock, Herbert William Purser Esq, A. C. Schaefer Esq. I also thank the staff of the Public Record Office and the London Library; as always, I can never express sufficient gratitude for the toil and trouble so ably lifted from me by my partner, my wife Betty.

Abbreviations

A/C   – Aircraft
AFV   – Armoured Fighting Vehicles
BEF   – British Expeditionary Force
CIGS   – Chief of the Imperial General Staff
CoAS   – Chief of the Air Staff
COS   – Chiefs of Staff
DeTe   – Decimeter Telegraphy: cover name for RDF (radar)
E/A   – Enemy Aircraft
GAF   – German Air Force
GHQ   – General Headquarters
HoFor   – Home Forces
JIC   – Joint Intelligence Committee
LCC   – London County Council
LDV   – Local Defence Volunteers: original name for Home Guard
NBBS   – New British Broadcasting Station: German propaganda
           radio
OKH   – *Oberkommando des Heeres*: German Army High Command
OKM   – *Oberkommando der Kriegsmarine*: German Navy High Com-
           mand
OKW   – *Oberkommando der Wehrmacht*: German Armed Forces High
           Command
R/T   – Radio Transmission
W/T   – Wireless Transmission

ⴢ

Deliverance

2–8 June

'Patrol over Dunkirk beaches – most amazing sight,' wrote Flying Officer B. J. Lane in his log. 'Thames barges, sailing boats, anything that will float, plus the Navy. God help them down there. They need more than we can give them.'[1] Withdrawal had continued for seven days and nights. Each morning saw a shrinking perimeter line and each hour the beaches became more crammed with British and French soldiers. 'There they stood,' commented one volunteer with a small rescue boat, 'lined up like a bus-queue, right from the dunes, down the shore, to the water's edge, and sometimes up to their waists beyond. There were bombers overhead and artillery fire all around them. They were hungry and thirsty and deadbeat; yet they kept in line.'[2] This volunteer and 202 other private boat-owners like him ferried a total of 5031 stranded men to the larger crafts: others were evacuated in yachts, trawlers and drifters, minesweepers, Royal Naval and Merchant Naval vessels.

At midnight on Sunday 2 June 1940, the commanding officer on the beaches, Major-General the Hon. H. R. L. G. Alexander, packed up his few items of equipment and made a final tour in a motor boat with the Senior Naval Officer, Captain W. G. Tennant. 'On being satisfied that no British troops were left on shore,' stated the official despatch, 'they themselves left for England.' About 225,000 British soldiers had been rescued. The operation, 'Dynamo', would continue to lift off French troops, bringing the total of men evacuated to 338,226 before the Admiralty declared the official end at 2.23 pm on Tuesday 4 June.

Britain's returning army caused chaos in south coast resorts. Ramsgate's sea-front was crammed with troops coming ashore: as they arrived they gave their names, dropped remaining rifles in a heap, and climbed into waiting buses or trains. The Ramsgate stationmaster, Mr S. W. Smith, flagged away eighty-two trains in one week carrying 43,000 troops. 'There were women volunteers bringing and sorting clothes, for many of the men arrived naked except for a blanket thrown round them, and others were all covered in oil... I remember one man went away in a college blazer, striped city trousers, and white plimsolls.'[3] Dover witnessed similar turmoil. 'The port presented an amazing scene,' wrote the Red Cross nurse Frances Faviell. 'The harbour itself was so thick with ships that it would have been possible to walk across it passing from one vessel to another. The place was one seething mass of khaki. Troops were lying about utterly exhausted all over the place... The misery and wretchedness of displaced humanity was one of sheer stark horror. And yet I could not look at all the faces of our own troops without intense wonder and gratitude that they were home.'[4]

Home, to a country threatened as never before. As Dunkirk finally fell, the enemy Chief of General Staff Franz Halder noted in his diary: 'Town and coast in our hands. French and English gone.' He stood on the littered beaches and looked across the Channel: on a clear day the Germans could peer through their binoculars and almost tell the time by Dover Town Hall clock. But for the moment the British could feel relief as the returning troops flooded away from the south coast across the Kentish countryside. 'It was a most lovely English spring morning,' wrote General Alan Brooke, recently commander of the BEF's 2nd Corps. He noted the 'contrast of this lovely sunlit country and its perfect peacefulness when compared with those Belgian roads crammed with distressed and demoralised humanity, horizons shrouded in smoke-clouds from burning villages, continuous rumbling of guns, bombs and aircraft, smashed houses, dead cattle, broken trees and all those war scars that distort the face of nature. To have moved straight from that inferno into such a paradise within the spell of a few anguished hours made the contrast all the more wonderful.'[5]

This inferno might now descend on England, even though Dunkirk could seem almost a triumph in the heady aftermath of evacuation. 'I was astonished to see the waving cheering crowds welcoming us home at Ramsgate,' remembered General Brian Horrocks. 'We might have been the heroes of some great victory instead of a beaten army returning

2

home, having lost most of its equipment. I could see the troops perking up all round me. In some mysterious way the letters BEF began to appear in chalk on the front of the steel helmets. I couldn't help smiling. Even in moments of disaster the British soldier always has an eye to the main chance.'[6] Horrocks' commanding general, Bernard Montgomery, reacted in different fashion. 'I remember the disgust of many like myself when we saw British soldiers walking about in London and elsewhere with a coloured embroidered flash on their sleeve with the title "Dunkirk". They thought they were heroes, and the civilian public thought so too. It was not understood that the British Army had suffered a crushing defeat at Dunkirk and that our island home was now in grave danger. There was no sense of urgency.'[7] Montgomery's observation was symbolic not only of his character but also of the confused feelings of the country as a whole. Dunkirk was indeed a defeat, but it was also a deliverance, and while this feeling of relief remained it would take time for the hard, harsh fact to be realised that the inconceivable might now be possible: those jackbooted German soldiers, who had stamped their way across Poland, Belgium and Holland, and who were now poised to trample France, might soon be stepping on to British soil.

In Whitehall, previous consideration of the possibility of invasion had been cloaked with an air of unreality. Existing plans were code-named after one of the only two completely successful violators of the country's independence, who had stepped ashore on the southern beaches almost 2000 years before – Julius Caesar. In October 1939 Neville Chamberlain's ministers had decided that the risk of a German landing during the long winter nights could no longer be completely ignored; the British Chiefs of Staff admitted that small raids were possible and an invasion attempt just conceivable, although the threat could not be considered serious. British forces judged necessary for the 'Julius Caesar' scheme totalled seven divisions. At the beginning of May 1940, after troops had been sent to France and the Middle East, nine divisions were available in the country, but these were mainly inexperienced; six more divisions were formed during May – all were untrained and ill-equipped for mobile warfare.[8]

General Sir Edmund Ironside, C-in-C Home Forces, could only employ his weak divisions in a totally inadequate fashion. A memorandum from his GHQ on 4 June attempted a confident tone: work had started on the most likely invasion beaches on the east, south-east and south coasts from Fraserburgh to Southampton, and reconnaissances were being carried out on other beaches. About 50,000 anti-tank mines had been issued and orders placed for a further 200,000. Every piece of ground in the Metropolitan area which could possibly be used for landing aircraft had been reconnoitred, and work to render each one unusable had started. 'Preparations for demolition of bridges on roads providing egress from selected ports on the east coast from Aberdeenshire to Kent are 90 per cent completed. Temporary road blocks on roads leading inland from ports are 80 per cent completed.' But despite Ironside's brave attempt, all defensive precautions taken so far were exceedingly flimsy and no match for élite German troops. Above all, weapons were critically short. Ironside's report specified that forty-seven batteries of two six-inch guns each were being installed on the east coast – but this meagre number had to be deployed on a line stretching from Amble in Northumberland to Newhaven. Only sixteen of these batteries were ready on 4 June. Anti-tank weapons only amounted to 120 two-pounder guns and a number of three-pounder, twelve-pounder and four-inch guns. These were being mounted on lorries. 'The first lot will be available in 3–4 days and the total number, 76, will be completed in about a fortnight.' The report said that instructions had been issued to all commands on the manufacture of Molotov cocktails; 50,000 Mills bombs had been allotted; recruitment of Local Defence Volunteers continued to be satisfactory.[9]

Eight of Ironside's fifteen infantry divisions at the beginning of June were devoted primarily to coastal defence, six of them in Eastern Command where, under the original Julius Caesar plan, it had been judged the German attack would most likely fall. These six were equipped with less than half their approved establishment of field guns and with only a bare minimum of anti-tank guns. The sector from Sheppey to Rye, in Kent, was manned by the 1st London Division equipped with twenty-three field guns instead of the establishment strength of seventy-two, no anti-tank guns, no armoured cars, no armoured fighting vehicles and no medium machine guns. The total number of armoured fighting vehicles in the UK on 1 June, including those in training units, was only 963, the majority – 618 – being light tanks.[10] The Chiefs of Staff, in an intensely gloomy report presented to the War Cabinet on 27 May, had admitted that: 'should the Germans succeed in establishing a force with its vehicles in this country, our armed forces have not got the offensive power to drive it out.' The War Cabinet had agreed with this report and with the COS recommendation that: 'The time has come to inform the public of the true dangers that confront us, and to educate them

4

on what they are required to do and what NOT to do if the country is invaded.'[11]

Now, after Dunkirk, only one fully equipped division, the 3rd under Montgomery, could be deployed in England until the losses of the campaign on the Continent could be made good. The Dunkirk evacuation added twelve divisions to the fifteen already in the country, but the returning units were completely disorganised and had left behind virtually the whole of their heavy equipment, including about 600 tanks, over 1000 field guns, 500 anti-aircraft guns, 850 anti-tank guns, plus 90,000 rifles, 120,000 vehicles, 8000 Bren guns and 400 anti-tank rifles, with 7000 tons of ammunition.[12] By contrast, the German army poised to inflict final defeat on France amounted to 114 divisions, ten armoured, four motorised, with nearly 2500 tanks.

On Tuesday 4 June, as the War Office appealed for cigarettes, handkerchiefs, foot ointment, shaving soap and razors for the returning troops, Flying Officer Lane again flew his Spitfire along the coast of France. 'Absolutely quiet at Dunkirk,' he noted. 'Returned to Tangmere as it was hopeless elsewhere.'[13] Two hours later Winston Churchill stood in the House of Commons to make one of his most famous speeches. His words placed Dunkirk in proper perspective: 'Wars are not won by evacuation.' He warned of the perils which might soon swoop on vulnerable Britain. 'We are assured that novel methods will be adopted, and when we see the originality of malice, the ingenuity of aggression, which our enemy displays, we may certainly prepare ourselves for every kind of novel stratagem and every kind of brutal and treacherous manœuvre.' He reached the climax to the speech in a passage which would echo round the world. 'We shall not flag or fail. We shall go on to the end. We shall fight on the beaches, we shall fight on the landing grounds, we shall fight in the fields and in the streets, we shall fight in the hills; we shall never surrender...'

The Prime Minister's message was intended to bolster the morale of those who considered Dunkirk a defeat, and to moderate the feelings of those who considered Dunkirk a victory. His sentences soothed Montgomery, so irritated by the lack of awareness on the part of the people: he wrote that Churchill's speech imparted a sense of urgency 'in words that rang and thundered like the Psalms'.[14] In addition, Churchill aimed at reassuring any overseas nations, especially the United States, which might believe Britain would bow to the threat. 'He spoke the language of Shakespeare,' commented the US broadcaster Ed Murrow, 'with a direct urgency such as I have never before heard in that

House... He gave the House of Commons a report remarkable for its honesty, inspiration and gravity.' Murrow ended his broadcast from London on this Tuesday, 4 June, by saying: 'There is a breathing space tonight, but no one here expects it to last long.'[15]

The length of this respite depended on one man. Adolf Hitler had mentioned plans for possible operations against Britain at a conference held just over a year before, on 23 May 1939. If Germany defeated Holland, Belgium and France, 'Britain can then be blockaded from western France at close quarters.' Hitler went into more detail in a memorandum on 9 October, which contained the statement that 'brutal Luftwaffe operations against the heart of the British will to resist can and will be carried out at the proper time.' The possibility of direct invasion, rather than mere strangulation, first received serious consideration by senior German staff officers on 15 November 1939 when Grand-Admiral Erich Raeder, C-in-C of the German Navy, ordered 'the possibility of invading England to be examined.' Preliminary considerations by the Naval Staff Operations Division were initialled by Raeder on the 29th.[16] In mid-December the German Army followed the Navy's lead in examining the invasion question. This document, dated 13 December, differed considerably from the naval memorandum produced at the end of November, and continuing conflict among this handful of top German army and navy officers would be an important factor in subsequent German actions, in turn a matter of life and death for so many British men and women.

The German Naval Staff laid heavy emphasis on the need for naval and air supremacy prior to the landing attempt. The November memorandum stated: 'Enemy naval forces must either be eliminated beforehand or be completely sealed off from the proposed landing area and the sea approaches to it; or the forces available for invasion must have great and clear superiority.' Yet the navy believed that if naval and air supremacy were obtained, a military landing might not in fact be needed. 'The achievement of these... conditions will in all probability result simultaneously in the complete collapse of her [Britain's] will to resist.' The naval staff pointed out grave difficulties that would arise should a landing be attempted, and the memorandum reached a hesitant conclusion, giving the clear impression that a full-scale occupation of Britain should not be considered; the most that should be contemplated was a smaller landing to give military backing to naval and air supremacy once these had been achieved.

But the German Army High Command, OKH, proved far more

6

ambitious in its mid-December study. This envisaged a three-phase assault aimed at the subjugation of Britain on land. First would be an initial assault to establish a bridgehead, preferably on the east coast between the Wash and the Thames and with Yarmouth, Lowestoft, Dunwich and Hollesley Bay among the primary targets. Secondly, a picked panzer corps would strike from the bridgeheads to cut communications between south and north England, helped by airborne landings in the Cambridge area. Thirdly, London would be captured, or the British Home Forces would be defeated. The Naval Staff prepared a paper in response to this army plan: this, despatched to OKH on 8 January 1940, once again stressed the need for naval and air supremacy, both for the initial assault and to secure continuous control of subsequent supply lines.[17]

No significant changes took place either in the German navy or army attitudes during early 1940. The blockade policy still stood in the absence of any other, more concrete consideration of the next step after the defeat of France. No time could apparently be spared for detailed studies of future operations, and soon all attention was focused on the Western offensive beginning 10 May. This strike into the Low Countries and France was, according to the German High Command, 'unexpectedly rapid'. Indeed, the speed of success seems to have taken Hitler by surprise, catching him off-guard with regard to plans for the next move. Raeder returned to the subject of Britain in an interview with Hitler on 21 May, mentioning the possibility of invasion – and probably repeating the naval estimate of the large difficulties entailed. Yet despite these difficulties, naval planners now devoted more time to contingency studies. These resulted in a memorandum, *Studie England*, drawn up on 27 May by Rear-Admiral Fricke, Chief of the Naval Staff Operations Divisions. This still expressed doubts over the enterprise and continued to insist that the RAF must first be grounded. The latest examination did not however stipulate that complete naval supremacy must first be achieved. Fricke seemed to assume that such supremacy at sea would be virtually impossible to obtain; instead, German planning must be directed towards a sudden, short-period naval strike in the hope that German warships could escape before the Royal Navy retaliated in force. The need for speed, and a short invasion route, led Fricke to alter the proposed invasion targets. Rather than the east coast, Fricke said that the general landing area should be in the south and south-east of England: he preferred the target to be somewhere between Portland and Yarmouth. Fricke's study, completed on the same day

7

that the British War Cabinet agreed 'our army forces have not got the offensive power' to drive out a German armoured bridgehead, stressed Britain's 'strong defences' and fierce determination to resist. According to Fricke: 'The ancient fear of invasion has again manifested itself and has grown into an almost hysterical anxiety.'[18]

At the end of May both sides overestimated the other's potential. Contrary to the German naval assessment, Britain's defences were far from strong; on the other hand, contrary to the British view, German plans were far from being worked out in any employable form. German naval and army thinking had still to be coordinated, and a critical lack of forward planning had become apparent. Among Hitler's prime characteristics was his opportunism: rather than working to a carefully planned, deliberate programme of expansion and acquisition, he seized his chances as they arose, reserving his options. But the unexpected speed of conquest since 10 May gave insufficient time for opportunism to be practised. Hitler had hoped, and half believed, that Britain would stay out of the war in September 1939. And now, with the fall of France imminent, Hitler still hoped, and half believed, that Britain might agree to end hostilities. Major-General Alfred Jodl, chief of operations staff of the German Armed Forces (OKW), noted in his diary at the end of May: 'The British can have a separate peace at any time after restitution of the colonies.'

Also at the end of the month the opposite attitude was expressed to Hitler by Field-Marshal Erhard Milch, Luftwaffe Secretary of State under Goering, who urged Hitler to attack Britain immediately, before the enemy – and especially the RAF – managed to prepare: a delay would be disastrous. Hitler, preoccupied with the astonishing campaign in France, with no plans for Britain prepared, and still hoping Britain would cease hostilities once her ally had been defeated, shrugged aside Milch's sound military advice. Nor did he even press on with contingency plans for an invasion of Britain. His lack of decisiveness and plans for invasion would perhaps constitute the greatest military mistake of his career.

An air of bewilderment spread over Germany, France and Britain during the turmoil at the end of May. Albert Speer, Hitler's confidant, wrote: 'I was firmly convinced that Hitler had already become one of the great figures in German history. Yet I wondered at the apathy I thought I observed in the public despite all the grand triumphs.'[19] William Shirer, the US journalist in Hitler's capital, witnessed this same German reaction. 'There is no real elation over the victory discernible in the people here,' he wrote in his Berlin diary. 'No emotion of any kind.'[20] A Berlin housewife, Else Wendel, remembered: 'England had asked for it and she had got Dunkirk. Feverishly we waited for the invasion of England. Some of us were astonished that it didn't come at once... We didn't hate the English so much now but just felt sorry for what was coming to them.'

In Kent, returning British soldiers had scrawled on railway carriages: 'Look out Hitler. We haven't started on you yet.' 'Back to Blighty – but not for long.' But despite such brave optimism, anti-invasion barricades were being thrown across country roads, some of them strange improvised erections. The first barrier at Chilham, Kent, comprised three tree trunks from the local saw mill; at Newingreen it included a plough, a boiler and iron water tanks plus some tip carts and an overturned car; at Farningham Hill the blockade included a four-furrow balance plough and steam tractors. Some were more substantial: concrete blocks were positioned so hurriedly at Maidstone that the defenders forgot to leave room for the British trucks and guns to pass through.[21] On 31 May orders were given for all signposts to be torn down, all milestones uprooted and names of streets, railway stations and villages obliterated. The Times declared: 'Citizens venturing off the beaten track will be able to experience the exhilarating feeling of being explorers.' 'Every signpost had been neatly beheaded,' wrote Mrs A. M. Peacock in the first entry of her 'war diary' on 1 June. 'We told the way by inn signs – "The Heart and Hand" – and by remembered trees, water and even flowers. Leafy Bucks, the only heavenly thing I have seen in the last fortnight...'[22]

Britain's Local Defence Volunteers, soon to be renamed the Home Guard, had expanded rapidly since the first broadcast appeal by War Secretary Anthony Eden during the evening of 14 May, and by the end of the month LDV personnel totalled about 300,000. They began to flex their muscles, sometimes with disastrous effect: on the night of 2/3 June four British citizens were killed in separate incidents when LDV men opened fire at roadblocks, after motorists had disobeyed or misunderstood signals to stop.[23] Jumpiness extended upwards, far beyond the local volunteer at his lonely roadblock. On the last day of May the Invasion Warning Sub-Committee, a branch of the COS Joint Intelligence Committee, considered a telephone report from Vice-Admiral Bertie Ramsay at Dover. According to Ramsay, heavily involved with his brilliant organisation of the Dunkirk evacuation, 'indications of numerous acts of sabotage and 5th Column activity [are evident] in

Dover.' Ramsay listed his evidence: communications leaks, sabotage, and even 'second-hand cars purchased at fantastic price and left at various parking places.'[24]

Confusion and uncertainty reached increasing proportions as Dunkirk ended and as Churchill made his 'we shall never surrender' speech in the crowded House of Commons on that gentle spring Tuesday 4 June. The weather would continue to add to the air of unreality. Later in June the temperature would reach 90 degrees; day after day dawned dry and sunny; LDV personnel sunbathed by their roadblocks. The climate seemed better suited for holiday than war and called to mind peacetime English summers. Mrs Peacock wrote in her diary: ' "Dada" from HQ Sussex Rgt writes he is busy barricading all roads from the coast and his spot when invasion starts is Bognor Pier ... Sounds queer that "Capt. Peacock will be facing the Hun at the other end of Bognor Pier" where once we watched the lady diver highdive and were asked not to forget her when the hat came round...'[25]

Early in the morning of 5 June the final phase of the Battle of France began. German units thundered forward in a massive assault on the Somme; soon they were attacking in overwhelming strength along a 400-mile front from Abbeville to the Upper Rhine. In Berlin, Hitler prepared to move his HQ forward into conquered territory. In London, news of the advance reached Winston Churchill during the evening. 'This was war on the largest scale,' he wrote.[26] France seemed increasingly doomed; Britain might be next.

Also during this Wednesday evening the C-in-C Home Forces addressed a gathering of LDV commanders. Until 27 May Ironside had held the most senior post in the British Army, Chief of the Imperial General Staff; replaced by General Sir John Dill, he had succeeded Sir Walter Kirke at the Home Forces HQ housed in the Army School of Music, Twickenham. 'He was powerful and impressive,' wrote Sir John Kennedy, soon to be Director of Military Operations. 'He had a more varied experience of the continental armies in Europe than his contemporaries.'[27] However wide Ironside's experience, the LDV officers now sitting before him represented a totally different kind of soldier. They ranged from shop-keepers, schoolteachers and clerks to retired senior regular officers. Among the latter was General Percy Hobart, perhaps Britain's greatest tank expert and shortly before that the commander of the Armoured Division in Egypt. Ousted after his methods had been criticised by his seniors, Hobart was now an LDV lance-corporal at the small Gloucestershire village of Chipping Campden.[28]

10

Faced by such a strange audience, Ironside made an uncertain speech. He seemed to find it difficult to judge at what level he should express himself. He attempted to reassure his listeners: however inadequately they might now be armed and equipped, prospects for the future were bright. In doing so, he revealed a horrifying picture of the present. 'You will be armed as required and you will be put into uniform,' he declared. 'We have already issued 140,000 suits of clothes and we are going to issue another 100,000. Perhaps we shall have up to half a million suits for you.' He continued in this slightly condescending tone: 'As regards arms: we have issued, I think, 80,000 rifles; more are coming; and I do not want you to misjudge the shot gun. I have now coming out over a million rounds of solid ammunition, which is something that will kill a leopard at 200 yards. It makes quite a decent bullet and you will have large numbers of them, though perhaps only three or four in the men's pockets to begin with.' Ironside described the required LDV attitude and role. 'I want you to know you have authority from us to get on with things. You will not be held responsible for anything except absolutely gross stupidity, and that I know I shall not get from you. The people of this country have not yet realised what this war means, and it will be for you, the cream of the leading population, to make them understand.' The LDV would have two main duties: static defence and the provision of information. 'Don't let us have among you people, what I shall call, county council rows. We are not going to quarrel with each other at all as to whether [a trench] shall be placed in front of somebody's shop or somewhere else. We don't want that; for goodness sake stop it if you can.'[29]

On the same day an order was issued from Ironside's HQ. 'On receipt of the code-word "Cromwell" troops will take up battle stations...' This code-word replaced 'Caesar', the existing signal to warn of imminent invasion. Issue of the word in an emergency would reduce the normal eight hours' notice down to 'readiness for immediate action'. Unfortunately, no provision existed for intermediate stages between the eight hours and immediate readiness. Moreover, the system was inadequately explained to units and formations which subsequently came under the command of Home Forces. Both shortcomings were to become fully noticeable on a grim night three months ahead.[30]

On Thursday 6 June, Hitler moved with his headquarters from Berlin to Bruly de Pêche, a small village on the Franco-Belgian border north of Rocroi. Over the frontier in France the German divisions were continuing to batter forward, with Fedor von Bock's Army Group B launching

11

vigorous attacks against the French 10th Army north of Paris. In London, the War Cabinet met at 12.30 pm to discuss increasingly frantic appeals for further British assistance received from the threatened French capital. The CIGS, Dill, warned that 'the enemy was probably testing the strength of the front all along before launching his main attack.' The Cabinet agreed that no further help could be sent, other than that already promised.[31] The British 51st Division, on the extreme French left, was likely to be hard-pressed and these remaining British troops, like their French allies, desperately needed additional fighter aircraft cover. Britain had no aircraft to spare. Already, according to Hugh Dowding, chief of RAF Fighter Command, too many had been sent and critical shortages might soon occur. During the day Churchill requested the Admiralty to transfer at least fifty trained and half-trained pilots from the Fleet Air Arm to Fighter Command; fifty-five would soon make the move.[32]

Typically, the Prime Minister also sought to be rid of an 'unduly defensive attitude'. He declared in a minute to General Hastings Ismay, his representative on the COS Committee: 'I look to the [COS] to propose me measures for a vigorous, enterprising and ceaseless offensive against the whole German-occupied coastline.' Churchill envisaged a 'butcher and bolt' policy aimed at German bases in occupied France, especially Calais and Boulogne.[33] On the same day, German naval planners studied possible operations using coastal artillery at these two French towns: the Naval Ordnance Office was requested to examine the feasibility of barring the Dover Straits through artillery bombardments; simultaneously, attacks would be made on British naval bases by the Luftwaffe, with both means being possible preliminary to invasion.[34]

'It is clear,' declared a report by the British COS Joint Intelligence Sub-Committee on 6 June, 'that as regards land forces Germany could attempt an invasion of this country at the same time as the renewed offensive on France now taking place.' The report continued: 'The invasion of this country will be for Germany her culminating effort of the war. She may be expected, therefore, to press it with the utmost intensity regardless of loss, and to throw into the balance all her available resources.' Nevertheless, this perceptive report stated that the Luftwaffe, unlike the German Army, could not undertake a full-scale offensive against both France and Britain. 'Moreover, German strategy has hitherto concentrated on one aim at a time.' The JIC gave details of the possible German offensive on Britain should France fall. 'An initial

12

air offensive, combined with sabotage and 5th Column activities would most probably aim at achieving the greatest possible degree of neutralisation of our fighter and bomber forces. A systematic attack must be expected on our defence organisation including aerodromes, storage and maintenance depots and the aircraft industry... A maximum total of 4800 tons of bombs per day must initially be expected.' German naval operations would aim at securing lines of communication for twenty-four hours; these assaults would be followed by full invasion. 'The main German objectives are likely to be the Kent and Sussex coasts and the east coast south of the Wash.'[35]

The COS studied this report at 10.30 next morning, 7 June. Dill and his colleagues – Admiral of the Fleet Sir Dudley Pound, First Sea Lord, and Sir Cyril Newall, Chief of the Air Staff – agreed with the JIC findings in general. But they also considered that 'in view of Hitler's tendency towards the unorthodox, and therefore the unexpected, it was... possible that a seaborne invasion (possibly in fast motor boats) might precede or coincide with other forms.' The COS also decided that a landing in the North of England or in the Shetland Islands might be attempted as 'an embarrassing diversion'.[36]

Already, the enemy had increased air activity over Britain. The Chief of the Air Staff reported to the War Cabinet at 12.30 pm that '168 enemy aircraft had been plotted over the UK and along our coasts between 10 pm and 3 am the previous night.' Damage had been slight and casualties very few, but the raids served to increase tension. The CoAS, Newall, said that 'police and Observer Corps reports of flares being fired from the ground while the raids were in progress were being investigated.'[37]

The Germans suddenly increased their pressure in northern France. Two armoured divisions drove towards Rouen to split the French 10th Army, separating the left French 9th Corps from the remainder of the front. Included in the threatened French 9th was the British 51st Highland Division. Under previous orders the movement of another British division to France, the 52nd, was scheduled to start that Friday, and these orders were confirmed despite the adverse situation. Montgomery's 3rd, the one remaining fully equipped division left in Britain, was also assigned to France. Yet until the BEF could be re-formed, expected to take at least three weeks, Britain's Home Defence army would consist of fourteen infantry divisions manned by inexperienced troops and with totally insufficient weapons. The latter included about 2300 Bren guns, barely enough for five divisions; only about thirty-three

13

heavy tanks would be available. By contrast, the JIC report of 6 June had pointed out that Germany had up to eighty divisions available for the present offensive in France, plus over thirty divisions in Central Germany. 'To oppose the troops in France the Allies have at present only some forty-nine divisions and of these the armoured and mechanised divisions are very reduced... Whether Germany attacks this country now or later, she will be able to make available for such an attack any numbers of divisions she may require.'[38]

But, as the JIC report also pointed out, first would probably come an air offensive. Initially, all depended on the RAF, now torn between the need to give support to the faltering French and the need to build up desperate defensive strength in the UK. And RAF Fighter Command was weaker at this moment than it ever would be again. On 3 June the number of Fighter Command serviceable aircraft had only amounted to 413 machines – seventy-nine Blenheims, 162 Spitfires, 163 Hurricanes and nine Defiants.[39] Many of these could be lost in the final battle for France: between 8–18 May, when intensive operations had been carried out against the initial German advance, a total of 250 Hurricanes had been destroyed; this had given an average of twenty-five a day, against only four a day received from production. On 3 June, warning against a despatch of further fighters to France, the Fighter Command chief Dowding had told the War Cabinet: 'If the enemy developed a heavy air attack on this country at this moment, he [Dowding] could not guarantee air superiority for more than forty-eight hours.' Four more squadrons were allocated to help the French on 5 June, but these would operate from bases in southern England.[40] The Air Ministry believed Luftwaffe strength to be about 1500 fighters and about 3000 bombers and dive-bombers, Of these, according to the JIC report of 6 June, 'it is estimated that about one-third, i.e. 500 of the German fighter forces would be available for escort [of bombers] purposes, approximately 300 Me 110s and 200 Me 109s. This number would not appear to be large enough to provide the numerical degree of protection already experienced in the battle area; on the other hand fighters could carry out more sorties than bombers, their bases being further west – resulting in a higher numerical degree of protection.'[41]

To many, the English Channel and the Royal Navy offered Britain her best defence. Yet plans drawn up by the Admiralty at the end of May had admitted that the Royal Navy would be unlikely to have the necessary strength to prevent the actual crossing of a German invasion fleet. Adequate warning could not be expected, and the Admiralty con-

14

cluded that the best hope would be an offensive against the enemy after arrival, severing supply lines. In addition to capital ships, at least four destroyer flotillas – thirty-six destroyers – would be required, plus supporting cruisers. The required number of destroyers might be available, but only after reductions in other essential tasks – mainly convoy duties – and in other respects the Home Fleet was weaker than at any time since the previous winter. Eight capital ships were deployed in home waters, yet of these the *Nelson* and *Barham* were refitting at Portsmouth and Liverpool, the *Hood* was under repair at Liverpool and was scheduled to move into foreign waters, and the *Resolution*, at present at Scapa Flow, had been ordered to the Western Approaches Command for convoy tasks. This only left the *Rodney, Valiant, Renown* and *Repulse*, all based at Scapa Flow.[42] By comparison, the JIC estimated the German Navy to have strong resources available for an invasion attempt, including the two battlecruisers *Scharnhorst* and *Gneisenau*, two old battleships, two eight-inch cruisers and four six-inch cruisers, plus a host of lesser vessels. The JIC report came to the gloomy conclusion that 'shipping will not be a limiting factor in conveying an expeditionary force.'[43]

On balance therefore, the situation in early June represented a clear weighting in Germany's favour: an overwhelming superiority in army strength, parity in air power and the strong probability that an invasion force could land without effective Royal Navy interception. Once Hitler had defeated France, all resources could be thrown against Britain if, as the British COS believed, plans existed for such an offensive. Britain had never been weaker.

15

∽

CHAPTER TWO

The Fall of France

9–18 June

'This may be the last opportunity,' declared the 1 pm BBC news on 7 June, 'for Americans to get home until after the war.' The warning, issued on behalf of the US Embassy in London, was ignored by many. General Wade H. Hayes had formed the 1st American Squadron of the Home Guard one week before, much against the wishes of the defeatist Ambassador, Joseph P. Kennedy. 'It might lead to all US citizens being shot as *francs-tireurs* when the Germans occupied London.'[1] Nor did the warning seem to affect the general calm throughout the country. 'I haven't heard anyone comment about this excited announcement,' wrote Mrs Peacock in her Sussex diary.[2]

On Sunday 9 June, the relatively obscure French general, Charles de Gaulle, arrived in threatened London. He noted 'a look of tranquillity, almost indifference. The streets and parks full of people peacefully out for a walk, the long queues at the entrance to the cinemas, the many cars, the impressive porters outside the clubs and hotels, belonged to another world than the one at war.'[3] During the day a flurry of excitement spread along the Embankment. A crowd gathered at Westminster Bridge, among them the Red Cross nurse, Frances Faviell. Up the Thames chugged a line of small boats, returning to their moorings from their Dunkirk rescue epic: 'those little dirty battered boats I'd seen like shrimps in Dover Harbour, their paint scraped and marked... They came in little groups of two and three, led by a tug with eighteen motor launches in tow, a lovely brave sight. Even now it brings a choking sensation when I think how I'd seen them... after the dangers they had faced to bring our boys safely home.'[4]

Yet at Southampton on that Sunday, troops of the 52nd Scottish

Lowland Division were boarding vessels to take them across to France. 'Our troops were mostly Territorials,' wrote John Kennedy, commanding the artillery, 'good, keen men, but undertrained and short of equipment... We continued to be confident until we had arrived in France.'[5] In France the British 51st Division was now cut off in the Havre Peninsula; Rouen had fallen during the previous day, 8 June, and now the trapped British troops fell back from Dieppe. Attacking from the east, the Germans reached the sea beyond the British line of withdrawal, cramming the bulk of the 51st in the St Valéry perimeter. Further south, enemy forces were being concentrated for the last push on Paris.

Also on 9 June the German Naval Intelligence Division produced a report forming a part of their detailed investigation of invasion problems. This twenty-page memorandum, handed to Rear-Admiral Fricke, comprised a study of the south and south-east English coastline from the Wash to the Isle of Wight. Possible landings were examined, and although the naval officers still stressed the difficulties involved, the information marked a further move towards the creation of a more definite German policy following France's defeat.[6]

In Rome, steps were also taken to steal advantage of the apparently inevitable German victory over the French. Benito Mussolini was determined to seize some of the spoils. At 4.45 pm next day, 10 June, the British Ambassador answered a summons from the Italian Foreign Minister, Count Ciano, and was informed of Italy's declaration of war. Sir Percy Loraine received the news in a 'laconic and inscrutable' fashion, according to Ciano, who revealed his own desperate thoughts in his diary. 'I am sad, very sad. The adventure begins. May God help Italy.'[7] Italy's entry into the war transformed the British position in the Middle East and imposed even greater burdens on her resources. 'Malta was isolated,' noted Ismay, 'exposed to attack by the Italian metropolitan air force, and in danger of invasion; Egypt, the Sudan, Kenya and British Somaliland were threatened by numerically superior enemy forces... The outlook was so bleak that many people thought that we should be attempting too much if we tried to hold the Middle East. But Churchill, with the full backing of the War Cabinet, the Chiefs of Staff and the commanders on the spot, was determined to fight it out to the very last ounce of our strength.'[8]

Yet at 10.30 am on this gloomy, overcast Monday the Defence Committee of the War Cabinet had heard an extremely depressing report from Ironside on the meagre resources available for Home Defence, even without further forces sent to the Middle East. First, Ironside

17

described the method being adopted to meet a German invasion. A complete system of coast-watchers had been instituted, and Ironside laid stress on the forward defensive positions. 'Thirty-two thousand men were allotted to holding of defensive positions in places where we could not afford to give up any ground to the enemy. Very rapid progress was being made in the preparation of beach defences.' Behind this defensive line would be the field force, organised into brigade groups to act as mobile columns to strike the enemy wherever he might land. Ironside declared: 'The arming of these divisions with rifles, Bren-guns, anti-tank rifles and armoured carriers, was on the whole fairly complete.' But he continued: 'There were, however, two chief weaknesses. First, the men in these divisions were not yet adequately trained for attack...Second, there was a great shortage of artillery and anti-tank guns.' The Home Forces Commander then described measures for static defence and protection of vital points further inland. 'Thirty-three thousand men of the Home Defence Battalions and 471,000 LDVs provided the static defence throughout the country, designed to defeat airborne attack. About 100,000 rifles and 80,000 shot guns were in the hands of the LDVs. 75,000 Ross rifles were being brought from Canada, of which 15,000 should now be arriving. One million "Molotov" cocktails had already been made, and were being issued to LDVs for use against tanks.'[9] So, even when the full amount of Ross rifles arrived from Canada, U-boats permitting, over 200,000 LDV soldiers would still be without rifles or even shot-guns. And, rather than anti-tank rifles, they would have to rely on the Molotov petrol bombs hurled against the advancing armour.

Any weapon seemed better than none. According to John Davey, North of England archery champion: 'Think of the effect on a group of Germans if one of them suddenly dropped with an arrow through him...They would be terrified.'[10] The Germans were also believed to be studying the possibilities of unusual weapons. An account had already been given to the War Cabinet, on 8 June, of intelligence reports that 'experiments had been conducted in Germany with bombs filled with very finely divided magnetic iron-ore. It was stated that by this means dust clouds of magnetic iron oxide could be created, which might put closely fitted moving parts out of action. It was suggested this weapon might be used against guns and tanks etc....' Ministers were also told of a report from a Spanish resident in Peru that 'he had overheard a German in Panama saying that the new weapon against England would be decisive and that it was a flying bomb.'[11]

18

Troops of the 1st Canadian Division were now landing at Brest – at the same time as elements of the British 51st were being evacuated from Le Havre. Other units of the 51st, cut off by the advancing army, retreated into St Valéry from which they hoped to be rescued. At 2 pm on the 11th Churchill was driven to Hendon airfield and flew for desperate talks with the French Premier, Paul Reynaud, at Briare on the Loire. Discussions continued into the night while 200 miles to the north thick fog swirled round St Valéry to prevent evacuation of the trapped 51st Division troops. These 8000 soldiers were obliged to surrender at 10.30 am next morning, 12 June, as Churchill held further talks with Reynaud, and as General Sir Alan Brooke crossed the Channel from Southampton in a 'dirty little Dutch steamer only capable of 12 knots with no arrangements for food on board.'[12] Brooke, knighted by the King at Buckingham Palace the previous day, had been ordered to take command of remaining British forces on the Continent.

All possible steps were being taken to increase British beach defences with the limited materials available. This Wednesday a first batch of forty-six new gun batteries, each comprising two six-inch guns and two searchlights, was added to the fixed defences. But in order to save critically short ammunition and conceal the battery positions as long as possible, the gunners were instructed to hold their fire until the enemy approached within four miles. This would limit the weapons to about half of their effective range, but would help off-set the inexperience of the aimers. Such batteries were woefully inadequate to prevent a determined invasion force from pushing ashore. Teams of engineers were erecting anti-boat booms at Dover, Harwich and Rosyth; about a hundred miles of lighter booms were being laid off designated open beaches, plus mines attached to jack-stays; about 300 miles of scaffolding, besides buried mines, would eventually be placed above high-water marks.[13]

During the afternoon of 12 June the Home Secretary, Sir John Anderson, told the House of Commons that the programme for provision of bomb shelters which bore his name, launched ten months before, had now been completed. Over half the civilian population could now find shelter space. Anderson's statement glowed with optimism. Yet although the supply of shelters did appear adequate, and those people below a certain income could qualify to have this protection free if they had a garden in which to place the corrugated iron construction, many were so far unwilling to spend the £8 needed to buy Anderson's device. Meanwhile, other civilians were attending first-aid classes ready to help

Blitz victims. 'Don't back away from dirt and filth – you'll see plenty,' warned a doctor lecturing to volunteer Red Cross personnel in Chelsea. 'Blood and tissues and spilled guts are not pretty, ladies and gentlemen – and they smell. You'll have to get used to that. If you come upon a casualty with half his stomach laid open and his guts hanging out thrust your hands unhesitatingly into the wound and pack them back. Hold your fists there to keep them in position if you have nothing else. The mess and smell may revolt you, but that man needs his guts.'[14]

'A chapter in the war was now closing,' declared Churchill at a War Cabinet meeting that Wednesday evening. Ministers had been summoned to 10 Downing Street at 5 pm to hear the Prime Minister's report of his latest visit to France. 'The French might continue the struggle- ...But effective resistance as a great land power was coming to an end.' Churchill continued: 'We must now concentrate everything on the defence of this island, though for a period we might still have to send a measure of support to France.' He viewed the new phase 'with confidence'. Earlier, the Vice-CIGS had informed Ministers that the French had fallen back onto the Marne, thus opening up a line of advance for the enemy into Paris. 'German advanced elements must be expected in the capital within the next 24–48 hours.'[15] Sir Alexander Cadogan, Permanent Under-Secretary at the Foreign Office, noted in his diary after this meeting: 'Awful nightmare... What a look-out! God give us courage.'[16]

Early next morning, 13 June, the evacuation of survivors of the British 51st Division was completed at Le Havre. About 2200 troops were brought back to England, yet other British soldiers were still arriving in Cherbourg to continue the hopeless struggle. In London the COS decided at 10 am to reverse the previous decision, made only the day before, to send two battalions for the defence of the Channel Islands. Troops on these islands would be extremely vulnerable, and the area would cease to be of strategic importance once the enemy reached the adjacent French coast. Removal of British forces would, it was hoped, demilitarise the islands.[17]

Churchill flew once more to France: it would be his last visit for four years. French forces were in tatters. At 4 pm the COS met again in London to consider the draft of a telegram to Dominion Prime Ministers; the subject of the message was Britain's position in 'a certain eventuality' – the euphemistic term still used to describe the defeat of France. The telegram declared: 'We estimate that without full economic and financial assistance of whole of American Continent our chances of

20

defeating Germany would be remote.' The COS continued: 'In situation envisaged, the first problem would be to secure security of the UK against concentrated German attack. This attack might take following forms: (a) breaking of public morale by unrestricted air attack; (b) starvation of country by attacks on shipping and ports; (c) occupation by invasion... We must expect widespread destruction, considerable dislocation of industry and communications, and heavy casualties. Chances of Germany achieving success depend mainly on our ability to maintain in being our air forces, their sources of supply and the fleet and its base.' The COS concluded: 'Providing we can prevent enemy gaining high degree of air superiority we think we should be able to prevent large-scale invasion of the UK. Our shortage of destroyers, however, gives us grave anxiety.'[18] The Prime Minister reported back to the War Cabinet at 10.15 pm. He described the terrible military situation in France and Reynaud's despondency. Ministers agreed to a statement from the British to the French Government, proclaiming the 'indissoluble union of our two peoples and our two Empires'.[19]

During the day a ban on church bell ringing had been announced. Bells would now only be rung by the police or military as a warning of attack by German airborne forces. The announcement was immediately criticised by the campanology journal *Ringing World* as 'a stunning blow... from which, even when the war is over, it will take a long time to recover.'[20] Also on the 13th it was decided to reverse previous instructions not to evacuate further children from cities prior to air raids: during the next five days nearly 100,000 boys and girls would be moved from the British capital.

Leading armoured units of the German 18th Army entered the undefended streets of Paris during the morning of Friday 14 June. Within an hour a giant swastika fluttered from the Eiffel Tower. In Berlin the German High Command announced: 'The second phase of the campaign is over with the capture of Paris. The third phase has begun. It is the pursuit and final destruction of the enemy.' William Shirer noted in his diary: 'Berlin has taken the news of the capture of Paris as phlegmatically as it has taken everything else in this war.'[21] Once again the question of the next step for Germany's armed forces needed urgent consideration. Admiral Raeder received a report from the Merchant Shipping Division: this stated that only forty-five seaworthy barges, essential for a landing on the English beaches, could be made available before mid-July. And, also on 14 June, it appeared that the German High Command of the Armed Forces had moved distinctly away from the army invasion idea. General Keitel, OKW Chief of Staff, issued a directive on war production which declared: 'The Navy and the Luftwaffe must be reorganised so that, after the defeat of France, the war against England will be continued by sea and air.' The directive therefore seemed to confirm a blockade policy.[22] Hitler, still at the small village of Bruly de Pêche, increasingly hoped for an early end to hostilities with Britain: on 14 June the *New York Journal-American* published an interview given by the Fuehrer to the Hearst correspondent Karl von Wiegand, in which Hitler publicly declared his earnest wish for a peaceful Anglo-German settlement as soon as possible.[23] And next day, 15 June, Hitler informed Halder that he wanted the Army partly demobilised.

British War Cabinet Ministers obstinately refused to abandon all hope for France. Urgent discussions took place on 15 and 16 June to carry further the proposal of 13 June for the 'indissolvable union' of the Anglo-French people. At the instigation of ex-Prime Minister Neville Chamberlain the War Cabinet agreed, on 16 June, to a declaration being sent to the French which, if the French would agree, would merge the two countries. The joint announcement would state that 'France and Great Britain shall no longer be two nations but one Franco-British union.'[24] Churchill prepared to journey across the Channel again.

But France's end came with terrible suddenness. Reynaud resigned on the evening of 16 June; at 11.30 pm the French radio declared that Marshal Pétain had been asked to form a new administration. In the early hours of 17 June, while British troops were moving towards the coast for their final evacuation, Pétain sought an armistice with the Germans. At noon of that day the new French leader announced over the radio: 'It is with a broken heart that I tell you today that fighting must cease.' In London, a message was hurried into the War Cabinet room during the early afternoon: most French troops had ceased fighting at 12.40 pm. Ministers had assembled to discuss the latest military situation, including the departure of remaining British troops from France and the defence of the UK against invasion. With the latter, Dill warned that 'the retreats and withdrawals which we had recently been compelled to carry out must necessarily have left their mark on the psychology of our troops.' A further warning came from Eden, War Secretary, who said that the LDVs were at the moment largely a 'broomstick' army.[25]

Ministers left Churchill alone in the quiet of the Cabinet Room at

10 Downing Street. He sat reading the latest telegrams. Then a signal informed him that over 3000 British troops had perished at St Nazaire earlier in the day when their rescue vessel, the 20,000-ton *Lancastria*, had been bombed. The Prime Minister forbade publication of this tragedy. 'The newspapers have got quite enough disasters for today at least.' At St Nazaire, General Sir Alan Brooke boarded the armed trawler *Cambridgeshire* for his escape from France; the vessel had rescued 900 men from the *Lancastria* and her decks were slimy with oil from the bodies of the survivors.

Soon after dawn next day, Thursday 18 June, Brooke set sail for England. As Brooke's evil-smelling boat throbbed slowly across the Channel and the last evacuation ship left Cherbourg, Winston Churchill sorted his notes and rose to his feet in the crowded House of Commons. Big Ben struck four o'clock as he adjusted his spectacles and began to speak.

'The Battle of France is over. I expect the Battle of Britain is about to begin.' Members of Parliament listened in absolute silence as Churchill's slurred, almost hesitant voice continued: 'The whole fury and might of the enemy must very soon be turned on us. Hitler knows that he will have to break us in this island or lose the war.' The Prime Minister's words grew louder and more assured; he reached his emphatic conclusion. 'Let us therefore brace ourselves to our duties and so bear ourselves that, if the British Empire and its Commonwealth last for a thousand years, men will still say: "This was their finest hour!" '

CHAPTER THREE

༄

Confusion across the Channel

18 June–2 July

'We were now alone,' wrote Ismay. 'So far from being alarmed, we were relieved, nay exhilarated. Henceforward everything would be simpler. We were masters of our own fate.'[1] Dowding, the Fighter Command chief soon to be plunged into the fury of the Battle of Britain, experienced the same reaction. He told Lord Halifax: 'When I heard of the French collapse I went on my knees and thanked God.' King George of England wrote to his mother: 'Personally I feel happier now that we have no allies to be polite to and to pamper.' Churchill's feelings were similar. Even before Dunkirk he had told the War Cabinet: 'The French are trying to get us on the slippery slope... Nations which go down fighting rise again, but those which surrender tamely are finished.'[2] He declared over the radio on the evening of 17 June: 'We have become the sole champions in arms to defend the world cause.'

Now, on 18 June, the 125th anniversary of the battle of Waterloo, the COS met to discuss the situation. Heading the items on the agenda was 'urgent measures to meet invasion'. The COS agreed that 'people living on or near the south-east coast were undoubtedly apprehensive... In the industrial North there was a more robust outlook. There was little realisation of the danger, but on the Tyneside and in Lancashire people were full of fight.' Response to the appeal to evacuate children from dangerous areas was considered unsatisfactory and 'there was a tendency for the danger of invasion to obscure the danger of the breaking of morale through intensive bombing. From the point of view of avoiding panic, the more men under discipline the better.'[3]

A massive increase took place in the flow of memoranda, orders and information between the War Office, the GHQ Home Forces and the

24

regional army commands – Northern, Southern, Eastern, Western, Scottish, Aldershot and the London area. These communications covered a multitude of topics. The War Office had signalled on 16 June: 'It has become evident that reports of parachutists having been seen dropping from aircraft have been due to individuals mistaking the white puffs of the bursts of AA shells for parachutes.'[4] On 17 June Northern Command had warned: 'As regards the ringing of church bells as an alarm signal for the LDV, it is pointed out that nearly everybody who rings a bell for the first time pulls the rope too hard, and finding it does not ring pulls it harder; the result is not to make the bell ring but to carry the would-be ringer up into the roof.'[5] On 18 June the Ministry of Information issued instructions on 'What to do if Parachutists should come.' The men and women of Britain were told: 'The order is to stay put... Do not believe rumours and do not spread them... Be calm, quick, exact. Keep watch. If you see anything suspicious note it carefully and go at once to the nearest policeman.' This leaflet suffered from an irritating condescending tone. 'When parachutists come down near homes they will not be feeling very brave. They will not know where they are or where their companions are... Do not give any German anything. Do not tell him anything. Hide your food, your bicycles, your maps...'

Exhortations to report anything suspicious led to police stations and military offices being flooded with tales of suspicious activities, and foreign nationals – many in British uniform and including Poles, French, Norwegians, Dutch, Belgians and Danes – experienced serious harassment. Nor did the British people as a whole react enthusiastically to lectures such as the 'Stay Put' leaflet. 'We British do not like scraps of advice and information handed out to us as pamphlets,' wrote Frances Faviell. 'I stuck the pamphlet on the wall and it never failed to amuse me when depressed.'[6] The British public refused to alter their life-style unless absolutely necessary and however grim the news the proper advantage had to be taken of clement June weather. 'All along the line,' wrote Mrs Robert Henry after a railway journey in southern England, 'young men in flannels were playing cricket in the sunshine on beautifully tended fields shaded by stalwart oaks and poplar trees.'[7]

'If London wants war it will be total war, complete, pitiless,' wrote Count Ciano in his diary on 18 June. The Italian Foreign Minister, attending talks between Mussolini and Hitler at Munich, believed the German mood towards England had changed. The possibility of invasion had apparently been discussed, but Ciano's diary entry

25

continued: 'Hitler makes many reservations on the desirability of demolishing the British Empire, which he considers, even today, to be an important factor in world equilibrium.' Ciano also noted: 'Hitler is now the gambler who has made a big scoop and would like to get up from the table risking nothing more. Today he speaks with a reserve and a perspicacity which, after such a victory, are really astonishing.'[8]

As Hitler dined with Mussolini at Munich during this evening, German aircraft once again prowled over England. Raids had diminished during the previous week; now, on this Tuesday, scattered bombs were dropped in the Midlands and East Anglia, and the first fell on Greater London, at Addington. The heaviest casualties were suffered at Cambridge where nine people died. In general, these and other raids during June caused minimal damage, and although they provided German aircrews with experience and navigational information, they also helped train British searchlight crews. Some officials suspected the Germans to be rehearsing for the dropping of parachutists as a prelude to invasion: Whitehall staff planners and officers continued to overestimate enemy preparations.

British counter-preparations were described in detail to the War Cabinet Defence Committee at 10 am on 19 June. 'Every bit of coastline would be seen every half-hour throughout the day and night.' Behind the coast watchers was the Observer Corps, covering most of the country. All-round defence was being organised in potential invasion areas. Inland, there would be 'lines of stops', and behind these barriers would lie the mobile reserves, although the Defence Committee learnt that mobility was extremely limited. 'Each division had enough transport for the conveyance of one brigade and it was hoped shortly that this would be increased to two brigades.' Troops would be rushed to the fighting in civilian transport – 'motor-coach companies were being organised as fast as drivers could be made available.' The search for bus drivers was in fact suffering from bureaucratic hindrance, even at this critical time. 'The civilian drivers of the coaches could not in all cases be taken, as many of them were over the age of forty-one and were therefore immune from conscription.' Ironside continued: 'Steps were being taken to inculcate throughout the army the offensive spirit which was so important; but it should be realised that effective counter-attack could not be carried out without the requisite weapons.' The latter were still in short supply. About eighty infantry tanks were now available; 710 field guns had been distributed representing only two-fifths of the establishment; preparations were being made for using

French 75 mm guns, of which Ironside commented: 'The ammunition would require reconditioning, as it was very old, but it would be quite good enough for use at point-blank range against tanks.' About 167 proper anti-tank guns were now available in the artillery of the various divisions.[9]

Meanwhile, Britain's primary weapon for counter-attack was RAF Bomber Command, although its effectiveness was inevitably limited. By early summer 1940 Bomber Command operated about 300 modern bombers, Hampdens and Wellingtons, which had sufficient range to penetrate deep into enemy airspace. In addition to these long-range bombers were about a hundred of the older Whitleys. A force of about 300 medium-range Blenheims could reach the fringe areas. But numerous problems had to be overcome. Daylight attacks required strong fighter escorts, and such aircraft were not available, yet darkness presented all the difficulties of location and navigation. Early raids were clumsy by comparison with later attacks, and crews in the old-fashioned Whitleys experienced all the defects of their antiquated aircraft especially through cold and shortage of oxygen.

'Such was the condition of the navigator and the wireless operator at this stage,' wrote the pilot in his report of a pamphlet-dropping excursion in October 1939, 'that every few minutes they were compelled to lie down and rest on the floor of the fuselage. The cockpit heating system was useless. Everyone was frozen, and had no means of alleviating their distress. The navigator and Commanding Officer were butting their heads on the floor and navigation table in an endeavour to experience some other form of pain as a relief from the awful feeling of frost-bite and the lack of oxygen.'[10]

Not until 19 March 1940 was the first bombing – as opposed to pamphlet – raid made on German soil, against the naval seaplane base at Hoernum. The War Cabinet in London was still hesitant to sanction full raids for fear that these would provide the enemy with a pretext for bombing civilian targets in Britain. The situation changed following the Luftwaffe attack on Rotterdam in May: ninety-nine RAF bombers attacked oil and railway targets in the Ruhr on 16 May.

But British bombing suffered from the lack of a clear policy. On 19 June, the Air Staff decided that the primary aim should be to reduce the potential scale of air attack on the UK, through striking at aircraft factories, communications, oil depots and airfields. This policy was laid down in instructions dated 20 June. Soon however other calls would be made on Bomber Command, chiefly for strikes against the German invasion preparations, but also including an ambitious scheme for burning German crops and forests. Throughout the summer, Bomber Command aircraft would be switched from one role to another, resulting in added strain.

On 20 June the German leader, now returned to Bruly de Pêche, received a visit from Raeder during which the German naval chief reported on naval planning for a possible invasion of England. Hitler discussed schemes for special invasion craft, but expressed no firm opinion on the operation as a whole. Raeder continued to emphasise the difficulties, especially the vital need for air supremacy and the need for airborne forces to assist in the formation of bridgeheads. He also repeated his anxiety to find adequate transport.[11] Moreover, the German Army General Staff had apparently come round to a similar view to that of the Navy regarding the operation's difficulties. Captain Loycke, naval liaison officer to OKH, reported next morning, 21 June, that 'the General Staff is not concerning itself with the question of England. Considers execution impossible... Presumably twenty divisions in England, i.e. at least forty divisions required by us. Is absolute air superiority attainable in view of very strong defence? General Staff reject the operation.'[12] Senior German army officers, like their British counterparts, were overestimating the enemy: the OKH erred by as much as five divisions over British home force strength, and made no allowance for seriously inadequate British equipment.

On this Friday Hitler had other matters to fill his mind. Early in the day he left his HQ at Bruly de Pêche and at 3.15 pm his big black Mercedes drew up in a small clearing in Compiègne forest. Nearby stood the railway-carriage used by Marshal Foch on 11 November 1918, when German generals had signed the surrender to end the First World War. The *wagon-lit* had been brought from its place of honour in a French museum to be placed in the same spot where it had stood twenty-two years before. Hitler walked the 200 yards from his car, passing the 1918 monument to Germany's humiliation. William Shirer, the US journalist present at the scene, vividly recalled the Fuehrer's face – 'afire with scorn, anger, hate, revenge, triumph'. Hitler stepped into the railway carriage, sat in the chair used by Foch and listened impatiently as General Keitel read the preamble of the armistice terms to assembled French generals.[13] The twenty-four-clause armistice treaty was transmitted through a specially laid cable running over German and French battle lines to the French Government at Bordeaux. Hopeless negotiations would continue next day until Keitel informed the French that they must sign within the hour. At 6.50 pm the signatures were written on the treaty marking the death of independent France.

British staff planners in Whitehall believed an invasion attempt might only be a matter of a few weeks, or even days, ahead. In addition to military personnel, about 150,000 British civilians were engaged on defensive works, and in general these preparations were being undertaken with a greater sense of urgency. But much remained to be done before even barely adequate defences could be erected at the most vulnerable points. Horrocks, now commander of the 9th Brigade in Montgomery's 3rd Division, had about 3000 men with which to protect the ten miles of densely-populated coast between Rottingdean and Shoreham. 'We wouldn't have stood much chance against a well-organised invasion, but even so this was probably one of the most strongly defended parts of Britain.' The air of unreality continued. Montgomery visited Horrocks at his Brighton HQ and pointed to an elegant seafront mansion partly blocking the fire from a machine-gun post. 'Who lives in that house?' he barked. 'Have them out, Horrocks. Blow up the house. Defence must come first.' Militarily, Montgomery was correct, but he was still demanding the impossible. Lieutenant-Colonel Selby Lowndes, the local gunner commander, complained to Horrocks in disgust: 'I never thought I should live to see the day when I occupied a battery position outside the Metropole on the front at Brighton.'[14]

It all seemed so strange and unnatural. The 52nd Division, just returned from France, was being deployed further north, based on Cambridge; General Kennedy toured the Norfolk coastline to examine likely landing areas and he wrote: 'I had often shot wild geese here, and watched birds, and sailed a boat, but never before had I thought of Norfolk as a possible battle ground. In the evening we dined with the dons [at King's College] and enjoyed their delicious wine and especially their excellent Château-Yquem, which they drank instead of port when the weather was hot. The dons did not regard the war as a serious business, or as an interesting subject of conversation; and that was most refreshing.'[15] On 21 June the *Spectator* carried an advertisement for the Aviemore Hotel in Inverness-shire. 'Today, more than ever, Aviemore will come as a haven of peace and rest. Here, among the tonic air of the pinewoods, you will find a sanctuary far removed from the rush and nerve-strain of the outer world...'

General R. H. Haining, Vice-CIGS, told the War Cabinet that up to the previous midnight a total of 122,006 British troops and 2174 casualties had been disembarked following the final evacuation from

France. Brest and St Nazaire were clear of British troops and 'evacuation might be regarded as complete.' Ministers were informed that the military evacuation of the Channel Islands had been carried out and 'that day would see the completion of evacuation of such of the inhabitants as wished to leave.'[16] The exodus from the islands would in fact continue until 24 June, numbering 29,000 people or over a quarter of the total population. Those remaining on the islands, which had been associated with the English Crown for almost a thousand years, were left to the mercy of the invading Germans.

'The near future will show whether Britain will do the reasonable thing in the light of our victories,' wrote General Franz Halder in his diary on 22 June, 'or will try to carry on the war alone. In the latter case the war will involve Britain's destruction, and may last a long time.'[17] Hitler informed Field-Marshal Walther Brauchitsch, C-in-C of the German Army, that Britain seemed to be 'coming down a peg'. His optimism stemmed from reports from the Swedish Minister in Berlin, who mistakenly believed that certain authoritative circles in London were inclined to negotiate.[18] In London next day the War Secretary revealed further evidence of Britain's weakness to withstand invasion. In a minute to Churchill written after a tour of the key counties of Kent, Sussex and Surrey, Eden reported: 'There is no anti-tank regiment nor anti-tank gun in the whole of this Corps area.' And tanks had still to be supplied.[19] On that Sunday, 23 June, Churchill was involving himself with protection plans for another vital district. Ismay sent a minute to General Bernard Paget, Chief of Staff at GHQ Home Forces: 'The Prime Minister is taking an active interest in the defence arrangements for the Whitehall area and I confess that I am not altogether happy about them.' The various Whitehall buildings were protected by respective bodies – Royal Marines, Guards and RAF personnel, plus LDVs. Ismay and Churchill believed the area should be manned by a homogeneous unit to prevent confusion. Paget convinced Ismay that the existing arrangement should continue.[20]

A multitude of other kinks had to be ironed out from the hurried defence arrangements. Existing arrangements for air raid warnings were inflexible: sirens sounded even when a district was not especially threatened; people hurried to shelters and there was dislocation of work in factories and offices. A total of seventy enemy aircraft flew over the country on 24 June: only Bristol was threatened by more than one or two raiders, yet the whole of the country below a line from Hull to Liverpool was under 'red' warning.[21] But the system did at least mean that men and women became used to the eerie, unnerving wail of the sirens, and organisations such as anti-aircraft units, Civil Defence services and hospitals were provided with the opportunity for many dress-rehearsals.

Churchill, in addition to concerning himself with details such as the defence of Whitehall, was also involved with hours of War Cabinet discussion over the question of the French Fleet. Three Cabinet meetings were held on 24 June in an attempt to find a way of preventing these invaluable warships from falling into the hands of the Germans. Moreover, the Prime Minister was looking even further afield: he drafted his first message to Stalin, despatched next day. Churchill appealed for better relations, hinting at the possibility of Russia's being Hitler's next target after Britain. 'The Soviet Union alone is in a position to judge whether Germany's present bid for the hegemony of Europe threatens the interest of the Soviet Union.'[22] Hitler had already given some thought to such a campaign against his Soviet ally. Russia's action in occupying the Baltic States of Lithuania, Latvia and Estonia on 14, 15 and 19 June had antagonised the Fuehrer still further. Soon Hitler would involve himself in planning for the German invasion of Russia, and already this possible step was adding more confusion to his thoughts.

General indecision spread throughout the German command. The draft OKH order for regrouping the German Army, dated 24 June, mentioned 'preparations against England', but this reference was omitted in final instructions issued on 26 June. A state of limbo existed between the France campaign and the next move. On 25 June, Hitler's HQ departed from Bruly de Pêche, but rather than transferring to a position where close contact could be established with army groups near the Channel, the *Fuehrer-Hauptquartier* shifted almost 200 miles south-west to the Black Forest. There, at Kneibis near Freudenstadt, code-named Tannenberg, Hitler's personal staff had to cram into an isolated inn in wooded country high in the hills. Hitler would arrive four days later. German activity against Britain was still limited to scattered air raids: about seventy aircraft were again active over the country on 25 June. But from this date onwards the raids seemed to be concentrated rather more on British aircraft industry plants and ports, perhaps indicating the start of a new trend.[23]

Also on 25 June, General Ironside appeared before the Vice-COS to describe latest progress in home defence arrangements. His exposition would cause severe alarm on the most important point of all: where, if the Germans attempted an invasion, should the main battle be fought.

'There were three main elements in the defence against seaborne invasion,' declared Ironside at this 10 am meeting. 'First, a crust on the coast acting as outposts. Second, a line of anti-tank obstacles running down the centre of England to the Blackwall Tunnel [in London], thence to Maidstone and southwards to the sea. Third, mobile reserves in the rear of this anti-tank line.' Ironside continued: 'Some 900 beaches on which landings might take place had been blocked and wired, and large numbers of anti-tank mines had been placed in position. Concrete block-houses were being put up by civilian contract. In Kent alone there were some 900... The frontages held by divisions on the coastline were admittedly very long indeed, but it would not be sound to lock up too many troops in a static role. Between the coast and the line of anti-tank obstacles were allocated mobile columns containing armoured fighting vehicles to deal with any tanks which broke through the crust.' Once again Ironside stressed the shortages of equipment.[24] The meeting ended at about noon and Ironside departed. The Vice-Chiefs discussed his remarks – and their scrutiny immediately led to doubts and misunderstandings.

The Vice-COS met again at 3.30 pm next day, 26 June. These three senior officers – Air Marshal Sir Richard Peirse, Vice-Admiral Tom Phillips and General Haining – expressed the 'gravest concern' at Ironside's dispositions: the coast was to be held by a 'crust' and it appeared the main resistance might only be offered after the enemy had overrun nearly half the country, obtaining possession of airfields and other vital facilities. The Vice-Chiefs declared that 'the only policy was to resist the enemy with the utmost resolution from the moment he set foot on the shore. Once he established himself firmly on land, experience had shown that the German was extremely difficult to dislodge.' The Vice-Chiefs also criticised the fact that Ironside had made very little mention of defence of the south coast, 'which was now quite as liable to attack as the east coast and south-east coast.' Ironside's plan was 'completely unsound and needed drastic and immediate revision.' They asked the COS to discuss this question with them as a matter of urgency.[25]

The COS obliged at a meeting beginning 9.45 pm that day. Prior to this late-night session the CIGS Dill, had hurried to Twickenham to see Ironside. The latter had always insisted that he would prefer a more offensive plan, but maintained his scheme of coastal defence was the most that could be done with his insufficient resources. Ironside pointed out that the ability of the forward divisions to counter-attack on the beaches was limited by their lack of artillery and training.[26] Dill supported Ironside at the 9.45 pm meeting. So too did Sir Cyril Newall, CoAS, who maintained he had received 'rather a different impression' of Ironside's plans than had the Vice-Chiefs. He understood that the coast would be defended by positions which would be as strong as possible, at least to check and delay landings. Behind these forward defences would be 'a mass of manœuvre'; the anti-tank obstacle running down the centre of England would only be used as a last resort. In the subsequent discussion it was agreed that Ironside's explanation had perhaps been badly worded. 'The beach defences... were referred to as outposts, giving the impression that at some time they might be withdrawn and might not be expected to resist to the bitter end.' Ismay, who had accompanied Churchill on a tour of East Anglia during the day, said 'the troops and commanders they had visited undoubtedly intended to fight on the seashore and had no thought of withdrawal.'[27]

All seemed well again: the COS were in agreement with Ironside that the main emphasis should be on the coastal battle, rather than further inland. A COS memorandum drafted after the meeting confirmed that Ironside's plan of defence 'appears to us to be generally sound. Nevertheless, we are not entirely satisfied that sufficient emphasis has been laid upon the paramount necessity of resisting the enemy by all means in our power, during that vital first phase in the operations.'[28] Once the necessary assurances had been given by Ironside, the COS believed, the home defence plan could proceed.

A dangerous lack of liaison nevertheless existed. The Whitehall emphasis on coastal defence was directly opposed by leading commanders in the field and these officers, regardless of the official directives from the War Office and HQ Home Forces, were clearly determined to plan their own tactics. Confusion was the inevitable result, which could have been disastrous if the Germans had been in a position to take advantage. On the same day that the COS met in London, 26 June, General Brooke took up his appointment as General Officer Commanding-in-Chief, Southern Command, the same post he had left in autumn 1939 to go to France. The coastline which Brooke was called upon to defend stretched from West Sussex round to Wales, with his HQ at Wilton. He was dismayed at the condition of defences in his area. 'The main impression I had', he wrote, 'was that the Command had a long way to go to be put on a war-footing... the shortage of trained men and equipment is appalling... There are masses of men in uniform, but they are mostly untrained: why, I cannot think after ten months of war. The ghastly part of it is that I feel certain that we can

33

only have a few more weeks before the *boche* attacks.'[29] Brooke immediately set about introducing improvements – especially through the formation of a reserve for mobile operations; this, rather than the actual coastal positions, appeared to him to be most important. Montgomery, a corps commander further east along the coast, held similar views. He wrote: 'I found myself in disagreement with the general approach to the problem of the defence of Britain and refused to apply it in my corps area... The accepted doctrine was that every inch of the coastline must be defended strongly... My approach was different.'

Churchill would soon involve himself in this difference of opinion. His visit to East Anglia on 26 June gave him much material upon which his ever-active mind began to work. Meanwhile, he addressed himself to other home defence topics. He insisted that air raids should be treated in calm fashion by press and people; he told Duff Cooper, Minister of Information: 'The people should be accustomed to treat air raids as a matter of ordinary routine... as if they were no more than thunderstorms.'[30] On 26 June the Prime Minister also sent a minute to Eden, War Secretary. 'I don't think much of the name "Local Defence Volunteers" for your very large new force. The word "local" is uninspiring... I think "Home Guard" would be better.'[31] Britain's civilian army would receive its new title on 31 July.

'If Hitler fails to beat us here,' wrote Churchill to Smuts, South African Prime Minister, on 27 June, 'he will probably recoil eastwards. Indeed he may do this even without trying invasion...' Churchill told his friend: 'Our large army now being created for home defence is being formed on principle of attack, and opportunity for large-scale offensive amphibious operations may come in 1940 and 1941.'[32]

In London, planners were still struggling to obtain some reasonable assessment of Germany's intentions – a task in fact impossible because these intentions were still undefined in Berlin. The New British Broadcasting Station, a German propaganda service claiming to be transmitted by agents from inside Britain, proclaimed on 27 June that the German offensive would be launched against twenty different points in Britain, including all large population centres. On the same day the COS intelligence section's weekly résumé attempted to discern sóme pattern from enemy activity over the last seven days. Fighter Command had flown 364 patrols, involving 738 aircraft, over the UK. 'Since the 21st there has been a very sharp drop in activity and it is probable that [enemy] units are being rested in order to consolidate and to retain a high proportion of serviceability.'[33] Next day the Fighter Command

34

Intelligence summary provided more details. 'Night attacks have never been an accepted part of German Air Force bomber tactics, because such attacks are not sufficiently accurate to permit bombing to destruction. The present phase, which has been on a restricted scale, compared with the strength available, has probably for its object...(i) to exploit nuisance value of night raids, which the Germans have learnt from our bombers; (ii) to train pilots on navigation for large scale raids if required.' The summary provided information for Fighter Command pilots, as an aid to interception: enemy aircraft seemed to fly in groups of three to four, which split over the target; the height favoured appeared to be between 10–15,000 feet.[34]

Hitler was enjoying his month of triumph and still neglected decision-making. At 5.30 am on 28 June he landed at Le Bourget, stepped into a waiting Mercedes sedan and drove off for a three-hour sight-seeing tour of Paris. First he visited the Opéra, his favourite building. Hitler, the amateur architect, had taken the trouble to study the plans before his visit and delighted in displaying his knowledge to his entourage. The tour continued past the Madeleine, down the Champs Elysées, to the Eiffel Tower and the Sacré Cœur. 'It was the dream of my life to be permitted to see Paris,' he told Speer. 'I cannot say how happy I am to have that dream fulfilled.' Speer felt almost pity for him. Hitler travelled back to his peasant's house at Bruly de Pêche. 'Wasn't Paris beautiful?' he exclaimed to Speer. 'But Berlin must be made far more beautiful.' He busied himself again with his scheme for reconstructing the German capital.[35]

While Hitler glowed with the rewards of conquest Churchill concerned himself with plans for Britain's defence. And the Prime Minister injected further confusion into the existing scheme. A memorandum drawn up by him on 28 June agreed with the official War Office view that the main German invasion attempt would most likely be made against the east coast. 'The south coast is less immediately dangerous.' But then Churchill declared that the main emphasis should not be placed on coastal defences, as the COS insisted. If the Navy failed to stop the invasion fleet the Germans might be able to make several lodgments. 'Once these are made all troops employed on other parts of the coastal crust will be as useless as those in the Maginot Line. Although fighting on the beaches is favourable to the defence, this advantage cannot be purchased by trying to guard all the beaches.' Churchill advocated coastal positions being manned by 'sedentary troops, well-sprinkled with experienced late-war officers'. He continued: 'The

35

battle will be won or lost not on the beaches, but by the mobile brigades and the main reserve.'[36]

Churchill's energetic intervention forced this vital issue to the front again. Ironside was summoned to a COS meeting at 11.30 am next morning, 29 June, where he was confronted both by the COS memorandum of the 26th and Churchill's paper of 28 June. Ironside, overworked and under extreme pressure, attempting to find adequate forces from untrained, ill-equipped divisions, once again explained his position: a note of exasperation crept into the official minutes. Ironside again emphasised shortages of equipment for a counter-strike against the invaders, and said the majority of the line divisions were only partly trained and had very little artillery. 'Formations in this condition were unsuitable for counter-attacks on a large scale.' Churchill's suggestion could not be taken up with these limited resources, and in answer to the Prime Minister's other main point, Ironside pointed out that allocation of troops to beaches had been very carefully considered in relation to the probability of landings in the particular area. 'If we had four armoured divisions in the UK the whole problem of the defence of the country would be solved.' Ironside therefore considered he was doing his best with the forces at his disposal.[37]

Divergences of opinion meant that the slender resources were being deployed in uncertain fashion. Churchill remained unsatisfied. So too did Brooke. In addition, the GOC Southern Command believed that the main German thrust would come across the Channel, not (as the COS and Churchill believed) across the North Sea against the east coast. Brooke, convinced that a major threat existed in his area, felt strong anxiety over the number of troops under his command. Late that evening, he received a telephone call from London with an invitation to lunch at Chequers; Ironside's chief of staff, Paget, would be present. Brooke declined to disrupt his hectic activity at Wilton and successfully suggested that Paget should come to see him instead. 'Had a long talk with him,' wrote Brooke. 'I rubbed into him the nakedness of this Command taken in relation to the new situation in western France.'[38]

'Certainly everything is as gloomy as can be,' noted Sir Alexander Cadogan in his diary. 'Probability is that Hitler will attempt invasion in next fortnight. As far as I can see, we are, after years of leisurely preparation, completely unprepared. We have simply got to die at our posts – a far better fate than capitulating to Hitler as these damned Frogs have done. But uncomfortable.'[39]

The enemy stepped closer to Brooke's weakly-defended command area. A Luftwaffe officer landed at Guernsey airport on 30 June, confirming that the Channel Islands were indeed demilitarised, and German occupation began. And, in the last days of June, German strategic plans were beginning to shuffle slowly forward. Hitler reached the 'Tannenberg' HQ in the Black Forest on 30 June. Dino Alfieri, Italian Ambassador at Berlin, telephoned Ciano in Rome to inform him that 'Hitler is going through one of his periods of isolation which, with him, precede the making of great decisions.'[40] The Fuehrer was in fact torn between total war with Britain and the hope that British politicians might still accept peace, even though the latter now seemed highly unlikely. Baron von Weizsäcker, State Secretary of the German Foreign Office, told Halder on 30 June that there was 'no concrete basis for any peace treaty...Britain will probably need one more demonstration of our military strength before she gives in and leaves us a free hand in eastern Europe.' Both the German military chiefs and the German Foreign Office impatiently awaited some decisive utterance from the Fuehrer's HQ in the secluded forest. In Rome, after a further report from Alfieri concerning Hitler, Ciano noted: 'I am convinced that there is something brewing in that fellow's mind, and that certainly no new decision has yet been taken. There is no longer that impressive tone of assurance which was apparent when Hitler spoke of breaking through the Maginot Line. Now he is considering many alternatives and is raising doubts which account for his restlessness.'[41]

In his pine-scented room at Tannenberg, Hitler studied a document drafted by Jodl, his personal adviser on military operations. The paper was titled 'The Continuation of the War against England'. German victory was only a matter of time, claimed Jodl, and this inevitability made it possible to choose a strategy which would economise forces. The aim should be to attack the RAF and the industry upon which it depended; simultaneous with these operations should be strikes against the flow of imports both at sea and in the ports, and on supply depots. Jodl declared: 'Linked with propaganda and periodic terror attacks, announced as reprisals, this increasing weakening of the system of food supply will paralyse and finally break the will of the people to resist, and thereby force the Government to capitulate.' A landing operation should only be attempted after air supremacy had been obtained; this would 'finish off a country economically paralysed and practically incapable of fighting in the air, if this is still necessary.' At least thirty divisions would be needed, and the necessary conditions for the landing

37

would not be attainable before the end of August.[42] But while Hitler considered this persuasive paper on 30 June and continued to hesitate, his second-in-command took a decision which threatened to force the Fuehrer's hand. Goering issued his 'General Direction for the Operation of the Luftwaffe against England'. As stated in Jodl's memorandum, the primary target would be the RAF, its ground organisation, and the industry feeding it. 'Acting in concert, the Luftflotten [Air Fleets] are to operate all out. Their formations, once lined up, are to be launched against defined groups of targets.' Attacks would also be directed against British shipping and ports.[43]

On 1 July, as Goering's staff worked out the details of this offensive, and as Halder embarked enthusiastically on more specific plans for invasion, in London the Air Secretary informed the War Cabinet of desperate steps being taken to find more pilots for RAF Fighter Command. Sir Archibald Sinclair said that training courses had been shortened, the capacity of training units increased, pilots transferred from the Fleet Air Arm and from non-operational units. Arrangements were in hand for training pilots of other Allied nations. Sinclair warned that more reliance must be placed on training facilities overseas, as the course of the war had made the UK less suitable.[44]

Britain's situation as July opened was only slightly improved from the position at the beginning of June. Defence plans in general still suffered from confusion and internal disagreements. With the army, the basic conflict was between static versus mobile defence; the Prime Minister, supporting the latter, now found a highly voluble ally in the field. On Tuesday 2 July, Churchill met Montgomery for the first time. The two men talked in the elegant Royal Albion Hotel, Brighton; Montgomery refused an alcoholic drink and proceeded to tell the Prime Minister his problems. 'The main thing which seemed curious to me was that my division was immobile. It was the only fully equipped division in England, the only division fit to fight any enemy anywhere. And here we were in a static role, ordered to dig in on the south coast. Some other troops should take on my task; my division should be given buses, and be held in mobile reserve with a counter-attack role. Why was I left immobile?' Montgomery claimed afterwards that his idea for buses seemed to appeal to Churchill like 'the cat's whiskers'.[45]

The other fundamental issue upon which Britain's defence rested was the question of the most likely target for a German landing. Churchill agreed with the COS: the east coast should be most heavily defended. But on 2 July Brooke sent a memorandum to GHQ Home Forces

38

objecting to the present policy. 'While admitting that from the German point of view it would probably be easier to organise and launch an attack from ports in Scandinavia and on the North Sea littoral, I consider that the threat to the south-west of England is as great, if not greater, than any of the northern portions of our east coast. At the present time I understand that six divisions are allotted to the Northern Command, whilst only three to the Southern ... This is not sufficient.'[46] GHQ replied that Brooke's comparison of the vulnerability of the south-west versus the northern east coast omitted three factors: '(i) The comparative ease of reaching London and the important industrial areas from East Anglia compared with the difficulties of an advance from the south-west. (ii) The fact that ... the Germans cannot yet force the Straits of Dover with large ships. (iii) The air factor.' Brooke's request for more troops was refused; he nevertheless continued to seek reinforcements.[47]

At least the army might have a while longer before the German invasion attempt could be launched. Respite for the RAF was likely to be far shorter. On 1 July the number of serviceable aircraft in Fighter Command totalled 602, an increase of 189 since 3 June.[48] These were organised in three groups: No. 13 Group for Scotland and North England, No. 12 covering the Midlands and East Anglia, and No. 11 south of London. A fourth group, No. 10, would later be formed for south-west England. Close cooperation between them and with Dowding's HQ at Bentley Prior, was clearly essential. Yet this cooperation would be hindered by disagreements among the senior commanders. Dowding was by no means an easy person to work with: nick-named 'Stuffy', he was austere and seemed unapproachable. Keith Park, No. 11 Group Commander, had previously worked at Fighter Command close to Dowding, and enjoyed a good relationship with him; he agreed with Dowding on most tactical aspects of Fighter Command operations. Park's group was likely to be at the forefront of the fighting. But he would need absolute support from No. 12 Group north of London, and his neighbouring commander, Trafford Leigh-Mallory, proved unsympathetic to Dowding's direction. Tactical methods did indeed have definite drawbacks. Originating from peacetime, they seemed based more on display formations for exhibition flying than on battle conditions: aircraft flew close together and pilots had to spend too much time keeping watch on their distance from colleagues, rather than searching the skies for the enemy. Dowding later admitted: 'I agree that at the beginning of the war we paid too much attention to close formation... There was tight wing-tip to wing-tip flying, with everybody looking round to keep the correct distance from his neighbour and that sort of thing... Circumstances forced us to relax that.'[49]

Beyond these problems of formation tactics, wider disagreements would emerge over the deployment of squadrons: these could either be sent up singly, as Dowding directed, and hence obtain a wider coverage, or as 'Big Wings', as Leigh-Mallory later advocated. The latter would enable RAF interceptions to be made at greater strength, but opponents argued that this concentration in the air would leave too few squadrons available for other tasks – specifically, airfield coverage. The argument would simmer throughout the Battle of Britain. Controversy would threaten to disrupt the vital cooperation needed between 11 and 12 Groups and, as conflict approached, Fighter Command squadrons as a whole were often raw and inexperienced for the task in hand.

Nor was the Royal Navy spared internal disagreements. By 1 July the Home Fleet situation showed only a marginal improvement since the beginning of June; fear that the French fleet might fall into German possession had led to a strong force being despatched to Gibraltar, and this left just four capital ships at Scapa Flow – *Nelson*, *Rodney*, *Renown*, *Repulse* – plus the *Barham* at Liverpool. Only three cruisers and nine destroyers were at Scapa, and two cruisers at Rosyth. Moreover, local striking forces to protect likely landing areas were extremely weak: only nineteen destroyers were deployed at Humber, Harwich and Sheerness, where the COS considered the strength should total at least forty. Dover and Portsmouth had five destroyers each. The Admiralty believed that the *Nelson* and *Rodney* should move south to Rosyth from Scapa, to be within easier reach of a German invasion fleet, yet Admiral Sir Charles Forbes, C-in-C Home Fleet, virtually refused. He preferred to keep the bulk of his capital strength in the greater safety of Scapa Flow, which was also nearer the convoy routes in the North-West Approaches, and he expressed concern at the rising losses of transport shipping owing to the diversion of convoy escort vessels to invasion waters; he believed that an enemy invasion attempt was not feasible until the Germans had acquired necessary air supremacy, and a move to the south would therefore be premature. At the beginning of July a situation of virtual stalemate existed between the Admiralty and the stubborn Admiral.[50]

'Most of the grumbling,' claimed *The Times* on 1 July, 'is about insufficient direction.' The air of uncertainty still spread over the country, from the politicians at Westminster and the officials in Whitehall, to the men and women in the street. No one could judge when or how, or even if, the German onslaught would come. If German plans had been previously prepared as part of an efficient forward programme, this would have been the moment of Hitler's greatest opportunity to defeat Britain through direct assault on her shores. Britain, her forces still disorganised and weak, vastly outnumbered by the enemy, her plans still confused, might have succumbed to a German invasion force launched without regard to cost.

Fighter Command Intelligence issued a new assessment on Monday 1 July. 'There are indications that a sea and airborne expedition is in an advanced stage of preparation.'[51] At 6.40 pm next day a signal flashed from GHQ Home Forces to all army commands. 'Parachutists have been captured in Reading area. All troops and local LDV to be warned that parachutists are expected.'[52]

Deep in the Black Forest, Hitler had come to a decision. During 2 July the OKW issued a top-secret directive. 'The Fuehrer and Supreme Commander has decided: That a landing in England is possible, providing that air superiority can be attained and certain other necessary conditions fulfilled. The date of commencement is still undecided. All preparations to be begun immediately.'[53]

✒

CHAPTER FOUR

Final Days

3–9 July

Hitler still had doubts, and his reservations would rob him of possible victory. Rather than an immediate all-out blow, he felt air supremacy must precede a seaborne invasion, and the concluding passage of his 2 July directive stressed: 'All preparations must be undertaken on the basis that the invasion is still only a plan, and has not yet been decided upon.' Yet the German air, army and naval staffs in Berlin now had something more definite upon which to work.

Simultaneous with this order from Hitler, the invasion scare continued to ripple through London. The COS met at 10.15 am on Wednesday 3 July, to hear a disturbing assessment from Major-General F. G. Beaumont-Nesbitt, Director of Intelligence at the War Office. The previous day's reports of enemy parachutists in the Reading area had been proved false, but Beaumont-Nesbitt commented: 'There was a considerable body of evidence which pointed to an invasion of this country at an early date.' These indications included an increase of German troops in south Norway, among them large numbers of parachutists; Norwegian craft of all types had recently been requisitioned and armed. 'We could not hope to get any long warning of an invasion from this quarter.' In addition, troops were concentrating in Denmark and large amounts of shipping were accumulating in Stettin and other Baltic ports. Troop concentrations were also reported in Holland, and two parachute regiments had been moved to Belgium together with special assault detachments drawn from units who had fought especially well in France. Beaumont-Nesbitt continued: 'A ceremonial parade in Paris, which had been fixed for 7 July, had been postponed until after 10 July. It was possible that Hitler was proposing to make his ceremonial entry

42

into Paris on this occasion and would then declare his intention of carrying the war into this country. The postponement of the date proposed indicated that the German measures were not quite ready.' The COS agreed that although they had previously believed an invasion would not be attempted until a 'large measure' of air superiority had been obtained by the Luftwaffe, 'it was possible that the enemy would throw in the whole of the resources at his command and hope to get ashore considerable numbers of troops in the general confusion.'[1]

A Fighter Command Intelligence summary issued that Wednesday morning underlined Beaumont-Nesbitt's warning. 'Enemy reconnaissance has shown a marked increase... Considerable movement of transport aircraft from Germany continued to be made to Antwerp and to a point south of Rouen... There is evidence that surface craft suitable for assisting landing parties have been prepared.'[2] Members of the War Cabinet assembled at 10 Downing Street at 11.30 am. Ministers had before them a COS memorandum referring to a War Cabinet decision on 27 June, which had postponed compulsory evacuation from nineteen east coast towns. The COS now asked for this decision to be reversed 'in the light of the indications that major operations against this country, either by invasion or by air attack, might now start.' Sir Cyril Newall, CoAS, and Dill, CIGS, stressed the danger of delaying the move until too late. But Sir John Anderson, Home Secretary, argued that 'whole families would have to be billeted...If invasion did not follow a difficult situation might ensue. Public opinion was already somewhat jumpy, and would become more so... Further, people on other parts of the coast would ask why they also were not being evacuated.' The War Cabinet agreed to adhere to the 27 June decision. But Churchill returned to this question of public morale later in the meeting: he was clearly disturbed by the reference to the 'jumpy' nature of public feeling, and he proposed to issue a letter to the fighting services and civilian departments. This communication was circulated later in the day.

'On what may be the eve of an attempted invasion or battle for our native land, the Prime Minister desires to impress upon all persons holding responsible positions... their duty to maintain a spirit of alert and confident energy... There are no grounds for supposing that more German troops can be landed in this country, either from the air or across the sea, than can be destroyed or captured... The Prime Minister expects HM servants in high places to set an example of steadiness and resolution... They should not hesitate to report, or if necessary remove, any officers or officials who are found to be consciously exercising a disturbing or depressing influence and whose talk is calculated to spread alarm and despondence.'[3]

Fears of invasion resulted in another decision taken at the 11.30 am War Cabinet meeting. Churchill believed that Bomber Command aircraft should now concentrate to a greater extent on ports from which the enemy might launch their attack, rather than on oil refineries, airfields and communications as laid down under the existing policy dated 20 June. The Chief of the Air Staff opposed such a switch. He said that invasion would constitute a serious danger only if the RAF had first been defeated, and that this defeat could only take place at the hands of the German air force. The main priority should therefore continue to be the attempt to reduce Luftwaffe efficiency by bombing such targets as aircraft factories, airfields and fuel supplies. Churchill argued that 'the coming week might well be so critical from the point of view of invasion that it justified transferring emphasis to the bombing of German ports.' The War Cabinet agreed.

Following this decision the Air Ministry gave formal new directions to Bomber Command to operate with Coastal Command against enemy ports and shipping. Such cooperation had of course already existed although on informal lines. In fact Coastal Command would continue to carry the main role in the RAF's anti-invasion activities, through observing enemy preparations, other reconnaissance and photographic flights, and even with bombing raids on its own account. Between mid-June and the end of August over 300 Coastal Command sorties were flown by aircraft of the Photographic Reconnaissance Unit. The thousands of photographs which resulted from these flights were studied with minute care for changes in the enemy build-up.

Meanwhile Bomber Command itself remained split between anti-Luftwaffe and anti-invasion roles, with a continuing imbalance towards the former. During July and August the Command dropped about 468 tons of bombs on Luftwaffe airfields and 1454 on German industrial targets and communications, compared with only about sixty-six tons on barges and shipping. Coastal Command, with its much smaller bombing ability, dropped about fifty-eight tons on dockyards, shipping, coastal airfields and invasion fuel-dumps.[4]

The Defence Committee met at 10 Downing Street shortly before midnight on 3 July, and again the invasion scare stood at the top of the agenda, Sir Cyril Newall reported the information given to his COS colleagues earlier in the day by Beaumont-Nesbitt. 'There was nothing that could be taken as definite evidence,' he added, 'but there were indications from a number of directions which pointed to the imminence of invasion which it would be unsafe to ignore.' Churchill asked for a detailed report to be prepared.[5]

At this moment of rising invasion fears Britain herself took the offensive – against her former ally. After long hours of War Cabinet discussion, it had been agreed to seize or destroy French warships to prevent them falling into German hands if no other course was possible. Early in the morning of 3 July, French warships at Plymouth and Portsmouth had been boarded; at 5.54 pm British vessels in the Western Mediterranean opened fire on the French fleet at Mers-el-Kebir. Negotiations, thankfully successful, opened with the French commander at Alexandria. Churchill, who had sat in the War Cabinet room throughout the afternoon in contact with the First Lord and First Sea Lord, believed this tragic episode underlined Britain's will to resist. 'It was made plain that the British War Cabinet feared nothing and would stop at nothing.'[6]

'It proves that the fighting spirit of His Britannic Majesty's fleet is quite alive,' commented Ciano in his diary next day. The Italian Foreign Minister had just received a report from Giuseppe Bastianini, recently Ambassador to London. 'Morale of the British is very high... Everybody – aristocracy, middle-class, and the common people – is embittered, tenacious and proud. Air and anti-aircraft preparations have been undertaken on a large scale, and are sufficient to repulse and greatly reduce the enemy offensive.' Ciano added: 'Hitler's indecision is thus explained.'[7] The Fuehrer's waverings were unsuspected in London. On 4 July the Joint Intelligence Sub-Committee completed its detailed report requested by Churchill at the Defence Committee meeting the previous night. This, titled 'Imminence of a German Invasion', repeated the JIC opinion that 'Germany's military superiority is such as to enable her to move in any direction she pleases with little or no warning.' The Intelligence experts then declared: 'We consider that large-scale raids on the British Isles involving all three arms may take place at any moment. A full-scale invasion is unlikely to take place before the middle of July.' The report included the item that the Luftwaffe in France 'is in process of being reorganised and regrouped and this process is nearing completion. Dive bombers are being concentrated in Belgium and north-east France.'This report was marked A-1 in terms of reliability.[8] The Air Ministry reached a similar conclusion in its situation report for the week ending 4 July. 'It is apparent that the main aim of the GAF High Command is as was expected, namely to build up and consolidate all formations after the damage and wastage which they had suffered in the Battle for France, and to complete the re-equipment of certain bomber units.' Technical overhauls would probably be finished by about 15 July.[9]

Only a few hours later on 4 July, enemy dive-bombers from Belgium and bases in north-east France initiated a new phase in the air war against Britain. Two *Gruppen* roughly equivalent to the RAF's Wings, of *Stukageschwader* 2 hurtled on to Atlantic convoy OA 178 off Portland. The Junkers eighty-seven 'Stuka' dive-bombers sank four vessels totalling 15,856 tons, including the 5582-ton auxiliary flak ship *Foyle Bank*. Nine other vessels were damaged. Goering had begun his offensive against British shipping in the Channel area; Dowding would soon find his precious fighter strength increasingly stretched by the need to provide convoy cover.

During the afternoon Churchill appeared at the House of Commons to explain his policy of attacking Britain's former friends, the French, and to bolster British morale. 'I leave the judgment of our action, with confidence, to Parliament. I leave it to the nation, and I leave it to the United States. I leave it to the world and history.' Members of Parliament listened to his speech in total silence. Until now the Conservative Party had treated Churchill with reserve – his warmest support had come from the Labour benches – and he awaited their reaction with some apprehension. Churchill's fears were unfounded; he wrote later: 'At the end there occurred a scene unique in my experience.' The whole House erupted in applause. Among those present was Harold Nicolson. 'The House is at first saddened by this odious attack,' he wrote in his diary, 'but is fortified by Winston's speech. The grande finale ends in ovation with Winston sitting there with tears pouring down his cheeks.'[10] Churchill hurried back to 10 Downing Street. In characteristic fashion he turned from broad strategic subjects to painstaking detail. A minute to Ismay asked: 'What is being done to encourage and assist the people living in threatened sea-ports to make suitable shelters for themselves in which they could remain during an invasion?'[11]

Nor did the Prime Minister overlook possible implications of the attack on the convoy off Portland. Early next morning, 5 July, he sent a probing minute to the Naval Staff. 'Could you let me know on one sheet of paper what arrangements you are making about the Channel convoys?... The attacks on the convoy yesterday were very serious and I should like to be assured this morning that the situation is in hand

and that the Air is contributing effectively.'[12] Churchill insisted Fighter Command should protect shipping in the Channel to the maximum extent; Dowding would soon insist that such a policy could be disastrous. Meanwhile, the Fighter Command chief was troubled by a totally different matter. He was scheduled to retire from the RAF on 14 July, barely ten days away, yet had still to receive the name of his successor and confirmation that he actually would depart. Now, in the midst of the invasion fear, he could tolerate the situation no longer: he telephoned the Chief of the Air Staff demanding some decision. Newall replied almost immediately, 'I am writing to ask if you will again defer your retirement...I would be very glad if you would continue in your appointment as AOC-in-C until the end of October.' Dowding protested over the incompetent handling of the affair, but agreed to stay.[13]

Invasion evidence continued to accumulate, with Fighter Command Intelligence reporting: 'Large-scale disembarkation was practised recently at Memel. Forty vessels... took part.'[14] During 5 July, British citizens were called upon to surrender fireworks 'capable of being used for giving visible signals to the enemy'. The redoubtable Lord Beaverbrook, Minister of Aircraft Production, issued a stirring appeal. 'Women of Britain, give us your aluminium. We want it and we want it now... We will turn your pots and pans into Spitfires and Hurricanes, Blenheims and Wellingtons.' The surrender of kitchen utensils and other articles, the aluminium content of which was small, was of doubtful military value, but psychologically the appeal was important. So too were similar calls from the Ministry of Supply: huge heaps of iron railings and gates were being accumulated and sorted out. Harold Macmillan, then Parliamentary Secretary at the Supply Ministry, described this sorting process. 'There was an old gentleman with a white beard, who was a great expert...It was quite a thrilling experience. He distinguished, for instance, the types, content and periods of iron railings with the reverence and knowledge of an art critic lecturing about drawings or paintings.'[15] The British people, young and old, were constantly ordered to make new sacrifices: on 6 July a Defence Regulation forbade 'any person, other than a servant of His Majesty' to fly a kite or a balloon.[16]

On the same day a signal from GHQ Home Forces informed Army Commands of the Admiralty's appreciation of most likely invasion dates. These, working on the assumption that the best time for a seaborne landing would be when high water occurred near dawn, with no moon, suggested any day after 8 July for the east coast and a period after the 11th for the south.[17]

For the past week Hitler had been in holiday mood. During his stay in the Black Forest he took leave from war; early each morning he drove off for sight-seeing excursions. He paid minimum attention to strategic planning and his staff enjoyed themselves at the two nearby inns, sampling the local brew of iced punch and wild strawberries. Virtually the only task which Hitler set himself concerned a victory speech which he intended to deliver to the Reichstag. And despite his directive of 2 July, Hitler still clung to the hope that Britain would accept Germany's overwhelmingly dominating position. Now, on 6 July, Hitler returned to Berlin. Crowds cheered his arrival; flowers fluttered on to his sedan and a massed girls' choir sang the popular song of the day – '*Wir fahren gegen Engeland*', 'We're going over to England'. Hitler drove to his Chancellery, studied the latest drawings prepared by Speer for the beautification of his capital, and examined the latest assessment of the situation regarding Britain. His enemy showed no signs of submission; the Royal Navy's action against the French Fleet displayed a foolish determination to resist. Yet Hitler could not bring himself to believe a campaign against Britain was unavoidable; indecision continued. Next day Ciano arrived in Berlin and immediately conferred with the Fuehrer. 'He is rather inclined to continue the struggle and to unleash a storm of wrath and of steel upon the British. But the final decision has not been reached and it is for this reason that he is delaying his speech [to the Reichstag], of which, as he himself put it, he wants to weigh every word... He is calm and reserved, very reserved for a German who has won.'[18] The Italian Foreign Minister then talked with Keitel, OKW chief, who believed a landing would be possible, but it was 'an extremely difficult operation, which must be approached with the utmost caution, in view of the fact that the intelligence available on the military preparedness of the island and on the coastal defences were meagre and not very reliable.' Keitel considered it would be easier, and also necessary, to launch a large-scale attack on Britain's airfields, factories and principal communication centres. 'But it must be borne in mind that the British air force is at present extremely efficient.'[19]

But next day signs were becoming apparent in London of the strain on the RAF caused by convoy protection. Between 9 am and 6 pm on this Monday – the daily period soon dubbed by pilots as 'office hours' – Fighter Command flew over 300 sorties, equivalent to the number flown each day during Dunkirk. Increased German attention to the con-

48

voys had already cost fifteen Fighter Command aircraft and twelve pilots since 29 June. Dowding warned the Air Ministry that the escort burden might become unbearable if the Luftwaffe also increased attacks on inland targets.[20]

For many young Fighter Command pilots these convoy escort duties in early July provided the first taste of aerial combat. Among those in action on the 8th was Pilot Officer Dowding, son of the Fighter Command chief. He and two other pilots from No. 74 'Tiger' Squadron had taken off from Manston before lunch to undertake a Channel patrol, during which the three pilots destroyed a Heinkel. Dowding's squadron shot down another German aircraft, an Me 109, during the afternoon.[21] Another young pilot now gaining vital experience was David Crook, whose 609 Squadron had been moved south-west to the Salisbury area. At 6.30 pm on Tuesday 9 July he and two other squadron members took off in their Spitfires to patrol the Weymouth region. Crook saw the enemy for the first time – at least nine Me 110s were diving down from behind. He shouted a warning to the others over his radio, but his inexperienced friends had left their R/T sets switched to 'transmit' instead of 'receive'. One was shot down in a flurry of enemy aircraft; the other barely escaped. Crook managed to open fire at close range and he now witnessed the deadly power of his Spitfire's eight ·303-inch Browning machine-guns, able to pump out 1350 rounds per gun per minute.

'Even in the heat of the moment I well remember my amazement at the shattering effect of my fire. Pieces flew off his fuselage and cockpit covering, a stream of smoke appeared from the engine and a moment later a great sheet of flame licked out from the engine cowling and he dived vertically. The flames enveloped the whole machine and he went straight down, apparently quite slowly, for about 5000 feet, till he was just a shapeless burning mass of wreckage. Absolutely fascinated by the sight, I followed him down and saw him hit the sea with a great burst of white foam ... I had often wondered what would be my feelings when killing somebody like this, and especially when seeing them go down in flames. I was rather surprised to reflect afterwards that my own feeling had been one of considerable elation – and a sort of bewildered surprise because it had all been so easy.'

Crook returned to base and made 'a perfectly bloody' landing. He found himself shaking, his voice unsteady, 'due, I suppose, to a fairly even mixture of fright, intense excitement, and a sort of reckless exhilaration.' These feelings would soon become commonplace, as would the emotion he felt when he went to his room which he had shared with the friend lost in the morning's dog-fight. 'Everything was just the same as Peter and I had left it ... His towel was still in the window where he had thrown it during our hurried dressing.'[22]

Hitler drafted and re-drafted the speech in which he planned to announce his intentions regarding Britain. His service planners continued their invasion preparations, as specified in the 2 July pronouncement. These preliminary moves would soon be further complicated by renewed disagreement between the German navy and army staffs. On 9 July the Naval Staff issued a memorandum stating that the most suitable invasion area lay somewhere between North Foreland and the western tip of the Isle of Wight. The Army Staff immediately took this to mean that plans should be made for landing along this entire stretch, from at least Ramsgate to Lyme Bay; the Navy, on the other hand, envisaged a narrower target within the region mentioned in their memorandum. Both staffs, however, agreed on one important point: the invasion should be directed against southern England, contrary to the view of British planners that the east coast was most menaced.[23]

In London, grumbles arose over the latest Government announcements. Tea would now be rationed. The US journalist Drew Middleton commented: 'A good part of the conversation was devoted to what "my old woman" had said about the Government as a result.' Middleton added: 'This was a period when the English habit of considering war as a series of small, personal affronts tried the nerves of foreigners in their midst.'[24] The War Cabinet met at noon to discuss the role of the public in the event of invasion. Dill pointed out that: 'It was essential to decide whether defence arrangements should include active resistance by the civil population.' Ironside believed that fighting should be left to the soldiers, and the War Cabinet agreed. 'Armed civilians acting independently might well upset the plans of a military commander by their unexpected and unorganised activities.' British Ministers then received some indication of the indecision in Berlin. A telegram had been received from the Ambassador in Switzerland, giving an account of talks which Dr Karl Burckhardt, acting President of the Red Cross, had had in the German capital. Burckhardt had discussed the situation with leading Germans, including Weiszäcker, and was informed that Hitler was hesitating before attacking England: he still hoped for a 'working arrangement' with the British Empire. German military chiefs were confident of their ability to defeat Britain, but 'they realise that it might involve greater sacrifices than had the defeat of the French.'[25]

Even more than usual in times of war, the opposing sides were groping in the dark. The German OKW complained of the meagreness and unreliability of intelligence available on British coastal defences; British intelligence sources still indicated increased German activity, yet Hitler, normally so decisive, seemed to be hesitating. Almost since Dunkirk there had been the peculiar waiting atmosphere. Within hours, this would end. Next day, 10 July, would be the date used by future historians to mark the official opening of the Battle of Britain.

CHAPTER FIVE

The First Phase

10–19 July

Thick cloud obscured dawn on Wednesday 10 July. Soon after 3.30 am, heavy rain was sweeping over much of England, brought by a low-pressure front from the North Atlantic. Sea winds broke some of the cloud cover over the Channel, swirling the cumulus up into towers, 10,000 feet high, but squally showers thrashed on to the sea beneath the lower banks of stratus. In southern England, pilots clustered in dispersal huts on forward airfields. Spitfires and Hurricanes had already been checked; each pilot had examined petrol levels and turned on the fuel, noted that the mixture control was on 'rich' and the airscrew in fine pitch, set the elevator trim, opened the radiator, switched on the oxygen, reflector sights and camera gun, checked the gun system air pressure. Now the pilots sat in their bulky Mae Wests around the stoves in the sheds, waiting for the telephone from control to ring. Across the Channel the German pilots also readied their machines and waited. They grumbled about the weather, and the thick mud which clogged their boots and which turned runways into quagmires.

But further up the Luftwaffe chain, action was being taken on Goering's directive of 30 June ordering an intensified offensive against the RAF and against supply convoys. Air raids during previous days, like that off Portland on 4 July, had marked the preliminary moves in this policy. Now the main effort would begin. Broken clouds provided protection for the Luftwaffe reconnaissance aircraft: soon after dawn a Spitfire patrolling from Coltishall managed to spot one such enemy aircraft near Yarmouth; the British pilot opened fire, but the German slipped into cover. At 3.45 am No. 74 Squadron Spitfires took off from Manston on dawn patrol: their leader, Flight Lieutenant Measures, sighted a large enemy formation over the Channel and the eight 'Tiger' pilots immediately dived into the attack. Flight-Lieutenant Mungo Park gained the first victim, shooting down a Dornier in a three-second burst, and five other Dorniers and Me 109s were damaged. So many machines were milling about that collisions were inevitable: two Messerschmitts dived earthwards, spinning viciously with their wings buckled upwards.[1] The 'Tiger' flight returned in victory to Manston for early breakfast.

At that moment a convoy was proceeding south off Yarmouth under Fighter Command escort, and events began to quicken. By 10 am the convoy had reached a point off Lowestoft, where Hurricane escorts spotted and drove off two German bombers. At noon an unescorted convoy in the same area came under attack from a further pair of German bombers, and suffered one vessel sunk. Another group of vessels was sailing off Margate: this attracted two more German bombers, escorted by fighters, which were successfully engaged by about twenty British aircraft from No. 11 Group forward airfields.[2] Still the enemy came. Spitfires from No. 43 Squadron, on their second patrol of the day, met about thirty Me 109s near Margate and once more plunged into the attack. The leader of the 'Tiger' Red Section picked out the leader of the enemy formation and opened fire at 300 yards, closing to 50 yards. His bullets literally tore the Messerschmitt to bits. 'It just dropped out of the sky,' he said later. 'What a thrilling sight!' Two more enemy aircraft were destroyed and others damaged.[3]

Shortly after 1 pm the telephone rang in the converted bus standing by the Cape Gris Nez airfield; the battered vehicle served as command post for Colonel Johannes Fink, the Luftwaffe 'Channel Zone Bomber Commander'. Fink received his orders and immediately contacted subordinate fighter and bomber *Gruppen* at Arras and St Omer. Soon afterwards seventy German aircraft were moving over the French coast and out above the Channel: twenty Dornier 17 bombers were escorted by one Me 109 squadron at close range and by another two squadrons flying above at heights up to 6000 feet. From another direction flew thirty Me 110s. At 1.30 pm a Channel convoy was steaming south-west through the Straits of Dover, escorted by six Hurricanes from No. 32 Squadron, Biggin Hill. At about the same time several radar stations plotted the enemy aircraft over the Calais area and the information was immediately transmitted to Park's No. 11 Group HQ, Uxbridge: four more fighter squadrons were scrambled – No. 56 from Manston, No. 111 from Croydon, No. 64 from Kenley and No. 74 from

53

Hornchurch. By 1.45 pm these squadrons were heading towards Dover.

The German aircraft were fast approaching the convoy not far from the coast. Captain Hannes Trautloft, commanding the escorting Me 109s, sighted the opposing escort of six Hurricanes, first three, then all six as they emerged from cloud. Simultaneously, these British pilots located the invaders; Lieutenant G. G. R. Bulmer, on loan from the Fleet Air Arm, reported: 'Waves of enemy bombers coming from direction of France in boxes of six.' For a moment the Hurricanes kept their altitude, watching the enemy fighters above for the first signs of a diving attack. Trautloft also held his hand: to engage the British escort might take his protective force away from the Dorniers, leaving the bombers a naked target for British reinforcements. Perhaps three minutes dragged by, during which six Fighter Command Hurricanes confronted seventy Luftwaffe aircraft.

Then tiny specks appeared from the cloud to the north: help from the scrambled 11 Group Hurricanes and Spitfires was arriving. 'Suddenly the sky was full of British fighters,' reported Trautloft later. 'Today we were going to be in for a tough time.' British odds had improved to thirty-two against seventy enemy fighters and bombers; the Fighter Command squadrons spiralled up to 15,000 feet to gain superior altitude, then peeled into the attack. The thirty Me 110s immediately curved into a defensive circle, each protecting the tail of the other; this only left Trautloft's twenty Me 109s to defend the Dorniers. Down flashed the Hurricanes and Spitfires, firing sudden, sharp bursts. Perhaps three Me 109s were destroyed in this assault, but other enemy aircraft dropped in pursuit of the British, and in a steep dive the heavier Me 109 had the advantage. First-Lieutenant Walter Oesau, one of the most successful Luftwaffe fighters, shot down two opponents in about two minutes; he chased after a third, only to see it crash at full speed into another German aircraft. Flight-Sergeant Dau destroyed a Spitfire, then turned sharply towards a Hurricane. The latter, piloted by Sergeant A. G. Page of No. 56 Squadron, flew directly at him. Both refused to swerve; both began to fire at the same moment. Dau's bullets streaked just below Page's aircraft, curving away into space; Page proved more accurate. The two aircraft missed each other at a distance of under ten feet, but then Dau felt his Messerschmitt shudder violently and a piece of one wing suddenly whipped away. His engine started to seize, white glycol coolant streaming behind; the temperature in his cramped cockpit soared to 120 degrees. 'The whole cockpit stank of burnt insula-

54

tion,' declared Dau. 'But I managed to stretch my glide to the coast, then made a belly-landing close to Boulogne. As I jumped out the machine was on fire, and within seconds ammunition and fuel went up with a bang.' Another Me 109 crash-landed near Calais. Flight Lieutenant Measures raced over the opposite coast, near Dover: he claimed that he outpaced six Luftwaffe fighters hanging on his tail.

BBC reporter Charles Gardner was standing by his car on the beach near Dover, shouting into his recording apparatus as dogfights took place above him; listeners could hear the stuttering of the guns. 'There's one coming down in flames – there's somebody hit a German – and he's coming down – there's a long streak ... Oh boy I've never seen anything so good as this – the RAF fighters have really got these boys taped!' By 2 pm the engagement had ended. A total of four Luftwaffe aircraft were lost and five British. One small vessel in the convoy had been sunk.[4]

Smaller-scale actions were being fought elsewhere along the coast. Considerable numbers of bombers were reported off Portland, and five Spitfires from 609 Squadron were scrambled to intercept. 'They saw the enemy while they were still some distance away,' wrote David Crook, absent from his squadron that day. 'The Spitfires were outnumbered by ridiculous odds, but Pip, who had never hesitated for one second at rugger or anything else in his life, did not hesitate now in this last and greatest moment of all.' The section leader detached two aircraft to try and hold off enemy fighters, which the British pilots estimated at about twenty, while he led the other two aircraft against the enemy bombers below. 'It was hopeless from the very start. The Messerschmitts dived down on top of our small formation and everybody was separated immediately.' Two pilots of 609 Squadron were killed including Pip Barran, the section leader; two enemy aircraft were claimed destroyed.[5]

Further west, a single German aircraft from Brittany bombed Falmouth, sinking one 6000-ton ship and setting two others alight. The Luftwaffe pilot escaped interception. The day's fighting in fact underlined the problem of responding with sufficient speed to reinforce convoy protection: no matter how rapidly they converged, the Fighter Command aircraft found the Luftwaffe there before them. The alternative was to increase standing patrols over the Channel, causing additional strain on Dowding's resources – precisely the German intention.

'This afternoon one of the greatest air battles of the war has been going on,' announced Sir Edward Grigg, Parliamentary Secretary at the Ministry of Information, in the House of Commons. 'At this moment it may be that bombers are over many of our towns. Tonight thousands of our soldiers will be on the alert waiting for an attack which may come in several places at dawn.' Grigg's statement, combined with reports of the day's aerial combat and a decision to stop all leave for those in the Home commands, immediately led to a renewed invasion scare throughout the country. Members of the public reported para-troop sightings and rumours multiplied. During the evening the Information Ministry was obliged to issue a statement declaring that despite these reports from the public, 'often accompanied by vivid and precise details', no enemy had yet descended.[6]

During the day Hitler ordered that all available artillery should be gathered as soon as possible, to provide frontal and flanking fire for an invasion; gun emplacements must be constructed along the Channel coast between Calais, Cape Gris Nez and Boulogne. Hitler therefore believed that if the invasion attempt were made, it should be against the British south coast. Yet he continued to hesitate. He had still to deliver his speech to the Reichstag and now, during the evening of 10 July, he again left Berlin, this time motoring to his 'Eagle's Nest' – his mountain retreat of Berghof near Berchtesgaden.

'It appears probable,' declared a British naval staff memorandum that Wednesday, 'that a total of some 100,000 men might reach these shores without being intercepted by naval forces.' The Admiralty, like the War Office, still believed that the primary German targets would be on the British east coast: of a possible 100,000-man force, up to 72,000 might be directed against this coastline, compared with 25,000 against the south with the remainder elsewhere. The naval staff considered that the Germans would avoid the south, in view of the increased likelihood of detection. But the memorandum added that if the Germans landed, either on the east or south, they would find that subsequent mainten-ance of the assault would be virtually impossible; the whole operation would therefore be 'a most hazardous undertaking'.[7]

Admiral Erich Raeder wholeheartedly agreed. The German naval chief had been summoned with other service leaders to confer with Hitler at Berghof; Raeder arrived on 11 July, before his colleagues, and immediately pressed his objections on the Fuehrer whom he found in a subdued mood. Hitler asked Raeder for his opinion of the planned address to the Reichstag – did the Admiral believe it would be effective? Raeder believed so, but added that the speech should be preceded by

56

a concentrated bombing attack on Britain. He was anxious for an intensified Luftwaffe offensive yet displayed extreme caution over a full invasion. Hitler apparently agreed that air supremacy was essential, and the Admiral noted 'the Fuehrer also views invasion as a last resort.' But the German army chiefs had still to arrive at Berghof: Hitler, wavering badly, might be swung further back to the invasion point of view.[8] All those at the German summit agreed on one aspect: the need to obtain ascendancy over the RAF. Goering remained highly optimistic. While Raeder conferred with Hitler, the Luftwaffe chief repeated the orders contained in his preliminary directive of 30 June: 'It is envisaged that the enemy's air armaments industry and the enemy air force will be destroyed at the earliest possible moment.'[9] RAF Fighter Command would be lured from their bases by continuing the convoy attacks.

'Increased preparations for a possible invasion of the UK have been reported,' declared the War Cabinet weekly situation report on 11 July, 'and it is possible that in Norway preparations for a seaborne expedition of two to three divisions, including some AFVs, must now be nearly complete.' The résumé stated that Fighter Command had flown 1040 patrols during the previous week, involving 3275 sorties. A total of forty-four enemy aircraft were claimed shot down, plus thirty-five unconfirmed; RAF losses totalled eighteen.[10] On the same day the Air Ministry claimed that overall German air losses in the period 10 May–9 July numbered 2264 confirmed, 922 unconfirmed.[11] All these enemy casualty figures were later proved highly inaccurate but at the time they boosted morale. Men and women in the street still lived with the constant threat of invasion, and were still being instructed on correct behaviour should such an attempt be made. 'What do I do?' declared an official advertisement in *The Times*. 'I remember that this is the moment to act like a soldier. I do *not* get panicky. I *stay put*. I do *not* say "I must get out of here." I remember that fighting men must have clear roads...' 'Will Hitler invade?' pondered Cadogan in his diary. 'I personally doubt it, but would never say so. Every day he gives us is a gain.'[12]

The air war continued above the Channel. Soon after 7.30 am the radar chain had detected two enemy formations assembling around Cherbourg; at the same time a convoy was moving eastwards across Lyme Bay. Park therefore despatched three Hurricanes from 501 Squadron, Warmwell, to engage the enemy while six Spitfires from 609 Squadron moved to patrol the convoy. Approaching from Cherbourg were nine or ten Junkers 87 dive-bombers, with these Stukas escorted by about twenty Me 109s. Just before 8 am the three 501 Squadron

Hurricanes clashed with this enemy force of about thirty aircraft. One Hurricane, piloted by Sergeant Dixon, was shot into the sea in the first burst of fire, and the one-sided struggle lasted for about five minutes; the Stukas began screaming down to unleash their bombs on the convoy. The six 609 Squadron Spitfires arrived, to be attacked immediately by the Me 109s diving from a superior altitude: two Spitfires were lost. Despite the wide disparity in numbers the RAF intervention disrupted the attack on the convoy, and the enemy turned for home without any ships being sunk.

Thick cloud settled later in the morning and restricted air activity. Then, in the early afternoon, six Hurricanes of 601 (City of London) Squadron were ordered from Tangmere to intercept a German reconnaissance aircraft; during the flight the section leader received fresh instructions to deal with a German raid, apparently by only one aircraft, in the Portland area. The Hurricanes found themselves confronting fifteen Junkers 87s escorted by up to forty Me 110s. The British pilots had two advantages: they were flying higher than the enemy, and the sun lay behind them. They immediately dived at maximum speed, slicing between the bombers and their escort before the latter could react, and shooting down two Stukas. Soon afterwards extra aircraft arrived to bolster the slender RAF force, and Portland escaped serious damage. But the day was far from over for 601 Squadron. A few minutes before 6 pm radar stations again reported an enemy force approaching from Cherbourg, and aircraft from 601 Squadron sped out to sea to meet them. The Hurricanes located the enemy – twelve Heinkel 111 bombers and twelve Me 110s – and split into two sections. One dived to engage the bombers; the other climbed in an attempt to gain height on the fighters. The bombers managed to reach Portland, where they dropped about twenty bombs, but another squadron, this time from Tangmere, entered the engagement in support of the 601 Hurricanes; the weaving, twisting aerial combat spread into the midst of the Channel. A number of German aircraft were reported shot down; miraculously, the British pilots emerged unscathed.[13]

Cloudy weather spread over the Channel next day, 12 July, again reducing enemy activity, but patrolling by Fighter Command sections nevertheless continued.[14] The pattern of fighting had begun which would continue into August. For the pilots, it contained a mixture of tense waiting, sudden action, frustration and fear. Above all, the British found themselves heavily outnumbered each time they met the enemy on a full bombing raid. No. 609 Squadron operation record book reported: 'The utter futility of sending very small sections of fighters to cope with the intense enemy activity in the Portland area is bitterly resented by the pilots... The situation is keenly felt by this Squadron whose "score" of enemy aircraft is in too close a ratio to its own losses.'[15] Dowding has been credited with pursuing a deliberate policy of despatching only limited numbers of aircraft to encounter the enemy, thus preserving resources for the main battle – hence the gap in respective strengths during those July duels above the Channel. In fact the situation arose more through circumstance than through Dowding's direction. Too few fighters were sent up simply because too few fighters were available to cover all the tasks which Dowding considered vital; these included protection of radar stations and airfields in addition to convoy duties. The Germans seemed to have all the advantages. They could choose the direction and nature of their attack; they could despatch far greater numbers of aircraft. Even the weather always seemed in their favour. Broken cloud gave them cover, yet so too did bright days of sunshine when they could lurk in the sun to pounce unseen on the convoys; and, when the weather was too foul for flying, the Luftwaffe could rest whereas Fighter Command pilots still undertook tense patrols. Moreover, the days were long at this time of year, with darkness only bringing respite between 11 pm and 3.30 am.

But Fighter Command pilots were gaining in fighting wisdom. 'Each combat,' commented Squadron Leader H. S. Darley of 609 Squadron, 'produced its own lessons, the fault of the past having been the inability to draw the correct conclusions.' Sometimes his pilots had been too eager. 'I made it abundantly clear that I would not welcome personal "aces". As far as I was concerned, the only figures that counted were Squadron ones.'[16] One of his pilots, Crook, described the faulty tactics from which the Squadron suffered owing to inexperience. 'We had not yet learnt that it did not pay to go out to sea to meet the enemy, but to let him come to us. Also we did not realise the importance that height meant. Afterwards we used to get as high as possible before going into action. This is the whole secret of success.'[17] Although this soon seemed elementary, the tactic marked a major step forward. Even as late as 2 June, Fighter Command Intelligence had offered the following advice to pilots which completely ignored this vital principle. 'Tactics adopted by enemy fighters are to form into a tight circle, line astern, and individually half-roll out, and dive to the attack. Evasion of this manœuvre might be to execute a steep climbing turn towards the enemy thus steepening his dive and making him overshoot.' Rather than this negative method, pilots soon learnt it was infinitely better to be above the enemy defensive circle and to dive direct into it. Fighter Command also advocated a 'he-who-dares' tactic. 'Two Spitfires...in line astern approach the Me head-on. The pilot of the Me holds his fire, waiting for the leading aircraft to turn and so present an easy target. When he can wait no longer, he pulls out and is then shot down by the second Spitfire who immediately pulls out and attacks from underneath.'[18]

But as Adolf Galland, the Luftwaffe fighter ace, wrote: 'The first rule of all air combat is to see the opponent first.' He also commented: 'In the opening encounters the English were at a considerable disadvantage because of their close formation. Since the Spanish civil war we had introduced the wide-open combat formation.' The Germans obtained greater air coverage, better freedom of manœuvre, and wider visibility. Galland added: 'The British quickly realised the superiority of our combat formation and readjusted their own.' Within a few weeks Fighter Command introduced 'Charlies' – two flanking aircraft flying slightly higher and to the rear of the main formation – to serve as extra eyes.[19] Moreover, from the very start the British had one extremely important advantage over the Luftwaffe: radar and the fighter control it offered. 'For us and for our Command,' commented Galland, 'this was a surprise and a very bitter one.'[20] So, while the pilots of Fighter Command could steadily learn from their enemy and from experience, the Luftwaffe could only continue to hammer at the British defences. In the long term, the balance would tilt towards the RAF – providing casualties in the first stage of the Battle of Britain could be kept as low as possible and providing the Luftwaffe activity remained temporarily at the existing level.

Fighter Command Intelligence commented on 12 July: 'A reliable source in a neutral country reports a marked change in highly placed Germans in that country during the last ten days, from one of extreme optimism to one of hesitation. Ten days ago the Germans were confident that England would be invaded almost at once and that we should quickly be compelled to seek an Armistice. However, they are now doubtful when invasion will take place, and are becoming increasingly doubtful whether, if attempted, the operation would succeed.'[21] In Berlin the chief of the OKW operations staff, Jodl, completed his 'First Thoughts on a Landing in England'. He gave the code-name 'Lion' to the operation – which he believed feasible. To overcome British ability to direct forces rapidly towards the invasion point, Jodl advocated the landings being made on a wide front: this would achieve strategic surprise.[22] Thus primed by the OKW staff expert, the two most influential German army officers journeyed to see Hitler at Berghof next day, 13 July.

Field Marshal Walther Brauchitsch, C-in-C, and General Franz Halder, Chief of Staff, smoothed away the objections to the invasion operation which Raeder had raised forty-eight hours before. At the end of the day's discussions Hitler approved the German invasion plan and ordered full preparations to begin at once. He wrote to Mussolini: 'I have made to Britain so many offers of agreement, even of cooperation, and have been treated so shabbily, that I am now convinced that any new appeal to reason would meet with a similar rejection.' While Hitler composed this letter during the evening, Halder was entering the day's events in his diary. 'The Fuehrer is obsessed with the question why England does not yet want to take the road to peace... He sees, just as we do, the solution of this question lies in the fact that England is still setting her hope in Russia. Thus he too expects that England will have to be compelled by force to make peace. He does not like to do such a thing, however. Reason: if we smash England militarily, the British Empire will disintegrate. Germany, however, would not profit from this...'[23]

Dowding was dining with Churchill at Chequers. He discussed the need to protect Channel convoys and mentioned the unfortunate treatment he had received from the Air Ministry concerning his retirement. The Fighter Command chief wrote to Sir Archibald Sinclair, Air Secretary: 'He [Churchill] was good enough to tell me that I had secured his confidence, and that he wished me to remain on the Active List for the time being.'[24] In official British circles the danger of imminent invasion seemed to have passed for the moment. Tidal conditions, especially on the east coast, apparently indicated a brief respite. The Combined Area HQ at Chatham had signalled the Home Commands during the day: 'The Admiralty opinion seems to point to July 27 and 28 as being the next most likely dates.'[25] The BBC nevertheless introduced another anti-invasion precaution: from that Friday the newsreaders announced their identities, to frustrate German plans for seizing broadcasting centres and issuing false information. 'The velvety voice of Bruce Belfrage or Alvar Liddell,' wrote one listener, Frances Faviell, 'would first tell us of some magnificent aerial battle – and in glowing terms state the number of enemy planes shot down. We soon got very accustomed to the quiet, "One of our aircraft is missing", or "Eight of our aircraft failed to return..." which ended the public announcement.'[26]

'And now it has come to us to stand alone in the breach.' No one could mistake the voice of Winston Churchill as he broadcast to the country on 14 July. 'We are fighting by ourselves alone. But we are not fighting for ourselves alone.' The magnificent sentences rolled on. 'Here, girt about by the seas and oceans where the Navy reigns; shielded from above by the prowess and devotion of our airmen – we await undismayed the impending assault. Perhaps it will come tonight, perhaps it will come next week, perhaps it will never come. We must show ourselves equally capable of meeting a sudden violent shock or what is perhaps a harder task, a prolonged vigil. But be the ordeal sharp or long, or both, we shall seek no terms, we shall tolerate no parley, we may show no mercy – we ask none.' Churchill's message was quoted in the regular nightly broadcast made by Ed Murrow to America. The US journalist commented: 'In those words Winston Churchill summed up the position of Britain tonight, and his listeners... know that so long as he's leader of this country, those words represent for them completely the fears and hopes of this Empire.'[27] And with such a leader it was inconceivable, even to hesitant Hitler, that Britain would ever seek peace on German terms. Next day, as attacks on the convoys continued in the Channel despite worsening weather, and as Fighter Command pilots continued to struggle against numerically superior numbers, Admiral Raeder appreciated that he must concede temporary defeat in the struggle to convince Hitler against the invasion operation. He received notification of the decision reached at Berghof on 13 July, and he issued instructions to his staff. 'The task of "Preparing an Invasion of England" takes precedence over all operational considerations. All other operational questions of the Naval Staff must now be subordinate to the most rapid and detailed preparation of the enterprise and to the examination of the feasibility of its execution.'[28]

On Tuesday 16 July Hitler issued his Directive No. 16 from Berghof. At last the Fuehrer seemed to be taking more positive action. 'Since England, in spite of her hopeless military situation, shows no sign of being ready to come to an understanding, I have decided to prepare a landing operation against England, and, if necessary, to carry it out. The aim of this operation will be to eliminate the English homeland as a base for the prosecution of the war against Germany and, if necessary, to occupy it completely.' Hitler added: 'The invasion will bear the cover name "Sea Lion".'

The landing, according to the Directive, would be in the form of a surprise crossing on a wide front from about Ramsgate to the area west of the Isle of Wight; possibilities should be examined of limited operations prior to the main assault. 'Preparations for the entire operation must be completed by the middle of August.' These preparations must also create necessary conditions for the landing. 'The English Air Force must be so reduced morally and physically that it is unable to deliver any significant attack against the German crossing'; mine-free channels must be cleared and German mines laid in return; strong forces of coastal artillery must be established and the Royal Navy tied down by air and torpedo attacks on bases.[29] The document therefore officially established that the invasion would be against the English south coast, not the east. But Hitler, despite his stern sentences, had carefully inserted the words 'if necessary' in two consecutive sentences of the introduction; and the prime condition remained – the RAF must first be beaten.

RAF Fighter Command Intelligence officers had accumulated enough evidence to obtain an accurate assessment of present Luftwaffe aims. 'Reports appear to indicate,' stated a survey on 17 July, 'that attacks by day on this country will be limited to aircraft operating singly and in conditions which provide adequate cloud cover against fighter attack. Attacks on convoys will be carried out in strength with strong fighter escort.'[30] Aircraft undertaking bombing raids on British towns might be small in number, but they still inflicted considerable damage and suffering. A few hours after the Fighter Command Intelligence survey had been issued a handful of bombers struck at the Medway Towns, Kent: four people were killed and nineteen injured. An eighteen-year-old Boy Scout, Donald James, became the local hero after he had wormed his way into wreckage until his body protected the upturned faces of two people pinned beneath the debris, shielding them from further falls for nearly four hours.[31] These raids in mid-July continued to provide the toughest kind of Blitz training for rescue and medical services. And although the strain on Fighter Command remained heavy, with forward squadrons operating three and even four patrols each day, this first stage of the Battle of Britain was also inflicting heavy casualties on the Luftwaffe. By 17 July many of the front-line German fighter groups had lost almost a quarter of their original strength; some had suffered even more – Captain Hannes Trautloft's *Jagdgeschwader Gruppe*, based at St Omer, was now reduced to fifteen serviceable Me 109s out of an establishment of forty.[32] Most of the casualties occurred through mechanical troubles rather than direct enemy action, but Trautloft and other commanders were by no means confident for the future. By that Wednesday, another day of bad weather which reduced activity, sixteen Fighter Command aircraft had been lost in action since 10 July, compared with about fifty-five Luftwaffe, and the RAF had a far better replacement record: the total of operational aircraft in Fighter Command was continuing to rise, despite losses.[33]

'The whole of England is trembling on the brink of a decision,' declared the Berlin evening newspaper *Nachtausgabe* on 17 July. 'There is only a slight possibility of England offering any military resistance ... The British people are in downright fear of forthcoming military and political events.'[34] The German General Staff issued orders allocating forces for the invasion operation: thirteen divisions forming troops for the first wave would now be transferred from various areas of France to the coast, with each comprising about 19,000 men; twenty-six other divisions would make up the successive waves.[35]

On the same day the COS in London approved a report by the Joint Intelligence Committee concerning the probable scale of a German attack. This severely underestimated the likely first-wave invasion strength and continued the incorrect assessment of the likely invasion area. In addition, the JIC still believed that substantial airborne forces would be involved in the assault; in fact, contrary to all British fears and defensive preparations, the Germans never placed the parachutists or glider troops in a prominent Sea Lion role. The JIC declared that the principal enemy objective would probably be the seizure of London, with the main seaborne invasion being launched against an area between the Wash and Newhaven: Southwold in Suffolk and beaches in north Kent were considered to be the most likely targets within this region. The Germans would attempt a pincer movement on the capital, with up to five divisions in the first wave. At the same time, three times as many enemy might be dropped from the air in East Anglia and Kent.[36]

General Brooke, isolated on the south coast, still disagreed with the Whitehall view that the invasion would most probably be directed against the eastern beaches. Equally, he continued to oppose the official policy of holding the beaches rather than creating a stronger reserve inland. On that Wednesday Brooke received a visit from the Prime Minister; this day would be amongst the most important in Brooke's life – and it carried with it fundamental implications for Britain's future military decision-making. Brooke met Churchill at Gosport then they spent the afternoon touring the command area, finishing at 8 pm. The two men immediately established an excellent relationship. They reminisced about the past – the Prime Minister had been a close friend of Brooke's two elder brothers – but they also discussed the present, with Brooke giving his candid opinions, and they considered the future; Churchill, according to Brooke, was 'full of offensive plans for next summer'. 'We were four hours together in the motor-car on this July afternoon,' wrote Churchill, 'and we seemed to be in agreement on the methods of home defence.'[37]

The Prime Minister addressed a memorandum to Ironside, Dill and Ismay immediately after his return from the coast. 'I find it very difficult,' he declared, 'to visualise the kind of invasion all along the coast by troops carried in small craft, and even in boats... A surprise crossing should be impossible, and in the broader parts of the North Sea the invaders should be an easy prey... it will be very difficult for the enemy to place large well-equipped bodies of troops in the East Coast.' The minute urged an end to defensive, static, plans. 'I hope... you will be able to bring an ever larger proportion of your formed Divisions back from the coast into support or reserve, so that their training may proceed in the highest forms of offensive warfare and counter-attack, and that the coast, as it becomes fortified, will be increasingly confided to troops other than those of the formed Divisions.' Churchill attached a copy of the earlier memorandum by the First Sea Lord, which had stated that although a total of some 100,000 men might reach Britain without being intercepted, the subsequent maintenance of this invasion force would be practically impossible. Churchill commented: 'I personally believe that the Admiralty will in fact be better than their word, and that the invaders' losses in transit would further reduce the scale of attack, yet the preparations of the land forces should be such as to make assurance doubly sure.' Churchill concluded with another statement entirely in line with Brooke's opinion: 'The sovereign importance of London and the narrowness of the seas in this quarter make the South the theatre where the greatest precaution must be taken.'[38] Although the Prime Minister still believed the heaviest attack would seem most likely in the east, his minute therefore marked the beginnings of his pressure to give greater priority to the south.

The day after his visit to Brooke, Churchill made a speeech to Parliament again stressing the difficulties facing the Germans. 'Even five divisions, however lightly equipped, would require 200–250 ships, and with modern air reconnaissance and photography it would not be easy to collect such an armada, marshal it, and conduct it across the sea without any powerful naval forces to escort it; and there would be very great possibilities, to put it mildly, that this armada would be intercepted long before it reached the coast, and all the men drowned in the sea or, at the worst, blown to pieces with their equipment while trying to land.' Churchill's opinion coincided exactly with that of the German Naval chief. Already, on 17 July, Raeder had warned Brauchitsch that the risk involved in Sea Lion was great enough to involve the loss of all invasion forces. Next day the Naval Staff was completing an appreciation which declared that the task was beyond the strength of the Navy, reiterating the need for air supremacy both before and after the landing date. The whole tone of the memorandum warned that if the invasion were attempted Germany might very likely suffer a disastrous defeat.[39]

But in Berlin the atmosphere was one of victory. For the first time since 1871, German troops marched in triumphant parade through the thick columns of the Brandenburg Gate. 'A holiday spirit ruled completely,' noted William Shirer in his diary. He added: 'Hitler will speak in the Reichstag tomorrow, we hear... There is some speculation whether it will be, as on the grey morning of September 1, an occasion to announce a new *Blitzkrieg* – this time against Britain – or an offer of peace.'[40]

While the crowds gathered in Berlin and while Hitler completed his preparations for his long-awaited speech, the lonely war continued in the clouds above the Channel. The morning of 19 July brought tragedy to one British squadron. Ten days before, No. 141 Squadron had moved from Scotland to Kent; the machines they flew were Defiants, of which only two squadrons existed in Fighter Command. These two-seater aircraft were slow and clumsy, with a hunch-back design caused by a bulging gun turret behind the cockpit. The gunners were unable to fire forward and relied instead on complicated manœuvring to bring their four rear guns into a favourable position. Shortly before noon, nine aircraft from 141 Squadron took off from the forward airfield at Hawkinge, ordered to patrol at 5000 feet south of Folkestone; three remaining aircraft had defective engines, thus escaping the fate of the rest. Off the coast lurked twenty Me 109s from Captain Trautloft's group, flying at 15,000 feet with the mid-day sun above them. And as the nine Defiants, commanded by Squadron-Leader Richardson, climbed slowly to their patrolling altitude, these enemy aircraft darted down for the kill: some Me 109s plunged directly on to the British aircraft while others approached their victims head-on. Within sixty seconds six of the Defiants had plummeted into the sea. Help from Hurricanes of No. 111

66

Squadron probably saved the others from similar destruction. The three survivors, including Richardson, made it back to base; within twenty-four hours the Squadron was ordered back to Scotland: clearly the Defiant was totally unsuitable for the battle over the Channel.[41]

RAF Intelligence officers in London believed the Germans were also suffering from their latest experiences. 'The GAF has come up against a thoroughly organised fighter defence system for the first time,' declared the War Cabinet weekly résumé issued this Friday morning, 'and therefore has little practical experience with which to tackle this new problem... Thus it seems that the operations against this country may perhaps be defined as tactical experiments on which future policy can be based.'[42]

General Brooke was inspecting defences on the Isle of Wight. As he sat with his staff to enjoy a sandwich lunch on the southernmost beach, a car drew up with a message from the War Office: Brooke must proceed at once to London to see Eden, War Secretary. He arrived at 7 pm to be informed that he was to take over command of Britain's Home Forces; General Ironside would be created a Field Marshal, presented with a peerage, and retired. General Auchinleck, at present commander of 5th Corps, would succeed Brooke as GOC Southern Command. Ironside had seen Eden at 2.45 pm. He wrote in his diary: 'Eden told me that the Cabinet wished to have someone with late experience of the war. I told Eden that he needn't worry and that I was quite prepared to be released. I had done my best.'[43] The Cabinet had not in fact been consulted; the decision originated from Churchill himself after his visit to Brooke two days before. Brooke, like Ironside, confided in his diary that night. He still believed that the Germans might invade, and his subsequent diary entries would reveal his constant expectation that the offensive was about to begin; he believed the hardest part of his job would be the 'absolute necessity' of submerging his own feelings and fears. 'I find it very hard to realise fully the responsibility that I am assuming. I only pray to God that I may be capable of carrying out the job.'[44]

As Brooke wrote these words top German officers and Nazi politicians were converging on the Kroll Opera House, Berlin. Hitler was about to make his important speech to the Reichstag, and the whole of Germany waited for his words: a decision had already been delayed too long.

CHAPTER SIX

ᔑ

In the Name of Reason
19–31 July

'Under one roof I have never seen so many gold-braided generals
before,' wrote Shirer in his diary on Friday evening, 19 July. 'Massed
together, their chests heaving with crosses and other decorations, they
filled a third of the first balcony.' Also present in the Kroll Opera House
was Ciano, who noted: 'It is solemn and theatrical.' Hitler walked
briskly to the rostrum, waited while the tumult died down, and began
to speak. Shirer continued his eye-witness account: 'His voice was lower
tonight; he rarely shouted as he usually does; and he did not cry out
hysterically as I've seen him do so often from this rostrum.'

During the day Hitler had received the German Naval Staff
memorandum concerning the difficulties of Sea Lion; Raeder warned
that the operation might mean utter defeat of the German forces taking
part; RAF Fighter Command aircraft still rose to defend Channel convoys; Britain's defences were being steadily improved and Churchill's
belligerence seemed greater than ever.

'From Britain I now hear only a single cry,' declared Hitler. 'Not of
the people but of the politicians – that the war must go on!... Believe
me, gentlemen, I feel a deep disgust for this type of unscrupulous politi-
cian who wrecks whole nations. It almost causes me pain to think that
I should have been selected by fate to deal the final blow to the structure
which these men have already set tottering... Mr Churchill no doubt
will already be in Canada... For millions of other people, however,
great suffering will begin. Mr Churchill ought perhaps, for once, to
believe me when I prophesy that a great Empire will be destroyed –
an Empire which it was never my intention to destroy or even to harm.'
Hitler was using all his best oratorical techniques. His hands moved

68

eloquently to emphasise his words; his body swayed in almost hypnotic fashion, and the crowded Opera House responded with cheers and out-stretched saluting arms. But the generals, politicians and diplomats fell silent as Hitler came to the core of his speech.

'In this hour I feel it to be my duty before my conscience to appeal once more to reason and common sense in Great Britain... I consider myself in a position to make this appeal since I am not the vanquished begging favours, but the victor speaking in the name of reason. I can see no reason why this war must go on.' And so Hitler made one last offer of peace. Shirer noted the reaction in the Reichstag: 'There was no applause, no cheering, no stamping of heavy boots. There was silence. And it was tense. For in their hearts the Germans long for peace now.' Hitler waited a moment to allow tension to build up, and then he added with subdued, almost sad voice: 'I am grieved to think of the sacrifices which it [war] will claim. I should like to avert them, also for my own people.'

'I believe that his desire for peace is sincere,' wrote Ciano. Shirer commented: 'As a manœuvre calculated to rally them [the Germans] for the fight against Britain, it was a masterpiece.'[1] Included in the Reichs-tag ceremony was the award by Hitler of Field Marshals' batons to twelve generals; Goering, already holding this rank, received the special honour of being named *Reichsmarschall*. Among those elevated was Kesselring, commander of Luftflotten 2; he wrote after the war: 'I am today perfectly convinced that none of us would have been made Field Marshals after the western campaign had Hitler not thought that peace was now probable.'[2]

Within sixty minutes of Hitler's speech the British reaction to the peace offer was announced by the BBC: the unauthorised statement amounted to a determined rejection. In Berlin, High Command officers and ministry officials were clustered round receiving sets at the broad-casting station when the abrupt BBC declaration came through; they exclaimed: 'Can you make it out?... Can you understand those British fools?... To turn down peace now? They're crazy!'[3] Ciano wrote in his diary: 'Late in the evening, when the first cold British reactions to the speech arrived, a sense of ill-concealed disappointment spreads among the Germans.'[4] Only the opening section of Hitler's address had reached London in time for the first editions of the next morning's newspapers; consequently Hitler's threats to Britain, contained in this early part of the speech, were quoted rather than the following offer of peace. The heading in *The Times* declared: 'Hitler's Threats to Britain'. Hitler,

69

despite the care and constant corrections with which he had prepared his text, therefore found his message had been distorted. He complained to Ciano in an interview next morning: 'The reaction of the English press to yesterday's speech has been such as to allow of no prospect of an understanding.' Ciano's account continued: 'Hitler is therefore preparing to strike the military blow at England...The air attack already began some days ago, and is continually growing in intensity.' Ciano also wrote: 'In the afternoon a visit to Goering. He looked feverish.'[5]

Hitler mistimed his speech in another respect apart from the newspaper deadlines. British War Cabinet Ministers had left London for the weekend. Ministers had been allowed a Saturday and Sunday free from meetings, for the first time since the start of the German attack on France and the Low Countries, and Hitler's speech was not considered sufficiently important to alter arrangements. Churchill sent a note to Chamberlain and Attlee on 20 July, suggesting that the speech might perhaps be answered by Parliamentary resolutions, but the War Cabinet would turn down this idea on 24 July, when Ministers also decided that newspapers 'should be discouraged from suggesting that there was anything in Hitler's speech which called for an official reply.'[6] Meanwhile, on the evening of 22 July a broadcast was made by Halifax, Foreign Secretary, in which he declared: 'We shall not stop fighting until Freedom is secure.' Ciano commented: 'Halifax makes an inconsequential speech about Germany, in which Hitler's vague proposals for peace are not taken into account.'[7]

Hitler held all the cards in his hand, yet found it impossible to play any of them. His forces had conquered Norway, Denmark, Poland, Czechoslovakia, Holland, Belgium, Luxembourg, France; his armies had introduced a devastating new form of war and had proved themselves masters in its application; the Fuehrer stood at the pinnacle of power. But Hitler was unable to bring war to a victorious conclusion. Britain remained fiercely stubborn; Russia, of whom Hitler had always felt hatred and suspicion, displayed disturbing signs of belligerence: on 21 July, forty-eight hours after the Reichstag speech, Soviet control over the Baltic States to Germany's north became complete, with respective Parliaments of these three countries voting for total incorporation into the USSR.

During this Sunday, Hitler summoned his service leaders to a conference at the Chancellery. He subjected Brauchitsch, Raeder and General Hans Jeschonnek to a long exposition which revealed his fumbling attempt to find a definite policy. Sentences seemed contradictory; decisions were qualified by objections raised by Hitler himself; his mind darted here and there seeking an answer to his dilemma. Russia, he declared, would 'make no effort to enter the war against Germany of her own accord.' Britain, relying on Russian help, was therefore in a hopeless position. 'The war has been won by us, and reversal of the prospects of success is impossible.' Yet how could the defeated be made to admit defeat? Rapid termination of the war was in Germany's interest, stated Hitler; then he added that there was no urgent necessity for such an early finish since Germany was in a favourable economic condition. Pressure must be brought to bear on Britain through the diplomatic sphere, by a union of Germany, Spain, Japan and Russia in a combined front; on the other hand, such a front would be difficult to obtain because the other countries concerned were 'waiting for a new miracle' – presumably an invasion of Britain. In spite of Germany's excellent economic position, Hitler then insisted that 'we should strive with every means to end the war in a short time and to exploit our favourable military and political situation as quickly as possible. The execution of Operation Sea Lion can be considered as the most effective means to this end.' Hitler's use of the word 'can' hinted at doubts in his mind over the project; almost immediately these doubts were revealed. Clearly, Hitler had paid close attention to Raeder's objections. Sea Lion was an 'exceptionally daring undertaking... This was not just a river crossing, but the crossing of a sea which is dominated by the enemy. This is not a case of a single crossing operation as in Norway; strategic surprise cannot be expected... Forty divisions will be required... The most difficult part will be the continued reinforcement of equipment and stores.'

Therefore, Hitler added, the invasion would only be undertaken 'if no other means are left for settling with Britain.' Yet time was limited for these 'other means' to be put into practice. 'The weather in the North Sea and in the Channel is very bad during the second half of September and the fogs begin in the middle of October'; if vital Luftwaffe cooperation for the landings was to be possible, then the main operation must be completed by 15 September. Hitler asked Raeder for a detailed study giving a timetable for naval preparations and examining the possibilities of naval protection for the invasion. But if Sea Lion did not prove feasible, what should be the alternative? Now, for the first time, Hitler raised the subject of an offensive in the east. 'Our attention must be turned to tackle the Russian problem.' He directed the General Staff to make

71

preliminary studies for war with the USSR, with hostilities possibly starting in the autumn.[8]

Yet the Fuehrer's second in command, *Reichsmarschall* Goering, had no doubts of his ability to defeat British opposition. His Chief of Staff, Jeschonnek, informed Hitler at the 21 July conference that Goering 'would soon like to be given freedom to launch attacks against Britain's fighter pilots, air force, aircraft industry, ports, industries, oil centres and the Channel area.' On the same day Goering summoned the Luftflotten chiefs to his headquarters: Kesselring, commander of Luftflotte 2 which spread over north Germany, Holland, Belgium and France north of the Seine; Hugo Sperrle, head of Luftflotte 3 in west France; Hans Juergen Stumpff, whose Luftflotte 5 covered Norway and Denmark. Goering told these three to work out detailed plans for the forthcoming all-out offensive; *Gruppen* must be brought to full effectiveness. The actual date for the intensified campaign would be announced as soon as possible.[9]

'Churchill means hunger and war,' declared the German propaganda broadcast to Britain on 22 July. 'When the capitalists set out to make this bloody war who did they call upon to fight it out for them? The working class of course... When the British working man sees his wife and children actually starving you'll be told to fire on the workers.' On that day Mr George Jarrett began employment as a tractor driver for the Somerset War Agricultural Committee, SWAC. He was typical of many thousands of British workers to whom the German propaganda broadcasts were directed. He was paid by cheque, not cash, and his wages amounted to £1 5s 8d at the end of his first week – 'which was about 50–52 hours and meant cycling eight miles to work, perhaps a little more, by 8 am. I believe my highest pay went to about £6 with overtime... I personally was never happier. Field work by day, Home Guard by night.'[10]

In Berlin, a Foreign Office spokesman announced: 'The Fuehrer is now considering whether he may not delay his action a little longer in case the British people should disavow their leader's answer to the Fuehrer's offer.' Admiral Raeder informed Hitler that naval preparations for Sea Lion could not possibly be completed by mid-August as specified in the 16 July directive, and that the time of readiness would be contingent on the achievement of air supremacy.[11] During the evening came the broadcast by Lord Halifax, virtually ignoring Hitler's peace offer. Officials in Berlin waited vainly for a more hopeful pronouncement from London during the 23rd, and on 24 July Ribbentrop's representative on Hitler's staff wrote: 'Halifax's speech has finally destroyed our belief in a party favouring an understanding over there ... If the English wish their destruction, they can have it.'[12]

The RAF Fighter Command intelligence report for 24 July commented that the Luftwaffe 'appear to be continuing their policy of confining heavy attacks to convoys.'[13] British pilots were in fact suffering from boredom. Action had dwindled during the last few days, and in comparison to the short, frightening bursts of activity, the waiting seemed to stretch the nerves. 'We had a private and somewhat jocular theory,' wrote Crook of 609 Squadron, 'that this unnatural peace was due to Goering having given the whole German Air Force a week's leave to get them fit for "things to come".'[14] During 24 July, aircraft from 65 Squadron, operating from Manston, were involved with enemy bombers and fighters while escorting a convoy in the Medway; the squadron record reported: 'This little shindy has eased the browned-off feeling and put our tails up and at least there will be a few Huns u/s for some time.'[15] A famous German pilot made his debut in the air war over England that day, when Adolf Galland led his squadron over the Medway Towns and attacked a convoy protected by Spitfires – probably the same engagement in which 65 Squadron eased its 'browned-off feeling'.[16]

For both sides this phase of the war had been accepted as almost routine. Two or three Luftwaffe sorties were flown each day, weather permitting; the enemy aircraft assembled over the French coastal area at an altitude of up to 18,000 feet, then moved over the Channel gradually climbing higher in order to gain the advantage over the RAF. 'In the attempt to outclimb the opponent,' wrote Galland, 'our dogfights occurred at ever-increasing altitude. My highest combat at that time took place at 25,000 feet. But at 27,000 feet and more – close to the lower limits of the stratosphere – one could usually see the vapour trails of German or English fighters.' Luftwaffe pilots were now instructed to undertake a 'free chase over south-east England' to weaken Fighter Command strength. But the Germans were already experiencing the range limitation of their aircraft which would be a crippling disadvantage in the main Battle of Britain phase. It took about thirty minutes from time of take-off to crossing the English coast at the Channel's narrowest point, yet the Me 109 had a tactical flying time of only eighty minutes, so, counting the duration of the return journey, Me 109 pilots had a mere twenty minutes to spare over England, or an operational range of 125 miles from their French bases. 'The physical as well as

73

the mental strain on the pilots was considerable,' commented Galland. 'The ground personnel and the planes themselves were taxed to the limit.'[17]

On 25 July the Air Ministry reported that in the period since 1 July the Luftwaffe had suffered 174 confirmed losses of aircraft and 120 unconfirmed. But during the day the Germans underlined RAF difficulties with a highly successful operation against merchant shipping in the Channel. A twenty-one-vessel convoy left Southend early in the morning; a Luftwaffe force of thirty-five aircraft attacked off Deal, and other strikes followed. Escorting Spitfires were heavily outnumbered; reinforcement Hurricanes were scrambled from Hawkinge, but these were unable to gain sufficient height before engaging the enemy – they had to climb in full view of the Luftwaffe and were hence placed in the worst possible position for action. Five ships in the convoy were sunk by nightfall and another six crippled, and of the latter, three were sunk soon afterwards by German E-boats. Fighter Command flew 641 sorties on 25 July, losing seven aircraft, and although German losses probably totalled about eighteen the day's events convinced Dowding that the situation must be changed as soon as possible; he prepared his papers for a confrontation with the Defence Committee in London.

In Berlin, Raeder was once again arguing against invasion. He saw Hitler during 25 July and put forward full details of the detrimental effect of Sea Lion on the German war effort. Withdrawal of merchant shipping was likely to prejudice the vital iron and coal traffic from Sweden; German inland shipping would probably be reduced by about 30 per cent; foodstuffs, unable to be carried along the canals, would rot in improvised barns; the supply of fish would virtually cease through trawler requisitioning.[18] But next day the German Army Staff reported to the OKW that 'the British operational command, possessing little flexibility, will not be in a position to master the difficult situations arising. The success of the German attacks is thus unquestionable.'[19]

The British COS met operational commanders at 3 pm to discuss anti-invasion measures. Brooke, the new commander of the Home Army, wrote afterwards: 'I came away feeling less confident... The Navy now realises fully that its position on the sea has been seriously undermined by the advent of aircraft. Sea supremacy is no longer what it was, and in the face of strong bomber forces can no longer ensure the safety of this island against invasion. This throws a much heavier task on the Army.' The naval problem, brought out at the meeting, arose from the need to undertake two equally important tasks: to repel invasion and to safeguard supplies. As Sir Charles Forbes, Home Fleet Commander, had already warned, a premature diversion of warships from convoy escort duties might have extremely serious results. However, the COS agreed at this meeting to approve an Air Staff paper: this maintained that invasion by sea was not a practical operation of war until Germany had defeated the British fighter force. Consequently the initial phase of the campaign against Britain was likely to include increasing attacks on fighters in the air, their bases, and the aircraft industry; a heavy air assault might simultaneously be directed against naval forces and naval bases especially on the east and south east coasts.[20]

Earlier in the day Dowding had appeared before the Defence Committee to warn that the existing situation imposed a heavy strain, and consequently serious dangers, on RAF fighter forces. Yet Churchill began the 11.30 am meeting by urging improved convoy protection. 'We could hardly go on allowing convoys to sustain casualties on the scale experienced on the previous day.' Admiral Sir Dudley Pound said that some of the latest Hunt class destroyers were now becoming available, which had much better armament and which would be employed as convoy escorts. 'It might be found that the Germans would concentrate on the destroyers and they might, or might not, succeed in withstanding these attacks.' Dowding then stressed the difficulties being experienced by his squadrons. 'At times there were over a hundred [enemy] aircraft over the Channel... This meant that most of the energies of our fighters were taken up in engaging enemy fighters, and the bombers often had a comparatively straightforward task.' The Fighter Command chief then declared: 'The Channel convoys consisted of small ships, mostly engaged in the coal trade on the south coast, and it would not be a national calamity if it ceased.' Dowding emerged from the discussions reasonably satisfied: it was eventually agreed that sailings of merchant ship convoys would be restricted, pending new Admiralty arrangements for passing them through the most vulnerable areas by night and escorting them more effectively by day.[21]

'There are indications that many fresh German troops are arriving in Holland,' stated the War Cabinet situation report issued on 26 July, 'and that Belgium, especially Brussels, is full of troops, of which a high proportion belong to the Air Force.' The résumé declared that enemy aircraft losses during the past week amounted to fifty-nine confirmed, forty-four unconfirmed; RAF losses totalled twenty-six fighters. British casualties from bombing comprised thirty-three people killed, 206 injured.[22] A more accurate figure for Luftwaffe losses was in fact about fifty aircraft.

The dangerous daily routine continued. Actions on 27 July included a strike against a convoy lying in Weymouth Bay, described by Crook of 609 Squadron. 'We went in to intercept it. A very confused action followed, in which most of us never saw or engaged the enemy, but we lost one pilot, Buck.'[23] This was the only casualty throughout the Channel area during the day; four German aircraft were destroyed. Next day, when clouds again dropped low, Major Werner Molders made his maiden flight across the Channel. 'He was the ace of all German fighter pilots,' wrote Galland. 'I followed him at some distance in constant rivalry.' Molders, like Galland, had fought in the Spanish Civil War and his figure of aircraft 'kills' had mounted rapidly during the offensive against France. But his career almost ended that day. 'North of Dover we met some low-flying Spitfires,' he reported. 'I shot down a Spitfire in flames. But now I found myself in the middle of a clump of Englishmen and they were very angry with me. They all rushed at me, and that was my good luck. As they all tried to earn cheap laurels at the expense of one German, they got in each other's way. Well, I managed to manœuvre among them and made them even more confused. Nevertheless, I couldn't avoid being hit. Bullets bespattered my aircraft. The radiator and fuel tank were shot up badly and I had to make a getaway as quickly as possible... Luckily my engine held out to the French coast, then it began to misfire. When I wanted to land the undercarriage wouldn't work. There was nothing to do but land without it. I made a smooth belly landing.'[24]

Another fighter ace had been in action in the Dover area at the same time as Molders. 'Sailor' Malan led a flight of forty-three Squadron Spitfires on an interception patrol which proved typical of his leadership and fighting skill. 'What I like about Sailor,' commented another of the brilliant forty-three Squadron pilots, Mungo Park, 'is his quiet, firm manner and his cold courage. He is gifted with uncanny eyesight and is a "natural" fighter pilot. When he calls over the R/T "Let 'em have it! Let 'em have it!", there's no messing. The b——s are for it...'[25] Now, soon after 4 pm on 28 July, Malan underlined the accuracy of this description. His subsequent flight report revealed his calm, business-like efficiency: during the next few minutes he shot down one Me 109 and damaged another despite being grossly outnumbered, before having to return to base with his ammunition expended.[26] About eighteen Luftwaffe aircraft were destroyed that day, against a Fighter Command loss of five machines.

Also on 28 July, advance parties of the thirteen German divisions intended for the first invasion wave began to arrive in the coastal area facing England. But Halder noted: 'We received a memorandum from the Naval Staff which upsets all previous calculations about the crossing.' He added in disgust: 'We can throw away the whole plan.' The naval paper, actually dated the following day, declared that preparations could not be completed until the last days of September, by which time the weather would impose great difficulties. Moreover, the German Navy believed that protection against the Royal Navy would be impossible in the invasion area. The memorandum therefore concluded that the naval staff 'must advise against undertaking the operation this year. In the event that the air war, in conjunction with various naval measures, does not induce the enemy to make peace, the preparations might be continued on a scale which the war economy can tolerate. Execution could then be considered in May 1941 or thereafter.' Admiral Schniewind, Chief of the Naval Staff, added a personal note: 'No responsibility can be accepted for execution this year. The possibility of carrying out the operation at all appears extremely doubtful.'[27] The conflict between the Army and Navy was clearly reaching a climax. The former was pushing ahead as quickly as possible – on 29 July detailed training instructions were issued by OKH, stating that tidal estuaries were to be selected on the French coast for training purposes, being chosen for their similar conditions to English estuaries. Yet the Navy continued to lag. All in fact depended on the Luftwaffe. Halder noted in his diary: 'In general, our Air Force feels itself superior in equipment, operational control, and general performance... Decisive results are expected.'[28]

On the same day RAF Fighter Command Intelligence reported: 'It is considered that the GAF, while still not brought up to full serviceability, is once more strong enough to begin a large-scale offensive, although it is doubtful whether advanced aerodromes have yet been supplied with sufficient stores of bombs, fuel and ammunition to carry out sustained operations.'[29] During the morning the War Cabinet had been given details of the previous day's engagement in the Dover Straits, and Ministers were told that further fighting was taking place at that moment in the same area. 'The latest report was that the enemy had lost eight machines for certain, eight more probable, and six possible. One of our pilots had been killed.'[30] That afternoon German bombers

77

struck at Dover itself, in the first concentrated attack on the town. An estimated eighty raiders took part, dive-bombing the harbour. 'The well-spaced ships in it bobbed about like corks,' said one eye-witness. RAF pilots and anti-aircraft crews claimed seventeen enemy aircraft destroyed.[31] Both sides were continuing to overestimate casualties inflicted on the other; next day the Air Ministry reported that since the beginning of the month a total of 261 enemy aircraft had been shot down for certain, plus 136 unconfirmed – about eighty-seven of the confirmed casualties occurring in the previous five days.[32] In fact about eight enemy aircraft were destroyed during the day's fighting on 29 July, and in the five days ending at dawn on 30 July about fifty-two Luftwaffe aircraft had been shot down. But this figure was still far higher than the Fighter Command casualty total – eighteen aircraft over the same five-day period – and the amount of convoy tonnage lost had dropped dramatically since the restrictions on sailing imposed shortly before by the Admiralty. This first phase of the Battle of Britain was becoming increasingly unprofitable for the enemy; new measures would have to be taken. On 30 July, Hitler instructed Goering that he should 'immediately and with great haste' arrange for the 'great battle of the German Air Force against England' to begin at a maximum notice of only twelve hours.[33] At the same time, Hitler summoned his military chiefs to a conference to take place next day at Berghof.

'Can't make out what the Germans are doing,' noted Cadogan in his diary. 'Various good indications that they *are* going to attack us. But why haven't they done so? And what are they doing with these costly and half-hearted air raids?... Must be something very deep.'[34]

German decisions taken on the last day of July were to be amongst the most important of the whole war. The day dawned with heavy cloud over the Channel. Air activity remained quiet, with only sporadic strikes against shipping and against the Dover balloon barrage, resulting in the loss of three RAF aircraft and five Luftwaffe. The record book for No. 65 Squadron was typical of others. 'A very quiet ending to the month, but taken all round we haven't done too badly and there were a few Huns less to knock off.'[35] Further west, pilots of 609 Squadron were also reflecting on the past month. Seven members had been killed at Dunkirk or after; others had been posted elsewhere, and there were many new faces in the mess. 'In less than a year 609 had altered completely its personnel and character,' wrote David Crook. 'We had a new CO and of the fifteen original members of the squadron, only four were now left.' He added: 'But the end of July came, and with it the end of our bad luck...I think that this influx of new blood played a big part in bringing to an end our run of bad luck, because from now onwards we started on an almost unbroken series of successes and victories.'[36]

During the afternoon Churchill addressed the House of Commons in secret session. He warned that a crisis might be imminent. 'Winston surpassed even himself,' wrote Harold Nicolson in his diary. 'The situation is obscure. It may be that Hitler will first bomb us with gas and then try to land. At the same time, Italy and Japan will hit us as hard as they can. It will be a dreadful month.' But Nicolson's diary entry continued: 'Hitler may feel that he cannot bring off a successful invasion and may seek to gain new, easy but sterile conquests in Africa and Asia. Were it not for this little island under a great leader, he would accomplish his desires. We may fail. But supposing we do not fail?...What a chance!'[37]

Pennanted staff cars drew up at Hitler's 'Eagle's Nest' high in the mountains above Salzburg. Officers crowded down the bare passage to the huge reception hall, then upstairs and through a long room decorated with paintings of nudes, and finally they crammed into Hitler's study. A wide window revealed the spectacular view of the valleys and snow peaks; the room itself was austere, and extra chairs had been fetched for the generals and admirals. Hitler's military conference began. The moment of decision could no longer be delayed. Soon the weather would worsen over the English Channel and fogs would shroud the British coastline. For almost two months the mighty German army had remained inactive; the soldiers, like the German people, were bewildered and uncertain in this situation of conquest without final victory. So too was Hitler. But the Fuehrer must now lead the way.

∽

CHAPTER SEVEN

A Programme Prepared

1–7 August

Grand-Admiral Raeder had made his reputation during the First World War when, as chief of staff to Vice-Admiral Franz von Hipper, he had watched the world's two mightiest fleets in a duel for supremacy. His periods of action covered sorties against the British Grand Fleet including Dogger Bank; the climax of his career at sea had been the thunderous clash at Jutland. Ten shells and a torpedo had smashed Hipper's flagship, the *Lützow*, and Raeder escaped by torpedo boat under fire with his commander, before boarding another battle cruiser to continue the battle. After Germany's defeat he believed his country would never again fight Great Britain. He became known as a strict disciplinarian and a hard worker; formal and distant, he suffered from a sense of insecurity which led him to believe rivals were constantly challenging his authority. Yet he also respected frank talk: he expected others to speak freely, as he did himself.

Now, in 1940, Raeder had lost none of his characteristic plain speaking and on Wednesday 31 July his frank attitude bordered on the brutal. Hitler began his Berghof conference by asking for Raeder's views: the Grand Admiral obliged at length. The German Navy, he declared, could not possibly execute Sea Lion until 15 September. Requisition of merchant ships would soon begin but conversion would take four weeks. Mine-sweeping would take three weeks; mine-laying was due to begin at the end of August, but both sweeping and laying would need prior acquisition of air supremacy by the Luftwaffe. Even the 15 September date might not be met: this target was contingent on no 'unforeseen circumstances due to the weather or the enemy'. Raeder delved into technicalities regarding the subject of weather. A landing would have to take place two hours after high tide to allow the ebbing sea to leave the barges well ashore: the Army insisted on a dawn landing and the night crossing would be best attempted in half-moon conditions; if these two requirements were to be met, then the invasion would have to be launched some time between 19 and 26 September – but this late start meant that weather conditions would be deteriorating, and a successful landing force might be stranded on the beaches.

'Even if the first wave crosses successfully under favourable weather conditions,' explained Raeder, 'there is no guarantee that the same favourable weather will carry through the second and third waves... We must realise that no traffic worth mentioning will be able to cross for several days, until certain harbours can be utilised.' Raeder objected strongly to the army proposal for a broad front stretching from the Dover Straits to Lyme Bay: such an extensive area would necessitate greater numbers of naval vessels to protect the invasion from the enemy. Transportation vessels would be extremely vulnerable during the first thirty-six hours when the first wave was being unloaded. Raeder therefore urged a shorter front, running from Dover to Eastbourne. 'All things considered,' concluded the gloomy Admiral, 'the best time for the operation would be May 1941.'

Hitler agreed that nothing could be done about weather conditions, but the consequences of losing time must be considered. 'Things will become more difficult with the passing of time.' While the British Army was at present in a weak position, by next spring it would have grown to thirty to thirty-five equipped divisions: this would amount to a formidable force in the restricted area of proposed landing operations. It was unlikely that the strength ratio between the German and British Navies would improve substantially by May 1941; moreover, the staying power of the Italians was questionable, especially in East Africa. Air and submarine war against Britain could take up to two years before becoming decisive – contrary to views earlier expressed by Hitler himself. Then Hitler reached his decision, recorded in notes taken by Raeder and Halder.

'Diversions in Africa should be studied. But the decisive result can only be achieved by an attack on England. An attempt must therefore be made to prepare the operation for 15 September.' Hitler added: 'The decision as to whether the operation is to take place in September or is to be delayed until May 1941, will be made after the Air Force has made concentrated attacks on southern England for one week. If the effect of the air attacks is such that the enemy air force, harbours and naval forces, etc, are heavily damaged, Operation Sea Lion will be carried out in 1940. Otherwise it is to be postponed until May 1941.' Hitler had been as positive as his doubts and hesitations would allow: his statement was an attempted compromise between the conflicting thoughts in his own mind and between the differing Army and Navy attitudes. Above all, Hitler's statement clearly revealed his frustration. Something must be done; the inactivity, with its constant drain on Germany's resources, could not continue indefinitely; a conclusion to the war must be obtained. But Hitler still had difficulty in seeing how this could be achieved. Nor did he apparently believe Goering's constant claims that an all-out aerial war would provide the answer – such an offensive could take as much as two years, according to the Fuehrer's statement. In effect the intensified Luftwaffe attacks on Britain, precipitating the main phase of the Battle of Britain itself, were seen in Hitler's mind not as a possible means of obtaining decisive victory, but simply as a means of occupying the time. Hitler had no real hopes of victory from the Battle of Britain; he could think of nothing else to do.

Admiral Raeder left the Berghof conference after Hitler's statement. But the Army chiefs, Brauchitsch and Halder, remained in Hitler's cold, bare study, and they heard the Fuehrer speak at length – almost as if he were voicing aloud his tangled thoughts. Halder jotted down his words. 'Britain's hope lies in Russia and America. If that hope in Russia is destroyed then it will be destroyed for America too because elimination of Russia will enormously increase Japan's power in the Far East.' Hitler became more excited; Halder's writing broke into shorthand to keep pace. 'Something strange has happened in Britain! The British were already completely down. Now they are back on their feet... Russia unpleasantly disturbed by the swift developments in Western Europe. Russia needs only to hint to England that she does not wish to see Germany too strong and the English, like a drowning man, will regain hope that the situation in six to eight months will have completely changed.' Halder stressed the following words in his scribbled account. 'But if Russia is smashed, Britain's last hope will be shattered. Then Germany will be master of Europe and the Balkans. Decision: in view of these considerations Russia must be liquidated. Spring 1941. The sooner Russia is smashed, the better.'[1]

Hitler believed he had found his answer. The end of the war would be obtained through the defeat of Russia. Fumbling and blundering to find a solution, his mind now rested on this new target; time would be needed to prepare for this ambitious offensive, and meanwhile the months would be occupied by continued operations against Britain. Increasingly, these operations would be a sham, emphasising the tragedy of the suffering involved. New instructions were issued from Hitler's headquarters on 1 August. 'I intend to intensify air and sea warfare against the English homeland... The intensification of the air war may begin on or after 5 August. The exact time is to be decided by the Air Force after the completion of preparations and in the light of the weather.' Hitler stipulated that attacks on south coast ports must be kept to a minimum 'in view of our own forthcoming operations'. Nor must the Luftwaffe expend all its energy in this phase of the campaign against England: 'It must also be ready to take part in full force in Operation Sea Lion.'[2] An OKW directive issued on 1 August, declared that 'if it is decided *not* to carry out Sea Lion in September, all preparations will nevertheless be continued, but in a form which excludes serious damage to the economy through the paralysis of inland shipping.'[3]

A strategic programme had at last emerged: first, unrestricted air war against the RAF and continued preparations for Sea Lion; second, invasion of Britain in September if conditions and preparations were after all satisfactory; if Britain were not invaded in 1940 the offensive might be launched in May 1941, or, far more likely, the campaign against Russia would begin. Although a compromise, this programme allowed maximum scope for Hitler's opportunism and it ended the state of limbo which had existed since the victory over France. Orders could be issued and forces trained and deployed with a more definite purpose in mind. The huge German war machine could begin to stir and shake itself from lethargy.

First of all, German aircraft flew over Britain on Thursday 1 August on a last mission of peace before the holocaust. They dropped leaflets instead of bombs. On these green and yellow slips of paper, fluttering down over Hampshire and Somerset, was printed the English text of Hitler's 19 July speech to the Reichstag; British newspapers immediately carried large photographs of housewives reading the message and treating the leaflets as something of a joke; some of the sheets were sold at local Red Cross auctions. So many German threats had been issued and so many invasion scares had come and gone, that to many British men and women the whole situation had become stale; at the beginning of August fewer evacuees were billeted away from their homes than there had been in January, with people drifting back into the supposed danger areas; gas masks were piling up in Lost Property offices; barbed wire barricades were used as washing lines in peaceful villages.

The artificial atmosphere would continue for a few more days, and the faintly theatrical feeling even spread to the front-line combatants of both sides. RAF fighter pilots were making the most of the latest lull which had fallen across the Channel. The number of daily sorties dropped, no RAF casualties were reported on 2, 3 or 4 August, and many British pilots were on leave in London, celebrating at the Trocadero and enjoying Leslie Henson's show. Across the water the fighter ace Adolf Galland was awarded the Knight's Cross by Kesselring; Galland had recently obtained his seventeenth kill. As Kesselring pinned the medal to the pilot's tunic two fighter aircraft flew over at great height. 'What are those?' he asked. 'Spitfires, *Herr General-Feld Marshal*.' Kesselring laughed and declared: 'The first to congratulate you!'[4] But the lull also enabled Fighter Command strength to be built up. The total number of aircraft operational in the command now stood at 675: twenty-five Defiants, sixty-three Blenheims, 239 Spitfires and 348 Hurricanes. The total represented an increase of seventy-three since 1 July, despite the losses over the month: Lord Beaverbrook, Minister of Aircraft Production since 14 May, was constantly improving output. His contribution to the Battle of Britain would soon become fully apparent, and his achievement cannot be overestimated, together with that of his valiant workers. The arrival of replacement aircraft would be a fundamental factor in the conflict, and production figures revealed Beaverbrook's domineering leadership: 141 new fighters in February 1940, 173 in March, 256 in April rising to 325 in May when Beaverbrook took over, soaring to 446 in June and 496 in July. As Dowding was later to write in his official despatch: 'The effect of his appointment can only be described as magical.' Beaverbrook, besides forcing a dramatic rise in production, was also pushing forward the essential repair organisation for damaged fighters. On 2 August Beaverbrook moved even closer to the centre of affairs, when Churchill invited him to enter the inner sanctum, the War Cabinet.[5]

Fighter Command was still heavily outnumbered. At the start of August the total number of operational fighters in Luftflotten 2 and 3 amounted to 929, the bulk of them Me 109s; in addition, these air groups included 316 dive-bombers and 875 long-range bombers. Luftflotte 5, on the edge of the Battle of Britain arena, had 34 Me 110 twin-engined fighters and 123 long-range bombers.[6] The Luftwaffe nevertheless suffered from a disproportionate lack of fighters compared with their

84

bomber strength: insufficient consideration had been given to the need for fighters, and too much emphasis had been laid on the potential of dive-bombers – in fact the latter, the famous Ju 87 Stukas, were to prove highly vulnerable in the Battle of Britain. Of the 1491 military aircraft produced in Germany in 1939, only about one third – 449 – were fighters; in 1940 a total of 6618 aircraft of all types were produced, but only a quarter – 1693 – were fighters. Simultaneously, the strength of fighter pilots available suffered from the need to find aircrew for the bombers and dive-bombers. The most important Luftwaffe aircraft in the Battle of Britain was the Me 109, yet at the beginning of 1940 the monthly production total for this type was only about 125. Not until 1941 would the production of Me 109s exceed 300 a month; by contrast, in autumn 1944, when Germany's fortunes were fast waning and when the country was being blasted by allied bombers, the Me 109 monthly production total reached a peak of 2500 machines.[7]

So, despite the numerical superiority of all types of aircraft in early August 1940, the Luftwaffe suffered acute problems and resources were by no means unlimited. A long, intense aerial campaign could have been just as intolerable for the Luftwaffe as it would have been for the RAF. The German Air Force already lacked sufficient fighters to escort large bombing raids; the total of Me 109s was by no measure excessive; fighter pilots might soon be in short supply. Above all, the Luftwaffe fighter force was being called upon to undertake a strategic role for which it had not been designed. Previously, it had been considered that the role of the fighters would be to obtain local air superiority over the Army front, assisting the Army in land operations in conjunction with ground support aircraft. Fighters had been seen as an integral part of *Blitzkrieg*. Now an entirely new role had been thrust upon them: they had been allotted the primary strategic task separate from a land offensive. This heavy responsibility would impose a severe strain on equipment, tactics and on the physical and mental make-up of the pilots themselves. And this strain was rendered even more unbearable by the inflated, false optimism of the Luftwaffe chief, Goering.

On 2 August Goering's Operations Staff issued instructions for the all-out battle against the RAF. The Luftwaffe would carry out the orders contained in Hitler's directive of the previous day. Goering believed the task of overpowering the RAF could be accomplished in just four days; the German forces given the honour of obtaining air superiority would initially be Kesselring's Luftflotte 2 and Sperrle's Luftflotte 3, after which the assault would be joined by Stumpff's Luftflotte 5 flying from Norwegian and Danish bases. On the first day the Spitfires and Hurricanes would be destroyed in the air, and their forward airfields, coastal radar stations and ground organisation would be eliminated. On the second day the attacks would be extended to airfields in the outer London area and to other parts of the country within the limited range of the German aircraft. These hard blows would be continued on the third day, leading to complete victory on the fourth. The programme was however conditional on good weather during the period; the German meteorological experts consulted their charts and declared that a fine spell would come within the next few days, yet the Luftflotten needed almost a week to prepare. Goering therefore chose 10 August as the date for the offensive to begin: he named it *Adlertag* – Eagle Day.[8]

Saturday 3 August saw the start of a British Bank Holiday weekend. The weather suited a holiday mood – sunny with a gentle north breeze. The RAF fielded a cricket eleven against the London Fire Service at Lords. Throughout the country myriad small groups of men took the opportunity of this day from work to undertake Home Guard practice – this force, which had changed its title from the LDV during the previous week, now numbered over one million men; from 3 August local units would be formally affiliated to the county regiments and permitted to wear their badges.

Churchill, at Chequers for the weekend, refused to allow the holiday spirit to predominate. He issued a warning statement: 'The Prime Minister wishes it to be known that the possibility of German attempts at invasion has by no means passed away. The fact that the Germans are now putting about rumours that they do not intend an invasion should be regarded with a double dose of the suspicion which attaches to all their utterances. Our sense of growing strength and preparedness must not lead to the slightest relaxation of vigilance.'[9] Churchill was preparing a long memorandum on the invasion situation which would be considered by the COS after the Bank Holiday. Meanwhile, the influence of Brooke was being felt at GHQ Home Command. During the 3rd a paper was sent from his HQ to the commands, compiled by representatives of the three services, which discussed the possible scale and direction of a German invasion. The assessment differed considerably from those made over previous months: possible points of departure for the German forces now included north-west and west France; a substantial attack might be launched against southern England; shipping available for German forces from Norway had risen to an amount sufficient to carry two divisions, rather than one as previously estimated. Concerning an air attack, the memorandum declared: 'The re-equipment of the German Air Force has not proceeded so quickly as had been anticipated. If the Germans have by now managed to complete the re-equipment of all their units, the bombers initially available could carry 2840 tons of bombs for one sortie, but this state of readiness has probably not yet been reached.' The paper still overestimated the numbers of airborne troops likely to be dropped in Britain and still underestimated the sea-borne strength. 'Air-borne troops of up to 15,000 lightly-equipped men might, given control of the necessary landing ground and local air superiority, be landed in one day in East Anglia or in Kent... This number includes some 5000 parachute troops... Sea-borne troops up to five divisions might be landed as an initial striking force.'[10]

Also on 3 August the thirteen crack German divisions intended for the initial striking force in Sea Lion completed their deployment in the coastal area facing Britain's south coast. Each totalled about 19,000 men; the complete force was armed with nearly 650 tanks. Every division had been split into two echelons, comprising a spearhead element of about 7000 men per division with the remainder acting as close support. The first echelon would carry the main striking power, including artillery, machine-guns, smoke-projectors and field-howitzers. Training had already begun and would now be intensified with field exercises and landing practice. Troops would spend many hours wading from rubber boats and landing craft – with the latter improvised somewhat inefficiently from Rhine barges. In fact, despite their strength on paper, the divisions were by no means as well-equipped as their commanders would have liked. Although the total force would be provided with up to 40,000 vehicles, this first invasion wave would also rely on nearly 26,000 bicycles and almost 4000 horses.

Hitler travelled from Berghof to Berlin on the same day and immediately received further reports from his Army staff on equipment deficiencies. Preparations were still a long way from completion, despite the order from Hitler that all should be ready by mid-August. Differences between the Army and Navy in France would soon emerge; meanwhile Hitler waited in his capital for the opening of the Luftwaffe's unrestricted offensive.

'This is August Bank Holiday,' declared Ed Murrow in his nightly broadcast next day, 'but it's a holiday in name only.' Murrow had spent the weekend at a Channel port. 'The coasts are deserted except for those soldiers, sailors and airmen who are preparing to fight unwelcome visitors from across the North Sea and the Channel... The white cliffs and the green fields of France were clearly visible on the other side. It almost seemed that we should be able to see the German planes taking off.' But nothing had happened except for the noise of the occasional high-flying aircraft. 'People who live in Kent,' continued Murrow, 'one of the most beautiful counties in England, tell me there isn't much talk of the war down there. Most of the talk is about this year's hop harvest, the heavy oat crop, the need for preserving fruit and vegetables for the winter...'[11]

On 5 August grouse-shooting began, brought forward from the traditional Glorious Twelfth because of the uncertain situation. Sportsmen bemoaned the fact that the weather, which the previous day had been clear and sunny, had now broken: clouds hung low and heavy showers drenched those waiting in the butts on the grouse moors. The deteriorating weather also affected conditions above the Channel, and Eagle Day, for which a fine period was essential, lay only five days ahead. Nevertheless, for the first twenty-four-hour period since 1 August the pilots of Fighter Command managed some success: they claimed four enemy aircraft shot down for certain and another four unconfirmed. One British pilot was reported missing.[12] The actual figures were probably one RAF and seven Luftwaffe aircraft destroyed.

On that day the Prime Minister completed his memorandum on the subject of invasion; the paper reflected his offensive spirit. 'The land forces and the Home Army are maintained primarily for the purpose of making the enemy come in such large numbers as to afford a proper target for the sea and air forces.' Churchill continued to insist that the emphasis on defence should not be placed on the beaches but on mobile reserves. The enemy's weakest moment was 'not, as is sometimes suggested, when actually getting out of his boats, but when sprawled upon the shore with his communications cut and his supplies running short.' He still believed the stretch from the Wash round to Dover, where the Germans would have the advantage of the narrow sea, to be the most menaced. 'This sector of the coast front is also nearest to the supreme enemy objective, London.' Churchill added a scale of relative degree of danger for various coastal regions: this gave a figure of five for the Wash–Dover section, three from Cromarty Firth to the Wash, one-and-a-half from Dover to Lands End, and only a fraction for the west coast.[13]

A Berlin conference on the same day revealed that the Germans were still contemplating landings west of Dover, rather than eastwards. But the discussions also confirmed the deep rift between the German Navy and Army over the width of the invasion area. Raeder insisted that the front should be concentrated in the Dover Straits between Folkestone and Beachy Head, whereas Brauchitsch maintained that an assault on this region alone would be highly vulnerable: the British would be able to bring superior forces to bear, and the Army must be allowed to plan an offensive on a wide front extending almost two-thirds along the south coast, from Ramsgate perhaps as far as Lyme Bay on the Devon–Dorset border. The respective Navy and Army chiefs could only agree to a staff conference to be held two days later, on 7 August, at Fontainebleu.[14]

Only one German aircraft was claimed shot down on 6 August; British casualties were said to be just one pilot injured. The lull seemed to offer some chance of slight relaxation for both pilots and workers, and Bevin, Minister of Labour and National Service, raised the subject of industrial holidays at the noon War Cabinet meeting. Bevin was clearly anxious to keep industrial morale as high as possible; he emphasised the need for a period of recuperation before the end of September, fearing that 'if no break was given, the effects on production would be serious, and the risk of labour difficulties would be increased when the days grew shorter and we got into the blackout period.' Beaverbrook strongly disagreed, seeking to keep production at fever pitch. He told the War Cabinet that he was 'very anxious to avoid any suspicion that the Government were encouraging the holiday spirit.' Ministers agreed that there should be no public announcement of any holiday break.[15]

Even apart from the weather restrictions, German units had other preoccupations to keep them on the ground: from western France up to Norway, airfields and aircraft were being prepared for Eagle Day. Goering summoned Kesselring and Sperrle to Karinhall, the luxurious hunting home which Goering had named after his first wife, Karin, and which so reflected the *Reichsmarschall*'s own character – extravagant to the point of being grotesque. 'The halls and rooms of Karinhall were sheathed with valuable paintings hung one above the other in three and four tiers,' commented another visitor, Speer. 'He even had a life-size nude representing Europe mounted above the canopy of his magnificent bed.'[16] Goering was constantly stocking his home with fresh art treasures filched from conquered territory; he confidently expected that fresh acquisitions would soon be obtained from England. He informed his Luftflotten chiefs: 'Providing the weather is favourable, launch the offensive in four days' time.' Details of the air campaign were discussed

89

and as always Goering oozed optimism; Kesselring exhibited his usual excitable, highly strung nature; Sperrle was typically frigid, with a disconcerting lack of emotion.

Next day the conference took place at Fontainebleu aimed at settling the German Naval and Army differences over the most basic Sea Lion issue – the landing areas for the invading forces. Discussions totally failed. Heading the respective staffs were Halder for the Army and Schniewind for the Navy; the latter continued to argue against the Army's wide-front proposal and urged a more concentrated target instead. 'I utterly reject the navy's proposal,' retorted Halder. 'From the point of view of the army I regard it as complete suicide. I might just as well put the troops that have landed straight through a sausage machine.' Halder pointed out that the narrow front would expose the invaders to a packed British defence in terrain which was extremely unfavourable for the attacker: the British must be thrown off-balance by threats on a multiple front. Schniewind declared that this would be 'equally suicidal... in view of British naval supremacy.' Halder wrote in his diary: 'The talk only led to the confirmation of an unbridgeable gap.'[17]

In London a COS meeting took note of a paper presented by Sir Archibald Sinclair, Air Secretary, dealing with the crucial subject of pilot strength. Sinclair, without the benefit of any intelligence reports indicating an imminent Luftwaffe offensive, displayed optimism. 'I am glad to be able to report that a material improvement has been effected in the crew strength of the RAF, notably in the Fighter Command; that a considerable accession of strength is to be expected from the allied air force personnel now in this country; that additional measures have been taken which will further speed up the output from the flying training organisation...' Sinclair pointed out that Fighter Command pilot strength had been a matter of 'grave concern' at the conclusion of the French campaign. 'The increase of the pilot establishment of each squadron of sixteen aircraft from twenty-one pilots to twenty-six had already been shown to be advisable, but had not proved possible to put into effect, and the unprecedented intensity with which the operations were conducted resulted in a most serious deficiency of pilots.' But the lull in late June and early July had been put to good use. 'Not only has the wastage been made good, but the strength of the fighter squadrons has almost been brought up to the new establishment, and a further four fighter squadrons have been formed. During the worst phase of the recent battle [in France] the pilot deficiency in Fighter

Command amounted to some 300. Now it is seventy-four on the increased total establishment of 1460. On the present rate of wastage this deficiency will, I hope, be overtaken by the end of this month.'[18]

So, as the end of the first phase of the Battle of Britain approached, Fighter Command was far more than holding its own: about eighty more pilots were serving in the squadrons than the desired establishment at the beginning of June, and, taking into account the replacement of pilots lost in the May–June fighting on the Continent, about 306 more pilots had been added to Fighter Command strength; four more squadrons were in operation than had been after Dunkirk; the number of operational aircraft stood at 714 – almost 300 more than on 4 June.[19] It seemed that Dowding's fears were groundless.

But Eagle Day approached. And even before the opening of Goering's main offensive, less than twenty-four hours after Sinclair's report was presented to the COS the Fighter Command pilots were engaged in their greatest battle so far, after which a total of sixteen would be reported dead, missing or wounded. On only six days during the entire Battle of Britain would this figure be overtaken.

✍

CHAPTER EIGHT

The Second Phase

8–12 August

First reports of air activity reached Whitehall as the COS met during the morning of Thursday 8 August, but so far the information seemed nothing unusual. The COS turned to a discussion of Churchill's paper on invasion, the one which, completed three days before, had included a ratio scale concerning the most likely German targets for invasion. The COS stated their entire agreement with the Prime Minister's assessment that the sector running east from Dover was the most menaced. The meeting also studied that latest War Cabinet weekly résumé, which revealed a significant drop in sorties: 3173 for the week just ending compared with 4606 during the period 25 July–1 August.[1] But the Air Ministry weekly situation report, also completed that day, warned that the lull might soon end and that the Luftwaffe seemed in excellent spirits. 'Almost without exception, prisoners of war say that the German people, and in particular the Fuehrer, still hope for peace, and wish to avoid total warfare. They almost pity us, because we do not realise to the full the terrific might of the attack when it does come. They think that the aeroplanes will come over in waves of at least 1000 at a time and that they will pulverise all objectives.' The Air Ministry assessment continued: 'The GAF appears to be maintaining its previous high standard of training, and, in spite of its losses, is giving no real evidence of a shortage in trained pilots.'[2]

Outside the COS conference room at the War Office the sky was clear and steel blue, with only occasional cloud. The same fine weather stretched along the Channel. Eagle Day was scheduled to begin in forty-eight hours, but now the German pilots took advantage of improved conditions to launch a preliminary offensive. Soon after dawn Spitfires from Britain's 609 Squadron had been ordered aloft to escort a convoy off the Needles. The twenty-five vessels had assembled the previous evening, and comprised the largest group to sail since the end of July. New protective plans had been prepared by the Admiralty: two destroyers would provide escort, and the vessels would sail through the most vulnerable area during darkness; specially modified ships carried barrage balloons. But during the previous night the convoy had come under attack from German E-boats, and now, with daylight, the Luftwaffe could take its turn.

The escort Spitfires from 609 Squadron located the convoy, which was already shaken from the night-time strikes – two ships had collided causing one to sink. 'It was a very clear day with a brilliant sun,' wrote the 609 Squadron pilot, Crook, 'just the sort of day that the Germans love.' He added: 'I remember thinking at the time that there was obviously going to be a lot of trouble that day, because this convoy was far too large a prize for the Hun to miss.' But nothing happened on this first 609 Squadron patrol; Crook and the other Spitfire pilots returned to base for breakfast.

Unseen by the Spitfires, a German reconnaissance aircraft had flown high over the Isle of Wight, and the enemy pilot pinpointed the convoy's location. His report soon brought results. Just before 9 am about 60 Luftwaffe bombers, including Ju 87s, assembled over the French coast and began moving across the Channel escorted by Me 109s. A few minutes later, Hurricanes of 145 Squadron took off from Westhampnett in the Tangmere sector, led by Squadron-Leader J. R. A. Peel and ordered to escort the convoy. The enemy arrived first. The Me 109 escorts climbed to about 20,000 feet, high into the sun, while the Stukas dropped one by one on to the vessels below. Huge columns of water began to erupt around the ships and destroyers. Then Peel's Hurricanes arrived. The British pilots, also with the morning sun behind their aircraft, noted the black dots of the Stukas beneath them and prepared to strike down into the vulnerable dive-bombers. But the Me 109s, at an even greater height, dived to intercept and the Hurricanes spiralled upwards to defend themselves.

'The enemy fighters, who were painted silver, were half-rolling and diving and zooming in climbing turns,' reported Peel. 'I fired two five-seconds bursts at one and saw it dive into the sea. Then I followed another up in a zoom and got him as he stalled.' The dog-fights swirled southwards over the sea; more aircraft fluttered and fell into the Channel. Then a burst of fire from a Messerschmitt ripped into the

93

fuselage of Peel's Hurricane, and his aircraft flipped forward with smoke pouring behind. It crashed headlong into the sea, but Peel escaped; aircraft from his squadron circled above him as protection until rescue boats arrived.[3]

The day had barely begun. At 11.30 am, six aircraft from 609 Squadron were ordered up for their second patrol over the British vessels; one of the Spitfires turned back with oxygen trouble, but the remaining five found the ships about twelve miles south of Bournemouth. They flew near a small layer of wispy cloud. 'I glanced out towards the convoy,' wrote Crook, 'and saw three of the balloons falling in flames. Obviously an attack was starting, and I climbed above the cloud layer and went towards the convoy at full throttle, climbing all the time towards the sun.' Crook could see a large number of enemy fighters circling above the ships 'looking exactly like a swarm of flies buzzing round a pot of jam.' Below, dive-bombers were flashing down and great fountains of white foam were again spurting skywards. 'I could see that one or two ships had already been hit and were on fire. I was now at 16,000 feet above the whole battle and turned round to look for a victim. At that moment, a Hurricane squadron appeared on the scene and attacked right into the middle of the enemy fighters.'

Among these Hurricane pilots was Pilot Officer J. L. Crisp. He had flown his first solo flight just a year before. Posted to 43 Squadron, Tangmere, on 5 July he had already survived numerous clashes over the Channel – on 19 July his squadron had met fifteen Me 109s off Selsea and Crisp was shot down, but he had returned to base, climbed into another aircraft and calmly flown off on another patrol later in the day. Yet Crisp still felt frightened as he flung his aircraft into the midst of the Me 109s. He jotted the following words in his Pilot's Log afterwards: 'Met large quantities of assorted Hun a/cs over convoys off I. of Wight, fired at some, no certs. (Very scared.)'[4]

Suddenly, the sky was empty again. Below, circles of widening oil on the surface of the sea showed where aircraft had disappeared beneath the waves. The pilots of 609 Squadron claimed four enemy destroyed;[5] the convoy sailed on, leaving two ships sunk. The same pattern was repeated during the afternoon: at 4.15 a strong enemy force appeared over the vessels and attacked from the cover of gathering clouds. British fighters sent up to intercept claimed that the Luftwaffe strength totalled as many as 130 aircraft of all types; RAF Hurricanes and Spitfires weaved and dived amongst them but were too few to give adequate protection for the vessels below, and the convoy dispersed during the late afternoon. Four ships had been sunk and another six damaged.[6]

Yet despite the loss of ships and despite the continuing disparity in aircraft strength over the Channel, many British pilots emerged from the 8 August actions even more confident than before. Aircraft from 609 Squadron again patrolled over the Isle of Wight during the evening, on their third operational flight that day, hoping to add to their total of four enemy shot down. The exuberant section leader, who had himself destroyed two of the four, scoured the skies for fresh victims. 'For the next few days he regarded the GAF rather as an organisation which provided him with a little target practice and general harmless amusement,' commented Crook.[7] A similar air of confidence was reflected in the report by the CoAS to the War Cabinet at 12.30 pm next day. The fighting off the Isle of Wight had been the 'biggest air action which had so far taken place off our coast,' said Newall. 'The enemy's main effort had developed into three successive attacks, involving at least 300 aircraft... Our fighters had achieved great success.' Losses were estimated at eighteen RAF aircraft for fifty-two German confirmed and fourteen unconfirmed. The War Cabinet 'congratulated the Secretary of State for Air and the Chief of the Air Staff on this fine achievement.'[8] Respective losses were in fact about thirty-one German and twenty RAF aircraft; two RAF pilots were reported killed, thirteen missing and one wounded.[9]

The weather again closed down. Limited air action took place on 9 August: five German aircraft were destroyed, but the RAF lost four. Across the Channel, all preparations had been completed for Eagle Day, scheduled for the next day. But Goering, after anxiously studying meteorological reports, postponed the operation at the last moment. The RAF would be reprieved until 13 August; Hitler once again left Berlin and travelled to Berghof. Goering's decision led to a sniping remark in the German Naval Staff war diary on 10 August, which revealed the lack of satisfactory relations between the two services: 'The Luftwaffe had missed opportunities afforded by the recent favourable weather.'[10] Nor had relations between the Navy and Army improved: the dispute still remained over the Sea Lion invasion area. During 10 August Brauchitsch handed a detailed memorandum to Keitel, Chief of Supreme Command of the Armed Forces, which explained the Army's views. Brauchitsch was 'very reluctantly' prepared to abandon the idea of a landing on the far west of the sector, Lyme Bay, but still insisted upon a far wider front than the Navy. An attack on the beaches around Brighton was considered especially important, because the terrain in this sector was ideal for mobile troops. A minimum of ten divisions must be put ashore within four days in the region between Ramsgate and Brighton Bay, with almost half this strength in the immediate vicinity of Brighton. A wide front would either compel the British to disperse their troops, or would allow the invaders to encircle the more concentrated defenders. 'Pressure will be brought to bear on the English, who may be rapidly forced to abandon the entire area south and south-east of London.[11] The Navy still maintained that the Army's ambitious scheme was completely impossible, and nothing could be done to sort out the differences until Hitler returned to Berlin.

Occasional bombing raids over England continued. These had been a constant feature of life in the south-east for over six weeks, especially in Kent – soon to be dubbed Hell's Corner. Maidstone had had its first air raid on 8 August, although no bombs were dropped on the town. On 10 August a lone Dornier raided West Malling airfield at 7.30 am, releasing a string of High Explosive bombs (HEs); the airfield buildings escaped damage, but workmen clocking in at the nearby contractor's office were injured by splinters and machine gun bullets.

Late in the evening the skies began to clear, and next morning, 11 August, the weather was again fine along much of the south coast. Fighter Command squadrons were once more ready for an upsurge of enemy activity. Spitfires from 74 'Tiger' Squadron, commanded by Sailor Malan, were patrolling off Dover at 8 am, and the day would later be referred to by the squadron as 'Sailor's August Eleventh'. He wrote in his report: 'I climbed on an ENE course to 20,000 feet into the sun, and then turned down-sun towards Dover and surprised eight Me 109s at 20,000 feet flying in pairs staggered line astern towards Dover.' The attack began in a flurry of Spitfires; other enemy aircraft dived to help their Me 109 companions, but all the British aircraft emerged unscathed. Malan shot down one Me 109, and seven others were claimed by the rest of his squadron.[12] Just over an hour later the Germans succeeded in a lightning attack on the Dover balloon barrage, and bombers struck at the harbour at about 10 am; once again Malan's pilots rose to intercept. His Red Section attacked, but his supporting Blue and Green sections, waiting above, failed to hear his R/T orders and stayed at a higher altitude. Sailor therefore climbed up to them and attempted to lead them back into the fight, but was unable to do so – his radio was later found to have been damaged by a bullet. 'I proceeded towards Dover by myself. I attacked two Me 109s at 25,000

96

feet about mid-Channel, delivered two two-second bursts with deflection at the rearmost one and saw my bullets entering the fuselage...
Eight Me 109s, who had previously escaped my attention, dived towards me and I climbed in right-hand spiral, and they made no attempt to follow.'[13]

Action spread westwards during the morning. At 11.30 am 609 and six other squadrons were patrolling Weymouth Bay, and as David Crook commented: 'Altogether it looked as though it was going to be a big show.' German bombers were already approaching, escorted by Messerschmitts at about 24,000 feet; the target for these aircraft, perhaps totalling 150 machines, was the Portland naval base. Hurricanes from the Tangmere sector were the first to see the enemy formations, and they immediately peeled into the attack. The Me 110s reacted with their usual tactic: they formed a tight defensive circle, flying round and round each other's tail and forcing any attacking British aircraft to come into the fire of the Messerschmitt behind. But the RAF squadrons had already found an answer to this defensive manœuvre, and now the Spitfires from 609 Squadron proceeded to put it into practice. They climbed to about 1000 feet above the enemy spiral, then the Squadron Leader banked his aircraft round, and down they dived. 'We came down right on top of the enemy formation,' wrote Crook, 'going at terrific speed, and as we approached them we split up slightly, each pilot selecting his own target. I saw an Me 110 ahead of me going across in front. I fired at him but did not allow enough deflection and my bullets passed behind him. I then closed in on him from behind and fired a good burst at practically point-blank range.' The British pilots claimed about five Me 110s destroyed, but the German bombers had meanwhile droned onwards: some reached Portland and caused considerable damage.[14]

Ninety minutes later German aircraft launched another raid, far along the coast to the east. A British convoy was proceeding off Norfolk when, at about 1 pm, twenty-four Messerschmitts appeared from the south. These enemy aircraft belonged to a special Luftwaffe unit, commanded by Captain Walter Rubensdörffer: the squadron had been given the title experimental *Gruppe* 210, and was the only one of its kind in the Luftwaffe at that time. Its unique feature originated from the 500-lb and 1000-lb bombs slung beneath the Me 110 fuselage, making these aircraft into fighter-bombers. The aim was to make up for the deficiency in German long-range bomber strength, and at the same time to overcome the difficulties being experienced by the bombers

97

through the lack of adequate fighter protection: the same aircraft could now, in theory, perform both roles. Yet the experiment was strongly disliked by many pilots. 'We fighter pilots looked upon this violation of our aircraft with great bitterness,' wrote Galland. 'The operative value of fighter-bombers cannot be denied, but only pre-supposing a surplus of fighter aircraft. To use a fighter as a fighter-bomber when the strength of the fighter arm is inadequate to achieve air superiority is putting the cart before the horse.'[15] But the raid by Rubensdörffer's aircraft on 11 August seemed to indicate that the experiment might be successful. The Messerschmitts dived into the attack on the Norfolk convoy, which failed to take necessary bomb evasion action and remained a concentrated target. Suddenly, the bombs dropped from beneath the Luftwaffe aircraft: two vessels were virtually crippled. The Messerschmitts curved south for their return home and had now become ordinary fighters again. Spitfires from 74 Squadron intercepted; the Me 110s formed a defensive spiral while the 109s held off the British aircraft, and the enemy eventually escaped without casualties.[16]

Pilots from 74 Squadron had greater success with another action during the afternoon of 'Sailor's August Eleventh', in an engagement described by Pilot Officer Mackay Stephen as 'a smasher... A hell of a dog-fight.' His account continued: 'We found forty Me 110s in three groups, getting into a position to attack a convoy. When the leader saw us approaching, he started forming into the Nazi's defensive formation circles. This suited us. Mungo Park, who was leading, and his merry Tiger boys carried out Sailor's diving-in-and-out-of-the-circle tactics. Nazis were tumbling into the Channel one after another. Ten went for certain.' Nor had the day finished for 74 Squadron: Malan led another patrol of eight Spitfires over Folkestone at 4 pm and himself shot down another aircraft. Results claimed for the 'Tiger' Squadron for the day's fighting, later shown to be over-optimistic, were twenty-three Me 109s and 110s destroyed, one Me 110 probable, and fourteen others damaged; the Squadron lost two pilots.[17]

As evening fell both sides assessed the day's activity and found reason for hope. Next day the Germans announced: 'The whole world is impressed by yesterday's great air battle at Portland, which... extended as far as Dover and in which the English lost 93 planes.' The announcement proceeded to give travelogue details of the target: 'Portland has 12,000 inhabitants. The naval harbour has existed since 1849... The well-known reformatory for young criminals is one of Portland's lesser attractions.'[18] At 12.30 pm the CoAS presented an equally optimistic account to the War Cabinet at 10 Downing Street. Although he admitted that as many as 150 German aircraft may have crossed the coast at Portland, Newall claimed that sixty Luftwaffe machines had been destroyed for certain, at a cost of twenty Hurricanes and five Spitfires.[19] A study of the records reveals that the respective casualty figures were more likely to have been about thirty-two RAF aircraft and thirty-eight Luftwaffe; sources for Newall's total are a mystery – Fighter Command's own estimate for German losses came nearer the truth, claiming thirty-two enemy aircraft destroyed for certain and forty-six unconfirmed.[20] British pilots were well aware of the difficulties in providing an accurate sum. 'It is almost impossible to stay and see definite results in the middle of such a mix-up,' commented Crook. 'All that you can do is to fire a good burst at some enemy and then, hit or miss, get away quickly.'[21] Two pilots often claimed the same machine destroyed; aircraft which seemed to be diving to destruction sometimes recovered at the last moment. More indicative of the true state of RAF affairs were the daily returns at the Air Ministry of aircraft strengths and pilot losses: these reveal that at 9 am on 12 August the number of operational aircraft in Fighter Command stood at 699, compared with 706 at 9 am on the 11th – all but seven of the lost aircraft had therefore been replaced. The number of Spitfires had actually increased, from 247 to 248.[22] The figure for pilot casualties seemed more serious. More men were lost in the twenty-four hours from noon 11 August to noon 12 August than on any previous day in the air struggle over England and the Channel: twenty-three pilots were listed as missing or dead, plus three wounded. And this total would never again be as high in the main Battle of Britain period.[23]

By noon on 12 August, battle had begun again. Newall told the War Cabinet: 'A number of enemy raids were in progress at that moment, including one at Portsmouth, but detailed information was not available.'[24] Early in the morning Goering had confirmed that Eagle Day would start the following day; final preparations were being made at Luftwaffe airfields. But German pilots were also seizing advantage of the excellent flying weather. Light cloud which had partly obscured visibility the previous day had now disappeared, and conditions were perfect. Soon after dawn the teleprinters at the Luftflotten 2 and 3 headquarters in Brussels and Paris began to click out an order from Jeschonnek, Goering's Chief of Staff. 'Known English DeTe stations are to be attacked by special forces of the first wave to put them out of action.' The code-name DeTe, standing for Decimeter Telegraphy, referred to

99

the RAF radar stations – the eyes of Fighter Command. Simultaneously, strikes would be made against RAF forward airfields.

At 9.30 am, Dorniers of Major Outzmann's bomber *Gruppe* appeared off the exposed coastal airfield of Lympne in Kent, covered by a strong fighter escort; a string of 100-lb bombs fell along the runway and struck nearby hangars. Meanwhile, at their French airfields the Me 110 and 109 fighter-bombers of Captain Rubensdörffer's experimental *Gruppe* 210 were taking off for another special mission; Rubensdörffer's three squadrons were assembled by 10.35 am and proceeded northwards over the Channel. Just before 11 am he spoke into his radio: 'Calling 3 Squadron. Proceed on special mission. Good hunting.' Rubensdörffer immediately swung south-west along the English coast with the twelve Me 110s of 1 and 2 squadrons, and the third maintained a steady course towards Dover. These eight Me 109s under First-Lieutenant Otto Hintze located their target: Dover radar installation. They dived to attack and at least three bombs exploded within the complex – but the vital 350-foot radar masts remained standing. Hintze's Me 109s, no longer able to undertake a bombing role, turned for home.[25]

Rubensdörffer had meanwhile struck further west. The two squadrons remaining under his direct control separated as they turned in from the coast, with six aircraft making for Pevensey radar station, near Eastbourne, and the others for Rye station near Hastings. Pevensey suffered hits from eight 1000-lb bombs which shattered the transmitters and put the station off the air. One of the most terrifying features of these raids was the fact that the radar operators, usually WAAF personnel, actually plotted the enemy as they moved nearer and nearer to their stations. This happened with the attack on Rye. Gradually the blips approached, until it became obvious to those watching the screens that they themselves were the target. 'I think it would be a good idea,' said the senior officer in the radar room, 'if we had our tin hats.' Moments later the enemy struck. 'A terrific explosion rocked the hut and the tube went flat,' wrote Corporal Daphne Carne, WAAF. 'The brilliant trace seemed to shrivel and then, as if in a final struggle for existence, flared up into a bright spot of blind light before it slowly faded away.' Outside she saw a sight which soon became painfully familiar to WAAF girls. 'Huge clouds of earth and mud covered the platform of the transmitter tower... The road was pitted with craters and great gaps were torn in the high steel railings enclosing the compound. Where the cook-house had been there was an enormous lake on which floated splintered planks of wood and all manner of kitchen utensils.' The 1000-lb and 500-lb bombs destroyed all the main buildings – but the station was in action again three and a half hours later.[26]

German aircraft were also moving towards the coast further west, in the Isle of Wight–Portsmouth area. This time Fighter Command squadrons were in a position to intercept. Pilots of 609 Squadron were called to readiness at 11 am and soon joined other aircraft above Portsmouth. Seventy-eight Luftwaffe bombers were approaching with fighter escort; battle began just before 11.30. 'I was staggered by the number of Huns in the sky,' wrote Crook. He muttered to himself: 'My God, what a party.' Someone else remarked: 'There was the whole bloody German Air Force, bar Goering.' Crook and his companions climbed towards the enemy and saw three formations of Messerschmitts circling at 20,000–28,000 feet. Crook decided to attack the middle layer and positioned himself about 2000 feet above the Me 110s; he dived straight into the middle of the circle. 'I selected a target and blazed away madly at him... But I could not observe any results as I flashed right through the enemy formation at terrific speed, narrowly missing a collision with one fighter and continuing my dive for some distance before I could pull out. I think I was doing well over 500 mph, and the strain of pulling out was considerable. I looked around to see what was going on, and at that moment an Me 110, enveloped in a sheet of flame, fell past within 200 yards of me.'[27]

Many of the German bombers turned back in the face of this Fighter Command opposition at Portsmouth, but some pressed on. Harbour works suffered damage, and warships came near to destruction from a brave raid by Stukas: these dive-bombers approached fast and low, using the gap in the balloon barrage at the harbour entrance. Once through the opening, the Stukas found an almost unbelievable target. One Luftwaffe pilot said afterwards: 'There was almost everything of which an airman dreams. Enormous ships lay at anchor and in the docks. The targets were so close together it was hardly possible to miss.' But the bombs fell wide. More accurate was another raid by fifteen aircraft which had fought their way from the main engagement near Portsmouth and turned on the Ventnor radar station, on the Isle of Wight. This attack proved the most successful of all the strikes against radar installations during the day: the equipment was so badly damaged that the station was rendered unusable – and a gap had been torn in Fighter Command's radar chain.

Only half the day had gone. Small, sudden bombing raids were spreading across southern England. 'We had four air-raid warnings in forty-eight hours,' wrote Mrs Peacock at Chichester; her diary entry continued: '"Moo" was just selecting a pair of shoes at the shoe shop and trying to decide between a high heel or a cuban one when the siren shrieked, the shop closed, and we left with others for a hole in the ground floor next door, which had been made into a modern crypt with *cement* seats very cold to the behind. When we got back to our rented house "Dada" had returned from barracks on his bike, and there was a bit of shrapnel in the bicycle basket.'[28] Further east, attacks were being launched at other RDF stations and a heavy bombing raid was in progress at Dover. Successive waves of aircraft swept over the town; two barrage balloons were shot down, and once again ships in the harbour bobbed like corks. Among the first civilian casualties was William Ransome, Dover's Deputy Town Clerk. 'I felt what I thought was a sandbag fall on my shoulder. I thought my neighbour was having some fun with me, until I put my hand behind me and felt blood.' Another victim, Mrs Emily Foster, said: 'I was up the stairs scrubbing the top floor, the next thing I knew I was lying in St James's Street, so I just picked myself up and walked away.'[29] Soon after midday twenty-two Stukas dive-bombed a convoy in the Thames estuary just north of Margate: these enemy aircraft were commanded by Captain von Brauchitsch, son of the German Army's C-in-C. Two small steamers received direct hits.

During this hot and sunny afternoon the enemy concentrated more on the Fighter Command forward airfields. Kentish radar stations hit in the morning were still not functioning at peak efficiency, enabling enemy aircraft to arrive almost without warning at Manston airfield at 1.30 pm. Responsible for this attack were the aircraft from Rubensdörffer's experimental *Gruppe*, with First-Lieutenant Martin Lutz's 1 Squadron leading the strike. His fifteen Me 110s appeared overhead; pilots of 65 Squadron had just sprinted to their Spitfires and the RAF machines were rushing down the runway in a desperate attempt to get airborne; only one or two managed to climb upwards as the Me 110s began their dive. Down they dropped to 1000 feet, levelled out, then released their 150-lb bombs. 'The fighters were all lined up,' reported Lutz. 'Our bombs fell right amongst them.' Below, Flight-Lieutenant Quill was among the Spitfire pilots struggling to escape. His Spitfire's engine noise was suddenly drowned by the shuddering crunch of the bombs and a nearby hangar was blasted into the air. Quill opened his engine to full throttle and the Spitfire leapt forward. Ahead, another Spitfire disappeared in a black cloud of smoke, then miraculously

At Compiegne to sign the Franco-German Armistice in June 1940, Hitler awaits the arrival of French delegates beside Marshal Foch's famous coach. With him are General Von Brauchitsch (right), Admiral Raeder (just visible above Hitler's shoulder), Rudolph Hess and Goering

Hitler, Major Deile and General Keitel (right) studying a map of England

The Dunkirk lifeline

The British
Expeditionary Force
arrives home. A
seething but
surprisingly orderly
mass of steel-hats, as
more and still
thousands more of
the BEF return to
England

Training school for the Home Guard

General Alan Brooke, C-in-C Home Forces paying a visit to the Scottish Command

Goering with a group of
German airforce officers
– and interrogating a
pilot just back from
England

appeared again on the far side. Quill felt his aircraft lift, and he banked away. Other Messerschmitts were bombing the airfield, this time from 5000 feet, and a total of 175 bombs struck the area. 'Direct hits... on hangars and billets,' reported the German section leader. 'Four amongst fighters taking off. Result: four Hurricanes and five other aircraft destroyed on the ground.'[30] In fact the majority of 65 Squadron aircraft – Spitfires, not Hurricanes as Lutz reported – had managed to escape, immediately climbing in pursuit of the enemy. Some of the Fighter Command pilots soon claimed revenge, among them Wing Commander B. E. 'Paddy' Finucane: 'After losing the two Me 109s at 24,000 feet I climbed up to 30,000 feet and sighted twelve aircraft... I dived into the foremost aircraft. It went into the sea, grey smoke pouring from it.' Finucane shot down another aircraft soon afterwards.[31]

By now the coastal airfield of Hawkinge had become the target. Three separate formations of Do 215s and Ju 87s struck at the station in mid-afternoon, flying at 2,000–3,000 feet with the dive-bombers above and the Dorniers below. Once again hangars were hit and the runway pockmarked by bomb craters. Fighter Command tried to organise itself against this new offensive; urgent orders were transmitted from the control centres to divert aircraft, and controllers and personnel of the WAAF worked to sort out the confusion. 'We tried to get the girls to leave those rooms in which R/T was broadcast from the aircraft during the air fighting,' wrote one senior officer, 'for the language was terrible. But it wasn't idle blasphemy or obscenity. It was the voice of men in the midst of fighting for their lives – and dying. The girls refused to leave their jobs.'[32]

Civilians clustered in the fields and streets to watch the dog-fights above them. 'It seemed impossible at first to believe that these were actual deadly battles and not mock ones,' wrote Frances Faviell. 'It gave one a strange, shaking, sick feeling of excitement to watch their every movement... Twisting, turning, their guns blazing, the sunlight picking them out in the clear sky, they would dive under, over, round, and then straight at their opponents until one would fall in a trail of smoke and flame, often with a gleaming parachute like a toy umbrella preceding the final crash to earth. It was horrible – but it had a macabre fascination impossible to resist.'[33]

Lympne, where workmen were toiling to repair the morning's damage, suffered again during the early evening. Fighting at last died down. Throughout the night the repair work continued at Manston, Hawkinge, and the Pevensey, Rye, Dover and Ventnor radar stations.

Fighter pilots returned to base, their clothes soaked with sweat, their legs and fingers stiff. Some of these youngsters then went on the town: a group of 609 pilots met at the Trocadero, among them David Crook. 'We had a hilarious dinner together, and parted in very good form about 11.30 pm. It seemed so funny to be dining peacefully in Piccadilly only a few hours after being in such a desperate fight.'[34] Meanwhile, the results of the day's battle were being assessed. Over the Channel, Goering was fed optimistic reports from the Luftflotten; senior officers in London felt similar confidence although with more justification. The radar stations at Dover, Pevensey and Rye, the latter with emergency equipment, were functioning again, plus two other complexes which had received minor damage. Ventnor was more seriously affected, and a gap would exist in the radar network at this point for eleven days; arrangements were on hand to send out impulses from another transmitter to mask this defect. These impulses produced no answering echo but they were picked up by the enemy and hence gave the impression that Ventnor had been repaired. A new station was eventually opened at Bembridge on the 23rd.[35] Of the airfields, Lympne, Manston and Hawkinge would be serviceable again by next morning, 13 August, although their efficiency had been impaired.

The RAF was by no means entirely on the defensive during 12 August. British aircraft also struck back at the Germans, in probably the most successful of all the anti-invasion attacks. The target was an aqueduct carrying the Dortmund–Ems canal over the Ems river to the north of Muenster, destruction of which would seriously hinder the movement of small craft to the invasion ports. Ten Hampdens took part in the operation, flown by specially selected crews from 49 and 83 Squadrons Bomber Command. Strong opposition was expected, since previous attempts against the aqueduct would have revealed Britain's interest in the target: five of the Hampdens were therefore ordered to create a diversion and draw enemy fire while the other five attacked.

Two of the five attacking Hampdens were shot down as they approached the target. The remaining three received hits, including the last aircraft flown by Flight Lieutenant Roderick Learoyd as it made a bombing run at 200 feet.

'Three big holes appeared in the starboard wing,' wrote Learoyd. 'They were firing at point-blank range. The navigator continued to direct me on to the target. I could not see it because I was blinded by the glare of the searchlights and had to keep my head below the level of the cockpit top. At last I heard the navigator say "Bombs Gone!"

I immediately did a steep turn to the right and got away, being fired at heavily.'

The bomb dropped from Learoyd's aircraft demolished part of the aqueduct embankment and water surged through the breach to render the canal inoperative for ten days. Learoyd managed to nurse his crippled machine back to his airfield at Scampton, Lincolnshire, where he found himself unable to land owing to damage to the hydraulic system. He circled until first-light on 13 August, then belly-landed. He was awarded the Victoria Cross for his courage.[36]

Newall informed the War Cabinet on 13 August that thirteen RAF aircraft had been lost the day before, with four of the pilots saved from these machines; sixty-two enemy aircraft had been destroyed for certain, and thirty-six probable, plus another thirty-nine damaged. Total service and civilian casualties during the twenty-four hours ending 6 am on the 13th were sixty-three killed and 155 injured.[37] Fighter Command Intelligence estimated that 102 enemy aircraft had been destroyed in the previous forty-eight hours, plus ninety probables; these intelligence officers also believed that about 1000 German aircraft were involved in the attacks on 12 August.[38] A similar overestimate was contained in the Air Ministry summary issued a few days later, which gave the total of German aircraft destroyed from 1 July to 12 August as 454 for certain and 275 probable; the total 'confirmed' German losses since 3 September 1939 was reckoned to be 3183.[39]

About 300 bombers and dive-bombers, plus no more than 200 fighters, were flown against England on 12 August – less than half the British estimate. After the day's battle the operational strength of Fighter Command aircraft numbered 678, a drop of twenty-one since 9 am – the Spitfire total had fallen from 248 to 226, and Hurricanes from 363 to 353.[40] To make good the deficiency in the southern area, and to be ready for the renewed onslaught which he now expected, Dowding ordered five squadrons in the North to be available for operations with No. 11 Group. The intensification of enemy activity on 12 August clearly indicated a new phase in the war. The COS were agreed that prior to the invasion the Germans would attempt to obtain air supremacy: this attempt had now begun. The preliminary stage in the Battle of Britain was over. This had lasted since about 10 July, when the Luftwaffe first began to concentrate on Channel convoys and ports. Pilots from Fighter Command squadrons were obliged to fly over 18,000 sorties between 10 July and 12 August, averaging about 530 each twenty-four hours.

But the results of this first period of the Battle of Britain represented a clear failure of German aims. Almost a million tons of shipping moved along the south coast each week, yet only about 30,000 tons were sunk over the whole phase. About 148 RAF aircraft were destroyed, but the Luftwaffe lost about 286, and despite the latest losses the flow of replacements had meant that Fighter Command total strength had continued to rise. The figure of 678 at 9 am on 13 August still represented an increase of seventy-six since 1 July. Pilot losses, although serious and tragic, were by no means critical: Fighter Command still had ample men to fly the aircraft. Even without recent replacements, the number of pilots was still only about 120 short of the 1460 establishment mentioned by Sinclair on 7 August, and in fact newcomers continued to arrive at the hard-pressed squadrons.[41]

By 12 August the Luftwaffe High Command had realised the vital importance of attacking RAF radar stations; but these raids should have been undertaken at the beginning of the Battle of Britain, and now Goering again switched direction. He judged the moment had arrived for the great Luftwaffe offensive. At 4.30 am on Tuesday 13 August dawned *Adlertag* – Eagle Day.

CHAPTER NINE

Days of the Eagle

13–15 August

Hitler had returned to Berlin late on 12 August. He would spend the following day listening to reports of the air offensive against Britain and studying plans for invasion; already, his attitude hinted that he did not hold strong hopes for decisive results on either score. Before long the autumn would come, and the Channel fogs; the days for Sea Lion preparations were fast slipping by, and soon it might be too late. The summer seemed to be ending, and the deteriorating weather affected Goering's great plans for the defeat of the RAF. During the night of 12 August the high pressure zone over the Azores had begun to disperse, and early on *Adlertag* the skies were grey and overcast, with mist lying over many German airfields and a thick cloud blanket stretching low over the Channel.

Goering, acting on the advice of his Chief of Staff, postponed the start of the offensive until 2 pm. General Jeschonnek immediately contacted the Luftflotten headquarters in Brussels and Paris, and these in turn teleprinted the delaying orders down to the groups in the field. But communications proved imperfect; the delaying instructions came too late. A number of aircraft were already in the air, and although some squadrons turned back to their airfields others continued to assemble ready for the move across the Channel. Among the latter were Dornier 17 bombers commanded by Colonel Johannes Fink; he had reached the rendezvous point where he would be joined by his fighter escort, but could only see a few Me 110s and these continually flew near to him then repeatedly dived, climbed, and dived again. Fink, unable to understand that the Messerschmitts were trying to tell him to return home, banked north over the sea with two other bomber *Gruppen* moving behind.[1]

107

Across the Channel, the assembly of the Luftwaffe formations had already been picked up on British radar screens: two forces, apparently totalling sixty aircraft, were detected over Amiens as early as 5.30 am and these began to move north at about 6.0 am; British radar then reported another concentration of about a hundred aircraft near Dieppe and a third just north of Cherbourg, this time about forty-strong. Soon afterwards a smaller force was contacted near the Channel Islands. All these German aircraft were unaware that the offensive had been postponed, and many flew without fighter escorts – their Messerschmitts, remaining longer on the ground because they took less time to take off and assemble, had heard the order from Paris or Brussels in those few extra minutes.

Fighter Command was fully alerted. Aircraft from 11 Group were in the air as the German bombers began to surge across the Channel. Men and women in the towns and villages, rousing themselves for work, heard the roar of the British fighter aircraft overhead. "It began with sixteen Spitfires which I watched from my bed streaking westwards,' wrote Mrs Peacock in her diary. 'A moment later siren and gunfire. I saw an old gentleman in the house opposite standing in his shirt only, waving madly. It was about 5.30 am.'[2] By 6.15 am two squadrons from Croydon and Hornchurch were patrolling near Hawkinge and Manston, another from North Weald was protecting a convoy in the Thames estuary, sections from two more squadrons had flown from Debden and Tangmere; soon afterwards another squadron took off from Tangmere, three more sections reinforced the strength over the Thames estuary, a section from Northolt had taken up position over Canterbury, and three more sections from Tangmere were patrolling the Arundel–Petworth area. Aircraft from 10 Group, further north, were also in the air patrolling the coast at Warmwell.[3] But despite these precautions, the RAF would still only have about seventy fighters to oppose approaching aircraft totalling over 200. Dowding was still attempting to husband his resources, and Park agreed that a commitment by a greater number of Fighter Command aircraft so early in the day could be disastrous. Yet the strain on the pilots was rendered even greater by the wide variety of targets against which those Luftwaffe bombers were now aiming.

Dorniers under Colonel Fink began the action. Soon after 7 am his bombers approached Kent from the south-east. Together with other German aircraft, totalling up to ninety bombers, the Do 17s made use of a thick bank of cloud lying over the Thames estuary, emerging near

108

Whitstable. Fink's fifty-five aircraft then separated from the others and dropped to 1500 feet, aiming for the Coastal Command airfield at Eastchurch on Sheppey. Roaring low over the villages and hop-gardens, the Dorniers reached Eastchurch without being intercepted; bombs fell across the runway and a number of buildings were destroyed; two fighter squadrons temporarily attached to Coastal Command were caught on the ground but escaped unharmed. Meanwhile, Spitfires from Hornchurch had moved to intercept. The rearmost bombers in Fink's group were blocked from reaching the target but managed to bank back into cloud, and Fink's remaining aircraft also escaped into this cover. Other bombers which had flown in with him were less fortunate. Aiming for Sheerness, they were engaged near the North Foreland by the squadron from North Weald, and soon afterwards by Hurricanes from Croydon; they were forced to drop their bombs haphazardly and scurry into the clouds. Four bombers were shot down in this first engagement of the day.[4]

Further west, bombers had entered Sussex and were heading over the rolling countryside of the South Downs. This time the targets were Odiham and the Royal Aircraft Establishment at Farnborough, but the invaders were harried from the moment they crossed the coast. The Northolt squadron patrolling over Canterbury immediately moved south-west to intercept the enemy near Bognor; further east the bombers were met by 43 Squadron from Tangmere and Nos. 601 and 64 Squadrons entered the fight soon afterwards. The Hurricanes and Spitfires dived into the enemy bombers, while the Luftwaffe fighter escort trailed too far behind to provide adequate protection – these Messerschmitts had apparently missed the planned rendezvous following the chaos surrounding Goering's delaying order. Low cloud hindered visibility for enemy bomb-aimers, and Odiham and Farnborough escaped damage; the bombers fled back to the coast under constant Fighter Command attack.[5] No sooner had these raiders disappeared at full speed than the RAF aircraft clashed with another enemy force, comprising dive-bombers with a strong fighter escort.

'We saw about twenty-four Ju 88s escorted by many Me 110 and 109s,' reported Pilot Officer Mayers of 601 Squadron. 'The fighters were stepped up into the sun. We flew alongside the bombers on the left until we were slightly ahead, when the leader gave the order to attack.' The British aircraft attempted to strike before the enemy fighter escort could dart down from the sun. 'I started to attack the bombers,' continued Mayers, 'but as the escort came down in a dive I made a climbing right turn into the 110s. I saw part of the roof and fuselage of one 110 break away as I fired one burst of about three seconds from almost head on. The enemy aircraft continued in a dive but I didn't see what happened to it.'[6] Despite this intervention from the escorts, the dive-bombers were beaten back without reaching their targets; also flying in this engagement was Pilot Officer Crisp, from 43 Squadron, who wrote in his log book: 'Met fifty Ju 88s and Me 110s, fired on one 88 and two 110s. Good Party.'[7]

Reports flooding in to Fighter Command HQ were studied by Dowding – who found a moment to acknowledge a letter from Newall, CoAS, confirming that he would stay as Fighter Command chief until the German air offensive had finished. Five major attacks had so far been launched, although none with any great degree of success; the time was still only 9.30 am. Simultaneously, intelligence reports revealed other German movements, indicating that the air actions might form part of an invasion attempt. Brooke was contacted by his GHQ Home Forces early in the day and told that 'Admiralty had received accurate information that Germans in Norway had embarked on the night of the 11th and that they expected invasion in the north.'[8] Yet final talks were being held in London this day on an Anglo-Free French offensive against Dakar in West Africa, and on the despatch of further forces to help General Wavell in Egypt which would be drawn from Brooke's over-stretched strength. Churchill sent a minute urging that these Middle East reinforcements must be sent through the Mediterranean, rather than the longer route round the Cape despite the added dangers; he then left for an inspection tour of south coast defences.

A lull had fallen in the air offensive. British pilots returned to their airfields, where mechanics hurriedly re-fueled and re-armed the Spitfires and Hurricanes. Pilots checked their machines, walked back to their nearby dispersal huts, and waited in silence for battle to resume. 'All the rest of the squadron who happened to be on duty were down there,' wrote David Crook of 609 Squadron, 'twelve of us in all, some writing or reading, some asleep, and the rest playing cards.'[9] The telephones in the dispersal sheds began to ring soon after 11 am and the pilots rushed to their aircraft: the Luftwaffe's next main mission had begun. This time fighters approached unaccompanied by bombers, probably aiming to draw out British defenders before throwing in bombers while the RAF aircraft re-fueled. The first attackers comprised twenty-three Me 110s led by Captain Liensberger, who had taken off from Caen with orders to make a landfall near Portland. British radar detected the enemy near Cherbourg, eighty miles away, and two squadrons from Warmwell and Exeter were immediately scrambled to patrol Portland; 11 Group despatched a squadron from Tangmere to the Swanage area. The enemy were tracked on their entire route to Portland, despite the loss of the radar complex at Ventnor, and instructions were radioed to the Fighter Command aircraft. The latter located the enemy and swung in to the attack. Liensberger's rearmost Messerschmitt immediately reported: 'Spitfires astern!' and the Luftwaffe commander banked to form a defensive circle; in stabbed the Spitfires to prevent this movement. 'I fired a short burst at one e/a head-on,' reported Flight Lieutenant A. P. Hope of 601 Squadron, 'and as I passed, I took another the same way. He tightened his turn and pulled straight up across me so that I could see all his pale blue underneath. I finished my bullets into his bottom.'[10] One Me 110 twisted violently to starboard and managed to escape; another German pilot attempted to dive to safety but a Spitfire followed him down and seconds later he flopped in flames into the sea.[11]

Twenty-thousand feet below, the battle was being witnessed by Churchill, Auchinleck, Brooke and Montgomery. 'We found a German plane which had just come down,' wrote Brooke. 'Pilot was all burned up, but as a 500-lb bomb was in the debris which was burning, we did not stop long.'[12] Above, Liensberger was retreating back across the sea with his survivors, leaving five aircraft behind; the Germans claimed two or three British aircraft had been damaged.

Once again the air battle quietened. At noon Newall reported to the War Cabinet that 'considerable enemy air activity' had taken place, including raids on the Thames estuary and another penetrating over Selsea Bill as far as Horsham. 'According to reports so far available, the casualties were ... our own aircraft, three crashed, two unaccounted for. Enemy – six confirmed, eleven unconfirmed, nineteen damaged.'[13] In Berlin, Hitler was discussing Sea Lion prospects with Raeder. He had just received a report from Jodl which, added to the unresolved dispute between the Army and Navy over the invasion targets, made extremely depressing reading. 'The landing operation should in no circumstances fail,' Jodl had warned in his paper. 'Failure can have political consequences far outreaching the military one.' If preliminary requirements could not be met, including the acquisition of air supremacy, then Jodl considered that the landing would be 'an act of desperation which would have to be chanced in a desperate situation, but which we have no cause to carry out now.' It would be better to defeat England by other

111

methods, including air and U-boat warfare, an Italian offensive in Egypt with German support, and an attack on Gibraltar.[14] Hitler now asked Raeder for his comments, and found that the Admiral's pessimism remained as strong as ever. Raeder saw no possibility of conforming to army demands: the supply of reinforcements could not be accelerated; Sea Lion should only be attempted as a last resort. Hitler again temporised, saying he would wait to see the effects of the intensified air offensive.[15]

Eagle Day continued to prove extremely unsatisfactory for Goering and his Luftwaffe. The *Reichsmarschall* had said the main attack would be launched at 2 pm, yet by then the weather conditions were worse than those in the early morning. Operations were again delayed, including the bombing attack to make use of the fighter missions flown earlier: casualties suffered by squadrons such as Liensberger's were therefore wasted. Not until about 3.15 pm did Luftwaffe aircraft begin to cross the Channel again, by which time Fighter Command squadrons were once more fully prepared. The enemy intended two main thrusts. First, aircraft from Luftflotte 3 would launch another blow against targets in Sussex, Hampshire and Dorset, ranging from the Bognor region through the Isle of Wight and Southampton to Portland; objectives would include port facilities and RAF airfields. Second, flights from Luftflotte 2 would return to the Kentish area, also aiming at airfields.

British radar picked up the enemy formations at about 3.30 pm with those of Luftflotte 3 being detected first, and within minutes extra Fighter Command squadrons were airborne to join those already patrolling the south coast and Thames estuary; these aircraft totalled up to seventy machines in the Sussex–Hampshire area, and about forty in Kent. Poor visibility reduced the efficiency of the enemy bombers and threatened to split them from their fighter escort. The first clash in the western region took place at about 4 pm off Portland, between Messerschmitts flying alone and British fighters from 213 and 152 Squadrons: the enemy were prevented from reaching the coast. But within thirty minutes came two or more waves of bombers still with fighter escorts intact. Hurricanes from 238 Squadron attempted to block the first formations but were unable to strike between the bombers and their Messerschmitts; a number of bombs fell on Southampton. Pilots of 609 Squadron had better fortune with the second bombing wave coming soon afterwards.

'We took off, thirteen machines in all,' wrote David Crook, 'with the CO leading, and climbed up over Weymouth. After a few minutes I began to hear a German voice talking on the R/T, faintly at first and then growing in volume. By a curious chance this German raid had a wave-length almost identical with our own and the voice we heard was that of the German Commander talking to his formation as they approached us across the Channel.' About fifteen minutes later the 609 aircraft saw the enemy: Ju 87 dive-bombers escorted by Me 109s above, with some Me 110s about two miles behind – apparently about sixty aircraft in all. Hurricanes from another Fighter Command squadron scythed in between the trailing Me 110s and the bombers while the 609 Squadron Spitfires, commanded by Squadron-Leader Darley, climbed up to 20,000 feet into the sun. Crook wrote: 'The CO gave a terrific "Tally-Ho" and led us round in a big semi-circle so that we were now behind them, and we prepared to attack.' As the Spitfire pilots dived they could still hear the German commander over the radio; he kept repeating: '*Achtung! Achtung! Spit und Hurri!*' Crook noted in his log book later: 'He sounded a bit fed up about something.'

'I managed to slip the Squadron through the fighters,' wrote the 609 Squadron commander, Darley, 'then went right back through the Ju 87 formation, taking pot-shots without throttling back. This enabled the chaps behind to position themselves without having to avoid me.' The result was devastating. One of the 609 pilots, a Pole named Novi, shot down two Me 109s; other enemy aircraft were plummeting down – a British pilot looked round in the midst of the action and in one small patch of sky he noted five German dive-bombers going down in flames 'still more or less in formation'. Crook opened fire on an Me 109 at close range and the enemy aircraft fell in a long trail of black smoke. 'I followed him down for some way and could not pull out of my dive in time to avoid going below the clouds myself. I found that I was about five miles north of Weymouth, and then I saw a great column of smoke rising from the ground. My Me 109 lay in a field, a tangled heap of wreckage burning fiercely, but with the black crosses on the wings still visible. I found out later that the pilot was still in the machine... I could see everybody streaming out of their houses and rushing to the spot.'[16]

Would-be spectators on the ground could see nothing of the dog-fights above the clouds. But they watched the burning wreckage of aircraft fall into view, and they heard the complaining whine and roar of straining engines, together with sudden, insistent bursts of fire sounding 'distinctly like a huge iron pipe being dropped on to concrete from a crane, the fire of the ·303s merging into a ringing clash.' This civilian, a member of the Royal Observer Corps, added: 'Some minutes after, a tinkling sound could be heard as spent cases fell on roofs and roads, fairy-like, quite detached from the high-flying aircraft.'[17]

The Luftwaffe bomber force wheeled back over the sea, their formations in tatters; pilots of 609 Squadron returned to their Middle Wallop airfield. 'All the machines were now coming in to land and everybody's eyes were fixed on the wing. Yes – they were all covered with black streaks from the smoke of guns – everybody had fired. There was the usual anxious counting... Thank God, everybody's OK. We all stood round in small groups talking excitedly, and exchanging experiences.' The squadron claimed thirteen enemy machines destroyed with six more probables or damaged – the Germans counted five of their aircraft destroyed. The only damage sustained by 609 Squadron was one bullet through an aircraft wing.[18] During the pilots' absence their airfield had received a sudden raid from six Ju 88s which managed to break through from the Southampton area, and the Luftwaffe commander, Captain Kern, reported hits on 'groups of tents and sheds along the edge', but no serious damage was inflicted; Middle Wallop, used by four RAF squadrons as a vital forward base, continued to function normally. During this late afternoon period bombs also fell at widely separated points in Wiltshire, Hampshire and Dorset, including a number of airfield areas, without sufficient accuracy to destroy important installations. Andover, near Middle Wallop, was attacked by a dozen bombers and suffered greater damage, but this was not a Fighter Command station. The Luftwaffe launched a final attempt in this western region at about 5 pm, when fifty-two Ju 87s escorted by Me 109s aimed at airfields in the Portland area. Dense cloud at 3000 feet virtually ruled out dive-bombing. 'The attack was a flop,' wrote General Wolfram Freiherr von Richthofen, commanding the 7th Air Corps. 'Thanks to fog our formations returned without releasing their bombs. The weather forecast had been false, and the attack ordered from "on high". It just couldn't be done.'[19]

The second prong of the Luftwaffe offensive struck at Kent while these attacks were taking place in the west. Results were very similar. Aircraft from 65 Squadron engaged the first raiders, a force comprising only fighters; bombers making for Rochford were prevented from finding their target by cloud. These aircraft were engaged by interceptors of 56 Squadron from Rochford itself, and they dropped their loads blindly near Canterbury.[20] Another raid was met by 74 Squadron aircraft over the Thames estuary, with the Do 17s suffering heavily from

'Sailor' Malan and his pilots. Soon afterwards other 'Tiger' pilots from 74 Squadron were in action over Dover, again with conspicuous success. But one of the 'Tigers', Pilot Officer Stevenson, barely survived. 'There were about twelve Me 109s diving at me from the sun and at least half of them must have been firing deflection shots at me. There was a popping noise and my control column became useless. I found myself doing a vertical dive, getting faster and faster. I pulled the hood back. I got my head out of the cockpit and the slipstream tore the rest of me clean out of the machine. My trouser leg and both shoes were torn off. I saw my machine crash into the sea a mile off Deal. It took me twenty minutes to come down. I had drifted eleven miles out to sea. One string of my parachute did not come undone, and I was dragged along by my left leg at ten miles an hour, with my head underneath the water. After three minutes I was almost unconscious, when the string came undone. I got my breath back and started swimming.' Ninety minutes later Stevenson was picked up by an MTB. The score claimed by his squadron for this and other actions during the day totalled six enemy aircraft destroyed, six probables and one damaged.[21]

The Luftwaffe obtained its greatest success of the day at Detling, south of the Medway Towns. Messerschmitts led by Major Gotthardt Handrick managed to sweep aside Fighter Command opposition, opening a gap for eighty-six Ju 87s. These bombers appeared over Detling airfield at about 6.15 pm and dived for the attack. 'We had no warning,' wrote one WAAF girl. 'I dashed down into our dug-out just in time. The noise was terrific, and I was deaf for two days afterwards. When I came out I shall never forget the sights which met my eyes.' The bombs had fallen across the runways and on to the buildings; Messerschmitts had circled in to machine-gun the area at low level. Casualties included many people having tea in the canteen.[22] But as with Andover, the effect of the raid was reduced through the airfield not being a Fighter Command base – like Andover it was used primarily by Coastal Command.

Air engagements ended at dusk. Night brought its own scares: the enemy flew over the Midlands and the Scottish Lowlands dropping a variety of objects – parachutes, wireless transmitters, small quantities of HE, maps, photographs, addresses of prominent people and instructions to agents. The operation, about which Goering claimed Hitler was 'very pleased', was intended to delude the British into believing that parachutists had landed and that a powerful Fifth Column was at work in the country prior to invasion.[23] During the day Churchill had already announced the formation of the Home Defence (Security) Executive – a committee to investigate the 'Fifth Column' possibilities; almost immediately the idea received strong criticism on the grounds of the prying, secretive nature of this body.

Eagle Day had been a failure. The offensive had barely scratched Fighter Command airfields and German casualties were heavy. Next day, 14 August, Newall reported to the War Cabinet that thirteen RAF machines had been lost the day before, with ten pilots saved, compared with seventy-eight Luftwaffe aircraft destroyed for certain, thirty-three probables and forty-nine damaged.[24] As usual, the figures for enemy losses were grossly over-optimistic: the Luftwaffe probably lost forty-five aircraft. Kesselring and Sperrle admitted thirty-four casualties, but tried to mitigate this loss by reporting that nine enemy airfields had been attacked, 'five of them to such good purpose that they could be considered to have been put out of action.'[25] In reality, the 484 bombers and dive-bombers which crossed the coast on Eagle Day, plus about 1000 fighters, managed to inflict damage to Andover, Detling and Eastchurch, none of which were Fighter Command airfields, plus some damage to Southampton and Castle Bromwich. Fighter Command, flying 727 sorties, had suffered a disturbing drop in operational aircraft available – the figure of 647 at 9 am on 14 August marked a decrease of thirty-one since 9 am the day before – but the deficiency would be made almost good during the next twenty-four hours. Five pilots were either killed or seriously wounded.[26] Moreover, many British pilots had received another boost to their confidence. 'The glorious realisation dawned on us,' noted Crook, 'that by using clever and careful tactics we could inflict heavy losses on the enemy and get away almost scot-free ourselves. Whenever in the future the squadron went into action, I think the only question in everybody's mind was not "Shall we get any Huns today?" but rather, "How many shall we get today?" There was never any doubt about it.'[27]

Goering must try again, but clouds still spread over the Channel on the morning after Eagle Day and most Luftwaffe units were grounded. The inactivity enabled replacements of Fighter Command aircraft and men to be rushed to the sector airfields. Pilot 'wastage' received attention at a 10.15 am meeting of the Defence Committee, and the cold dispassionate calculations revealed the anxiety felt at the time over the potentially dangerous loss of young lives. Air Ministry figures were produced which showed that training establishments were being programmed to produce a maximum of 746 pilots a month to cover losses

116

in the intensified air war; the figure of 746 could be reduced to an estimated 650, taking into account operational pilots who returned to active duty after recovery from wounds. Defence Committee members were informed that the actual figures for pilot losses, in action and accidents, had been 318 killed, forty-three wounded in June, giving a total of 361; and 208 killed and seventy wounded in July, a total of 278. Churchill disputed the terrifying estimate of future losses; he appreciated 'the need for planning on a general scale, but it was important not to overdo this process, otherwise we would be presented with training problems which would be too great for us to solve.' He asked for detailed figures to be prepared, ready for another meeting as soon as possible, showing how the figure of 746 could be justified.[28]

Reports were being received in London of the German parachute drops made the previous night; the German propaganda radio, NBBS, announced that parachutists had landed near Birmingham, Manchester and Glasgow 'in civilian clothes or British uniform'. The Air Secretary, Sinclair, gave the announcement some credence at a War Cabinet meeting held at 12.30 pm. Forty-five parachutes had been found, he said, apparently abandoned by the enemy in various districts of Scotland, Derbyshire, Staffordshire and Yorkshire. 'Two parachutists were reported to have been captured, one in civilian clothing.' The War Cabinet considered whether a reward should be offered for the capture of paratroops, but decided against it. 'The widest publicity, however, should be given to the landings of enemy parachutists, if confirmed, so as to enlist the help of the civilian population.'[29] The reports were not confirmed and the feint was soon shown to be a fake: one clue which gave the German game away was the absence of tracks in the dew leading away from the 'Fifth Columnist' litter left in the fields.

The only serious action of the day was taking place as the War Cabinet met at 10 Downing Street. Just before noon about ten Me 110s from Rubensdörffer's experimental dive-bomber *Gruppe* made use of cloud cover to slip over the Kent coast. They turned north towards Manston, where they suddenly burst from the cloud south-east of the airfield and split into three formations of three aircraft. Each section dived to less than 1000 feet and released their bombs: four hangars were destroyed or damaged, but light anti-aircraft guns brought down two of the attackers. About twenty-five minutes later German aircraft shot down seven balloons at Dover and penetrated as far as Ashford before retiring. Bombers from this force destroyed the unarmed Varne lightvessel, despite vigorous protection from Spitfires based at Kenley. Small-scale actions took place elsewhere in the Kent area. During the afternoon, aircraft from Luftflotte 3 attempted a different tactic in the west – one which would be criticised by Goering himself. Rather than try to penetrate with large raids escorted by fighters, bombers came over on their own or in small unescorted groups, relying on surprise and cloud cover. The operations, directed mainly against airfields or rail centres, failed completely. Bombs were dropped at Swingate, Cardiff, Colerne, Kemble, Yeovilton and Middle Wallop, but generally without causing significant damage.[30]

Middle Wallop, soon christened 'Centre Punch', was the most important of these objectives; David Crook described this new Luftwaffe tactic. 'We heard the unmistakable "ooma-ooma" of a German bomber above the clouds. I immediately signalled to my ground crew to stand by ... I kept my finger on the engine starter button and waited expectantly.' Almost immediately a Ju 88 broke out of the clouds to the north, turned slightly to correct the course, and dived at high speed; four bombs were released at about 1500 feet. The Spitfires were racing to get airborne and other Spitfires already aloft were engaging the enemy. The Junker 88 fell in flames about five miles away with the loss of all the crew. 'I certainly admire that German pilot for his coolness and determination,' commented Crook, 'because he made his attack despite the Spitfires that were closing in on him. It was a very daring piece of work, even though he only lived about thirty seconds afterwards.'[31] Two more attacks were made on Middle Wallop, involving three aircraft, one of which was shot down. Fighter Command claimed a total of thirty enemy aircraft destroyed on 14 August, plus eight probable; RAF losses were eight machines, with three pilots saved.[32] More accurately, the Germans lost about nineteen aircraft – still over twice the RAF total and with a far higher percentage of pilots killed.

Goering, with some justification, blamed the weather for the inadequate results so far; as soon as the clouds lifted, he declared, a greater effort would be made, and he remained supremely confident. Other German service chiefs were watching the weather with increasing anxiety: these overcast August days provided a portent of autumn. 'The airborne troops can influence neither the weather nor the sea,' declared a naval memorandum on Sea Lion. 'They cannot prevent the destruction and incapacitation of the few harbours, nor hold off the enemy fleet.'[33] These dangers were evidently on Hitler's mind when he presented the new Field Marshals with their batons during the day; Raeder noted: 'The

Fuehrer does not propose to carry out any operations whose risk is too great: he advocates the view that the aim of defeating Britain is not dependent on the landings alone.' Nevertheless, during these discussions on 14 August Hitler confirmed that landings would not be attempted as far west as Lyme Bay, owing to difficulties of naval cover, and the invasion would instead be concentrated further east, perhaps with a single crossing in Brighton Bay. This was far more acceptable to the Navy, but the Army and Navy Chiefs had still to agree on the size of the force. Both services were agreed on the need for maximum air effort during the invasion, and the Luftwaffe had already prepared a memorandum which was studied by Hitler during the afternoon. 'Special effect is anticipated from a ruthless air attack on London,' declared this document, 'if possible on the day preceding the landing, as this would certainly cause countless numbers of people to stream out of the city in all directions, thereby blocking the roads and demoralising the population.'[34]

Dawn broke on Thursday 15 August with the clouds still obscuring the Channel and southern England; once again it seemed that air activity would be restricted. The commanders of the Luftflotten and the air corps flew to Karinhall for a conference with Goering, expected to last for much of the day. In London, a staff memorandum was issued from GHQ Home Forces during the morning which attempted to analyse German intentions; this, clearly influenced by Brooke, recognised that the south coast might be the most likely target for the main invasion attempt. The GHQ staff officers had at last produced a British assessment of German invasion plans which found the correct answer. But all still depended on the conflict between the RAF and Luftwaffe.[35] The War Cabinet met at noon to hear optimistic figures from the CoAS on the previous day's fighting. Ministers also heard that the news of parachutists being captured were now known to be untrue. 'At least eighty parachutes had been discovered, but there was no evidence that any parachutists had descended with them.'[36]

The weather began to clear over London and south England while this War Cabinet meeting took place at 10 Downing Street. Activity suddenly increased at numerous airfields on both sides of the Channel. For the first time, these preparations for combat were also being undertaken at Luftwaffe bases in Norway and Denmark: today the attempt would be made to coordinate operations by all the Luftflotten units, including those of Stumpff's Luftflotte 5 in the north. Britain would be assaulted from the north-east, south-east and south-west; hopefully, the attacks would be almost simultaneous, and would thus impose an intolerable strain on Fighter Command. But as had happened early in the morning of Eagle Day, 13 August, the offensive on 15 August began with confused orders. Instructions from Berlin reached the Luftflotte 2 forward HQ at about 11.30 am: owing to the bad weather no raids would be undertaken. The order arrived too late to prevent the departure of two Stuka groups; the dive-bombers collected their fighter escort over Calais at noon, and this force of about sixty aircraft crossed the coast near Dungeness. The formation immediately turned north towards the airfields at Lympne and Hawkinge. Spitfires and Hurricanes managed to destroy at least two dive-bombers, but the vast majority reached the targets. Lympne was so badly damaged that it was put out of use for forty-eight hours, but Hawkinge – the more important – was barely touched.[37]

Only a few minutes later the improved weather situation led to the despatch of urgent orders to all Luftflotten HQ units: the main attacks would now begin. The first move was made by two bomber forces of Luftflotte 5, one from Stavanger in Norway and the other from Aalborg in Denmark: these aircraft were airborne shortly before 1 pm, heading in a diagonal line across the North Sea towards Northumberland and Yorkshire. The operation involved considerable risks. The total flying distance, including time spent in take-off, assembly and return landing, represented over 1100 miles – far beyond the range of most fighters; the bombers would therefore have to fly with only flimsy escort support. Stumpff aimed to distract the RAF attention by despatching about twenty seaplanes on a mock attack in the Firth of Forth region. These departed before the main bombing formations, and the deception apparently proved successful. Just after 12.15 pm the northern RAF radar stations detected a force of about twenty aircraft approaching east of the Firth of Forth, and within fifteen minutes Spitfires of 72 Squadron from Acklington were in the air, proceeding northwards to intercept the enemy out from the Farne Islands. Other aircraft from 13 Group were also scrambled: 605 Squadron flew to patrol near Tyneside, 41 and 79 were airborne soon afterwards, joined shortly by 607 Squadron from Usworth. This meant that nearly forty fighters had been ordered into action, even though the original radar contact had only indicated an enemy force of about twenty, later raised to 'forty-plus' approaching from a more southerly direction than first thought.

The confusion arose from the feint by the Luftwaffe seaplanes towards the Firth of Forth, combined with the approach of the actual raiders comprising sixty-three He 111s from Stavanger. These were escorted by thirty-five Messerschmitts equipped with special long-range fuel tanks; the attackers would therefore still outnumber the defenders almost two-to-one. Moreover, a navigational error brought the German aircraft to a landfall seventy miles further north than intended – to the area where British fighters had been concentrating to intercept the mock attack. 'Thanks to this error,' commented Captain Arno Kleyenstüber, staff officer in Norway, 'the mock attack achieved the opposite of what we intended. The British fighter defence force was not only alerted in good time, but made contact with the genuine attacking force.'

Spitfires from 72 Squadron made the first sighting of the enemy about thirty miles east of the Farne Islands, with pilots reporting massed German bomber formations flying at 18,000 feet in a broad reverse wedge, escorted by two waves of Messerschmitts at 19,000 feet. 'There must be hundreds of them!' exclaimed a Spitfire pilot over his radio. These first British aircraft were vastly outnumbered, but had the advantage of the sun behind them and an extra 3,000 feet of altitude. Four Spitfire pilots immediately engaged a section of the Messerschmitts while the rest of 72 Squadron dived on the bombers from the rear. Many of the Heinkels immediately jettisoned their bombs and scuttled into cloud safety, but vigorous fighting took place between opposing fighters. The Luftwaffe formation divided, one bomber section heading for Tyneside and the rest turning south. Spitfires from 79 Squadron joined those of No. 72 in their attacks on the fighters and claimed an unknown number of enemy aircraft shot down with no British losses. The Germans, whilst admitting to six Me 110s lost, claimed two Spitfires destroyed. Flight-Sergeant Linke, a Messerschmitt pilot, described in his combat report how he approached within fifty yards of a Spitfire 'and did some good deflection shooting. The Spitfire reared up, then spiralled vertically down.' Moments later Linke's Me 110 was riddled by bullets from a British aircraft, and his port engine seized. 'I pushed the stick and dived vertically through the clouds with the two Englishmen on my tail. After 2000–3000 feet I pulled out below the upper layer, having meanwhile varied my course. Going down through the lower layer I saw two Spitfires hit the water. Time about 13.58.' Linke managed to struggle back across the North Sea with only one engine. Another Messerschmitt pilot, Corporal Richter, also had a narrow escape. Hit in the head from British fire, he lost consciousness and his aircraft plunged out of control towards the sea. His radio operator baled out and was never seen again, but Richter recovered at the last moment, pulled hard on his stick and

121

levelled out; he managed to re-cross the North Sea and made a forced landing near Esbjerg in Denmark.

Meanwhile the most northerly bomber wing approached Newcastle, harassed by British fighters. Most of the bombs dropped in the sea. The southerly section made a landfall in the Seaham area, but again caused minimum damage. Neither force found their intended targets – the British airfields at Dishforth and Linton-upon-Ouse – and only at Sunderland were houses destroyed. Luftwaffe losses probably totalled eight bombers and seven fighters; Fighter Command still claimed no RAF casualties. Soon after 1 pm the second German attack in the north, by about fifty unescorted Ju 88s from Aalborg, had approached the coast some ninety miles further south aiming at Driffield airfield. The first radar contact indicated an enemy strength of only six aircraft, soon uplifted to thirty. Spitfires from 616 Squadron, flying from Leconfield, first sighted the enemy off Flamborough Head; the squadron banked east and dived to intercept about five miles from the coast. The Ju 88s, approaching in irregular formation, darted into clouds and crossed the coastline. Despite attacks from 616 and 73 Squadrons over half the enemy bombers managed to make use of cloud cover and penetrated the ten miles to Driffield; bombs landed on the runways leaving craters thirty feet across and ten feet deep, and about a dozen Whitley bombers were destroyed on the ground plus four hangars and three groups of buildings. More bombs were dropped at Bridlington. But the British aircraft continued to harass the invaders, with the defenders including Blenheims from Catterick and Defiants from Kirton-in-Lindsey, and six enemy bombers were brought down plus two more probables. Once again, Fighter Command claimed to have escaped with no aircraft lost in the air.[38]

But battle was only just beginning further south. Soon after 2 pm enemy aircraft were detected approaching Essex, Suffolk and north Kent. Aircraft from over seven squadrons were ordered to intercept, but this operation was rendered even more difficult than usual by the confused, scattered nature of the attacks, coming from a variety of different directions. RAF fighters which did manage to intercept the first enemy aircraft found themselves outnumbered and often badly positioned – sometimes still climbing from their airfields. Nine Hurricanes from No. 1 Squadron, scrambled from North Weald, encountered nearly forty Me 110s and Me 109s ten miles out from Harwich harbour. The Hurricane flight leader, 'Hilly' Brown, immediately attacked but his pilots found themselves in desperate danger. The enemy force comprised the Me 110 fighter-bombers of Captain Rubensdörffer's experimental *Gruppe*, aiming for the fighter airfield at Martlesham; the escorting Me 109s reacted vigorously to the British interception attempt and wild dog-fights broke out with the Hurricanes attacked from all sides. Bullets slashed into the cockpit of Hilly Brown's aircraft and his face and hands were lacerated by splinters; his aircraft lurched out of control, and he pulled back the battered canopy to bale out, landing in the sea – and was fortunately rescued by a trawler. Two other pilots in his section were killed as the enemy raced the few miles inland from Harwich and dived low over Martlesham. The attack on the airfield began at 3.26 pm and lasted five minutes: at least fourteen bombs of about 500 lb each were dropped from under 3000 feet, plus several incendiaries, and craters up to twenty feet deep were carved into the runways; two hangars were set on fire and workshops, stores and communications destroyed. Hurricanes from 17 Squadron, based at Martlesham, were recalled urgently from patrol duties over the Thames estuary, but they arrived to find their airfield shrouded in black smoke and the enemy gone.[39]

Other British aircraft chased the enemy back out to sea, shooting down one Me 109. Meanwhile about a hundred Do 17s and Messerschmitts were approaching the Kent coast to the south side of the Thames estuary. Four Fighter Command squadrons were patrolling the area, but the superior number of Messerschmitt escorts held off the British aircraft while the bombers droned through to strike at Eastchurch, Rochester and Hawkinge – the latter for the second time that day. Rochester received most damage. Attacked by thirty Do 17s led by Colonel von Chamier, the runway was severely hit and showers of 100-lb fragmentation bombs crashed into the Shorts aircraft works on the northern boundary where Stirling bombers were under construction. 'Aero-engine works repeatedly hit,' reported von Chamier. 'Copious flame and smoke.'[40] This raid into Kent cost the Luftwaffe four or five aircraft – but Fighter Command lost nine.

The balance had swung towards the enemy during this second major offensive, and Sperrle's Luftflotte 3, farther east along the coast, had still to be committed. Already, Fighter Command was suffering from considerable over-stretch: at 2–3 pm the 'state of readiness' board in Park's underground operations room at 11 Group HQ had shown many squadrons unavailable owing to engagements. But now came a lull. Fighter Command aircraft were rapidly re-fueled and re-armed, and lights began to spread on Park's 'immediate readiness' panel. Once again Fighter Command pilots were prepared for action as they sat near their machines and waited during this sultry August afternoon.

Churchill had been anxiously studying latest Fighter Command reports throughout the day. He broke off to address the House of Commons, where he had to face criticism over his announcement of a Home Defence (Security) committee. For once, the Prime Minister revealed signs of strain. 'Mr Churchill lost his temper,' wrote the *News Chronicle*'s political commentator A. J. Cummings, 'and his hold on the House, for the first and only time since he became Prime Minister.' But Cummings continued: 'Nobody will be inclined to rebuke him for an occasional touch of testiness... The surprising thing about Mr Churchill is that, though anything but a model of human patience, and in spite of the terrible responsibility he now carries, he has not only borne himself (as one would expect of him) with high courage, but has shown high good humour.' Immediately after undertaking his unpleasant duties in the House, Churchill hurried out of London to visit Park's Operations room. He reached Uxbridge just as battle began again, and now the activity rose to such intensity that Ismay, accompanying Churchill, felt 'sick with fear'.[41]

Sperrle's Luftflotte 3 began its part in the supposedly coordinated offensive just before 5 pm. Junker 88s took off from Orleans at 4.45, joined a few minutes later by Ju 87s from Lanion in Brittany; these dive-bombers began to move northwards under a strong Messerschmitt escort aiming at the Portland area and totalling over 200 aircraft. The invaders were detected by British radar soon after 5 pm and Nos 10 and 11 Groups responded by sending airborne the largest force so far used against a single enemy attack, eventually amounting to six squadrons and a section from Brand's 10 Group combined with seven squadrons from Park's 11 Group. The leading Luftwaffe squadron commander, Captain Jochen Helbig, sighted the English coast at about 5.20 pm. His rearmost dive-bomber crews suddenly shouted into the radios: 'Spitfires to port... Fighter attack from astern... Am being attacked!' These interceptors belonged to a squadron from the Middle Wallop sector who dived out of the sinking sun on to the Ju 88s, in an attempt to destroy this enemy bomber formation before the Messerschmitt escort could react. The Ju 88s were forced to break and bank to either side, whereupon the Spitfires concentrated on single enemy machines using their advantage of superior speed. Flight-Sergeant Schlund, Helbig's radio operator manning his single backward-firing gun, reported over the intercom: 'Spitfire astern and to starboard... 400

124

yards...300...250.' Schlund held his fire until the last moment then opened up a split second before his opponent; simultaneously Helbig wrenched over the control and the Ju 88 lurched to starboard in a tight turn. The Spitfire flashed past, suffering hits from the German machine-gun in its belly, and Helbig saw it disappear smoking out of sight. But only Helbig's aircraft plus one other from his squadron emerged from the dog-fights: five were shot down in as many minutes and other Fighter Command aircraft were swarming up to attack. Only three air-craft from the *Gruppe* to which Helbig's squadron belonged, totalling fifteen machines when the flight began, managed to reach their target: the naval airfield at Worthy Down. Heavy enemy casualties were suffered elsewhere along this section of the coast: some aircraft managed to drop bombs on Portland, but the majority jettisoned their loads and banked hard for home. Only twelve Ju 88s pressed further inland, form-ing part of a force of thirty or more which came under repeated attacks from some seven British squadrons. Despite the blocking attempts the dozen Ju 88s headed for the Middle Wallop airfield, where some aircraft of 609 Squadron were still on the ground.

'We got off...only a few minutes before they arrived at the aero-drome,' wrote Crook, 'and were unable to intercept them, or even to see them until they were practically over the aerodrome, as they dived out of the sun, dropped their bombs, and then streamed back towards the coast as hard as they could go.' Two hangars were hit and one air-craft destroyed before it could lift off; five others were damaged. 'But we were attacking them the whole time,' commented Crook, 'and shot down at least five.'[42] Flight Lieutenant Howell, also of 609 Squadron, reported: 'I easily caught up one Ju 88 doing 320 mph which dived for cloud...R/T talking in German was very loud indeed, with excellent modulation. One voice was speaking the whole time in a very excited manner. Machine-gun and cannon burst audible between what sounded like almost hysterical orders or swearing.'[43] The attack marked the fourth on the airfield in three days, yet the German pilots were unaware of the target's true identity: they reported it as being Andover.

As battered German formations were hurrying back over the Channel still chased by Fighter Command squadrons, other enemy aircraft were preparing to launch another thrust against Kentish airfields. These latest attacks marked the most critical moment of the day. Radar stations reported the approaching waves at about 6.10 pm, with the enemy force believed to number up to seventy machines; in fact this attempt by Luftflotte 2 totalled nearly a hundred aircraft, aiming for

Redhill, Biggin Hill and Kenley, sector stations for 11 Group. Many of Park's aircraft had been on patrol or had been supporting 10 Group further west, and these squadrons were still being readied for further battle; some aircraft were still airborne but would soon need to return to base. The Luftwaffe, as planned, was about to catch the fighter defence system of south-east England at its weakest moment.

The attackers reached the coast near Dungeness at 6.30 pm, and exhausted pilots of 501 Squadron immediately dived to intercept. Park had hurriedly ordered four squadrons from his easterly sectors down in support, later summoning up more squadrons for reinforcements from the western flank. Churchill and Ismay sat at Park's HQ staring at the plots in front of them. 'At one moment every single squadron in the Group was engaged,' wrote Ismay. 'There was nothing in reserve, and the map table showed new waves of attackers crossing the coast.'[44] In the sky above Kent the strained RAF fighter pilots repeatedly threw their aircraft against the enemy, the wings of their Spitfires and Hurricanes already blackened from the fire of their guns in previous engagements during the day. One youngster described a typical experience. 'I began to close in on him and found I was travelling much too fast. I throttled back and slowed up just in time. We were frighteningly close. Then I swung up, took aim, and fired my eight guns. Almost at once I saw little flashes of fire dancing along the fuselage and centre section. I closed in again, when suddenly the bomber reared up in front of me. It was all I could do to avoid crashing into him. I heaved at the controls to prevent a collision, and in doing so I lost sight of him ... I dived from 30,000 feet to 3000 feet at such a speed that the bottom panel of the aircraft cracked, and as my ears were not used to such sudden changes of pressure I nearly lost the use of one of the drums. But ... I had to get that bomber. Then as I came nearer I saw he was on fire. Little flames were flickering around his fuselage and wings. Just as I closed in again he jinked away in a steep climbing turn. When he got to the top of his climb I was almost on him. I took sight very carefully and gave the button a quick squeeze. Once more I saw little dancing lights on his fuselage, but almost instantaneously they were swallowed in a burst of flames. I saw him twist gently earthwards and there was a spurt of fire as he touched the earth. He blew up and set a copse blazing.'[45]

Torn by these terrier-type tactics, and confused by the chequer-board pattern of the Kentish fields and woods below, enemy bombers erred in their navigation. They failed to find Biggin Hill, Redhill and Kenley; one group flew north to Maidstone and bombed the airfield at West

126

Malling, while others made an even more serious mistake. These aircraft, fifteen Me 110s and eight Me 109s of Rubensdörffer's *Gruppe* 210, ranged north-west looking for Kenley and Redhill. Instead they found Croydon, London's airport and on the fringe of the city's southern suburbs.

London had so far been spared direct enemy action, and the air of unreality continued in the capital. Cinemas, restaurants and theatres seemed more crowded than ever; the bustle and the August heat made the city an unpleasant place to live in. 'London was hot, dirty and airless,' wrote Frances Faviell. 'The sand blew about from bursting sandbags, and the streets did not get the same cleaning as they once had.'⁴⁶ At 7.10 pm the air-raid sirens sounded, the first daytime warning for many weeks. The journalist H. R. Pratt Boorman was eating in the Lyon's Corner House, Charing Cross. 'As soon as the siren went almost all the "Nippies" disappeared into their shelters, leaving their customers at their tables. One or two stayed behind, apparently quite against orders, and tried to carry on, with the result that bills got hopelessly mixed up. The orchestra, which was playing, immediately switched over to community singing, but it was half-hearted. Soon after the "Raiders passed" sounded, and the band struck up "After the ball was over".'⁴⁷ During this ten-minute interval, the reality of the air war had reached the streets of south-east London. Britain's capital was marked as a prohibited zone of Luftwaffe operation maps: Hitler had ordered that the area should not yet be attacked. But Rubensdörffer's Me 110s and 109s, searching in vain for their correct target, had located the Croydon airfield and had looped northwards for their bombing approach. The fighter-bombers evaded a first interception attempt by Hurricanes from 111 Squadron and released their loads. Bombs ripped open hangars, and up to three dozen training aircraft on the ground were destroyed or severely damaged. The bombs spread beyond the airfield and into the nearby neat lines of houses: about 200 homes were affected by the explosions and sixty-two people were killed.

Pilots from 111 Squadron again intercepted as the enemy climbed from Croydon. The last Luftwaffe bomber came under fire from Squadron Leader Thompson's Hurricane, and chunks of the Messerschmitt's wing were ripped away. The pilot managed a forced landing and he and his crewmen were immediately seized by civilians. Above, the Me 110s and 109s moved into defensive circles but more Hurricanes, 32 Squadron from Biggin Hill, joined the attack. Rubensdörffer tried to break away with others from his *Gruppe*; according to his unit's combat report: 'The four other aircraft of the staff flight followed him in a shallow dive for home. They disappeared into the mist and were not seen again.' Rubensdörffer probably died after a further interception by Spitfires from 66 Squadron; besides the *Gruppe* 210 commander, his unit lost five other Me 110s and one Me 109.[48]

Dusk at last began to fall on Thursday 15 August, and fighter pilots returned to base. The WAAF girls ceased to move the counters on the plot at 11 Group headquarters, and Churchill and Ismay stood to go. They climbed into their car to drive to Chequers. 'Don't speak to me,' said the Prime Minister to Ismay, and then he added: 'I have never been so moved.' Ismay's account continued: 'After about five minutes he leaned forward and said: "Never in the field of human conflict has so much been owed by so many to so few." The words burned into my brain.'[49]

~

CHAPTER TEN

The Few

15–25 August

'This was the day Hitler was to be in London,' wrote Cadogan late on 15 August. 'Can't find him ... BBC announced we had shot down eighty-eight today, and lost nineteen, pilots of five of which had been saved. Marvellous!'[1] After further reports had been received, the total of German aircraft destroyed on 15 August was said to be 156, with another fifty-nine probables.[2] The Luftwaffe made similar extravagant claims: 111 British fighters destroyed, fourteen 'questionably'.[3] A more accurate figure for German losses was probably about fifty-five, compared with thirty-four British. Once again, a good many of the latter were immediately replaced: Fighter Command had 672 serviceable aircraft at 9 am on 15 August and 653 at 9 am the next day. According to the official daily returns only two British pilots were reported killed in action in the twenty-four hours starting at noon on 15 August, and a further eight were missing; three had received serious wounds.[4]

Fighter Command Intelligence staff summed up the situation on 16 August: 'Recent activities of the GAF suggest the opening phase in an attempt to gain air superiority by a process of exhausting attacks on fighter defences. This policy is not proving successful and the GAF has suffered heavy casualties; on 11, 12, 13 and 14 August approximately 50 per cent of the total German strength of dive-bombers and fighters was probably employed together with about 15 per cent of the long-range bomber force.'[5] The War Cabinet situation résumé agreed with this assessment but added: 'It is believed that the GAF is not yet in a position to begin and maintain full-scale attack against this country.' This résumé also stated that Fighter Command had flown 4475 sorties during the week ending noon 15 August – before the main actions on that day.[6] Luftwaffe sorties during 14 August were believed to have totalled about 1786 – this figure is probably about 200 too low.

On the morning of Friday 16 August there seemed grounds for considerable satisfaction: the enemy had suffered heavy losses since 8 August and the effect of raids was well within acceptable limits. Of the targets attacked during 15 August, significant damage had only been caused at Driffield, Middle Wallop, West Malling and Croydon, but none of these airfields had been completely put out of action and the most important, Middle Wallop, was functioning normally after only an hour. Yet the Luftwaffe High Command still insisted that the offensive was achieving success. On the morning of 16 August the Intelligence Branch of the German Air Staff calculated that heavy losses since the beginning of July had reduced Fighter Command to about 300 serviceable aircraft – less than half the correct figure. Goering believed that Fighter Command's back would soon be broken.

Goering's pilots knew better, and the differences between the *Reichsmarschall* and Luftwaffe airmen would soon become serious. The stress on pilots on both sides was in many ways similar: this comment by Galland was echoed by many of his RAF opponents: 'We saw one comrade after the other, old and tested brothers in combat, vanish from our ranks. Not a day passed without a place remaining empty at the mess table. New faces appeared, became familiar, until one day these too would disappear.'[7] Morale among RAF pilots in mid-August was by no means universally high. Some squadrons, such as 609 down at Middle Wallop, were tired but elated; others were weary and despondent. No. 1 Squadron at Northolt, for example, had suffered heavy casualties during recent days, and the squadron historian described the feeling after the fighting on 15 August: 'The atmosphere at Northolt that night was not a happy one. None of the pilots felt like going up to London after duty, for the loss of three of their number in five days seemed to tell them that the squadron's good luck was beginning to run out. When morale started to flag there was plenty to grouse about. Although most of the boys had lost all their personal kit in France, the Air Ministry was still arguing over the £60 replacement allowance due to each man. It had even been wryly suggested that the authorities were trying to save money by waiting until they had all been killed before authorising the payment.' But the historian, Flight Lieutenant Michael Shaw, pinpointed the remedy: 'A classic and successful battle was obviously needed to revive the squadron's flagging spirits.'[8] The majority of RAF fighter pilots were extremely resilient: a victory

130

by the squadron, a personal triumph in the sky over southern England, could transform morale. For the Germans the situation was far more difficult, and failing morale sapped strength at a much deeper level. Galland wrote: 'We complained of the leadership, the bombers, the Stukas, and were dissatisfied with ourselves.' Luftwaffe pilots were given a false propaganda treatment, yet were berated by Goering for not achieving better results, to which Galland and other air leaders replied that fighters could not obtain a greater number of kills while tied to the bombers. 'In those days,' wrote Galland, 'all the loud-speakers of the "Greater German Reich" from Aachen to Tilsit, from Flensburg to Innsbruck, and from the army stations of most of the occupied countries, blared out the song: "*Bomben auf En-ge-land*". By beating the big drum in strong and martial rhythm and blending it with the roar of aircraft, they expected a mass psychological effect. We pilots could not stand this song from the very start.'[9]

The British fighter pilots' defence of their homeland gave justification for their treatment as heroes and provided them with infinitely more determination. And a deeper reason existed for their greater resilience. The RAF, formed in April 1918 by the amalgamation of the Royal Flying Corps and the Royal Naval Air Service, was young enough to be proud of its independence, yet old enough to have firm traditions and stability. The Luftwaffe by comparison had only been developed as a separate service for seven years: its growth had been astonishing, but insufficient time had been possible for the establishment of tradition and for a general feeling amongst pilots that their squadron was a home for them, as it had been for others in the past. German commanders often lacked experience of modern war; the disruption of the German air force's history after 1918, caused by the scrapping of this service in the Versailles Treaty, had destroyed continuity in leadership. German fighter pilots, like the British, were usually very young – Dowding declared: 'Only exceptionally should officers over twenty-six years of age be posted to command fighter squadrons' – and they were equally brave. But the Germans often lacked that indefinable spirit which went beyond sheer courage and which could not be artificially created. Ed Murrow, an eloquent outsider, captured something of this spirit when he visited a Fighter Command airfield. 'As we sat there, they were waiting to take off again. They talked of their own work; discussed the German air force with all the casualness of Sunday-morning half-backs discussing yesterday's football. There were no nerves, no profanity, and no heroics. There was no swagger about those boys in wrinkled and stained uniforms...When the squadron took off, one of them remarked quite casually that he'd be back in time for tea.'[10]

But the strain would continue. On the morning of 16 August those young pilots fully expected the high fighting level of the previous day to be repeated. For the first four hours after dawn enemy operations were virtually restricted to reconnaissance flights. Then at about 11 am activity began to increase. Once again Goering had issued orders for attacks on airfields and a series of raids were launched in three areas: at 12.15 enemy aircraft flew over North Foreland after attacking a convoy off Orfordness; ten minutes later three waves of aircraft, estimated at forty-five machines, crossed the coast at Yarmouth. Squadrons were ordered to intercept by 12 Group, but no contact was made through poor visibility – the same clouds also prevented the Luftwaffe from effective bombing attacks. Five minutes later, at 12.30 pm, three waves of twenty aircraft each arrived from the Cherbourg area to strike at Portsmouth and Southampton, and at the same time a succession of sudden, smaller-scale strikes began on targets in Kent. A total of twelve squadrons were despatched by 10, 11 and 12 Groups.[11]

In Kent the airfield at West Malling, hit by mistake the evening before, received considerable runway damage, but cloud continued to hinder German bombers and most of the planned targets in the area were spared. Bombs were dropped haphazardly instead, and once again these reached close to London: some landed in the Thames and the sticks spread into nearby Northfleet. Further west, the cloud layer began to thin as the raiders arrived. Among the first Fighter Command aircraft to intercept were Hurricanes from 1 Squadron, based at Tangmere and still demoralised from the recent run of ill-luck. Fortune had still to favour them. They dropped down on a small group of Me 109s, probably acting as an advance for the main wave approaching from Cherbourg, but failed to inflict damage; instead, two of the 1 Squadron aircraft were destroyed although both pilots survived. The remaining pilots from the squadron returned to refuel and within minutes were airborne again. Now, soon after 12.30 pm, the main enemy raids began. The principal attack was suffered by Tangmere, struck by a Ju 87 and Ju 88 *Gruppe*. The enemy aircraft approached from the south in successive waves, each dive-bombing the runway and installations in turn, and this time the bombs were accurate. 'The following buildings were destroyed,' declared the official report. 'All hangars, workshops, stores, sick quarters, pumping station, Y hut officers' mess, Salvation Army hut...' Fourteen aircraft on the ground were demolished or seriously

132

damaged, including seven Hurricanes and six Blenheims. Casualties included the American volunteer pilot 'Billy' Fiske, who returned to Tangmere in his Spitfire already damaged from a dog-fight, and who found the airfield still under heavy attack. He was forced to attempt a landing with his wheels jammed up and with smoke pouring from his engine. Fiske's aircraft hit the runway on its belly and slithered forward, skidding between one bomb crater then another; it had almost come to a stop when the aircraft suddenly burst into flames and exploded. Fiske died later from his injuries and a tablet was placed in St Paul's: 'An American citizen who died that England might live.'[12]

The battle still swirled around Tangmere when pilots of 1 Squadron returned to base in mid-afternoon from patrols elsewhere. They flew low through the smoke to examine the damage, then sighted another raiding force approaching from the sea. Squadron Leader Pemberton gathered his aircraft around him and the six Hurricanes climbed for height. Confronting them were an estimated 120 Heinkels and Me 110s with a further formation of Ju 88s close behind. Pemberton's pilots attacked immediately, diving in from the beam. The Squadron Leader opened fire at close range and his victim, a Heinkel, dropped in flames; then bullets shattered into Pemberton's engine, and he was forced to leave the fight. Another pilot, Peter Matthews, led the section into the Luftwaffe escorts and shot one into the sea; a Hurricane pilot with Matthews in this dive had to curve away from the dog-fights with glycol pouring from a punctured tank – this airman, Peter Boot, made a forced landing on the Hogsback but his aircraft was completely ruined when it ploughed through anti-invasion spikes. Above him, the flight continued. Another Heinkel went down, attacked by Sergeant Clowes. The latter then swept below a cloud layer and expended the last of his ammunition on a Ju 88, causing damage; the Luftwaffe pilot crash-landed after further harassment from Spitfires which had appeared from the east. Pilots from 1 Squadron converged on Northolt, claiming the certain destruction of four Heinkels, one Ju 88 and one Me 110. At last the run of bad luck had apparently ended.[13] Also involved in the air actions around Tangmere were pilots of 43 Squadron; one of them, Pilot Officer Crisp, described his experience succinctly in his log book: 'Beat up with five 109s. Baled out over Bognor and broke leg (Starboard).' Crisp would be unable to return to duty until June 1941; he scrawled across the pages in his log book 'Interval for repairs to undercarriage'.[14]

During these engagements over the fields of Sussex and Hampshire, a British pilot was earning himself the only Victoria Cross to be awarded

133

for air fighting in the Second World War. Flight Lieutenant J. B. Nicholson, with other pilots from 249 Squadron, dived on three Ju 88s near Southampton, only to see them shot down by intervening Spitfires before he could approach sufficiently close. Then, climbing again to join other sections of his squadron, Nicholson came under sudden attack from an unseen Me 110. Shells ripped into his Hurricane: one struck his spare petrol tank, causing an immediate fire; another pierced his cockpit and tore away part of his right trouser leg; another shattered his left heel. Jagged splinters struck his face, nearly severing his left eye-lid. Blood gushed from his eye and forehead, but almost instinctively Nicholson jerked the controls of his aircraft in evasive action. The Messerschmitt roared past, overshooting the burning Hurricane. Nicholson immediately attacked. Flames were licking around him, his skin was already blistering and his vision was almost obscured by blood, but he kept on his enemy's tail and fired. Nicholson was too blinded to see the result, but eye-witnesses on the ground noted the Messerschmitt as it swung violently upwards almost on its back, then hurtled into the sea. Nicholson hauled himself out of his wrecked aircraft and plummeted downwards – his hands were so badly burnt that he fell thousands of feet before he managed to pull his parachute rip-cord. As he swung down to safety, pretending to be dead to avoid being attacked by enemy aircraft, he noticed blood seeping through the lace-holes of his flying-boots.[15]

Seventy-five enemy aircraft were claimed shot down by Fighter Command that Friday, plus twenty-nine unconfirmed: the actual total was forty-five.[16] Operations were soon resumed from the bombed RAF airfields. At Tangmere, which had suffered most, some buildings were 'promptly made fit for habitation' as soon as the attack ended, and the official report continued: 'The depressing situation was dealt with in an orderly manner and it is considered that the traditions of the RAF were upheld by all ranks.'[17] Fighter Command Intelligence stated: 'Croydon, Manston, Redhill, Lympne and Tangmere are only unserviceable at night through enemy-damaged equipment.'[18] But the number of serviceable aircraft in Fighter Command had suffered another drop, from 653 to 631 including the loss of aircraft destroyed on the ground, and at least seven more pilots had been killed. Moreover, Fighter Command Intelligence issued a sober warning a few hours after the fighting on 16 August: 'In spite of heavy losses large-scale attacks by GAF on airfields and industry are likely to continue, though... it is impossible that heavy sustained operations can be maintained from present bases in occupied territory for more than a brief period. The High Command probably overestimates considerably our own losses, and in view of the numerical superiority of GAF is prepared to suffer heavily in the attempt to obtain air superiority. It would be contrary to their doctrine to desist from these attacks, to which they are now committed.'[19]

The German propaganda radio stated that the intensified air raids on south-east England foreshadowed surprise landings by enemy troops, possibly in the north-east. The threat of invasion remained. Brooke was spending his time on a rapid tour of Britain's coastal defences; he fully expected an invasion attempt once the Luftwaffe had managed to obtain an edge in the air war, and he wrote: 'The pilots of Fighter Command were putting up a performance for which they will remain famous throughout history. There were, however, grave doubts as to whether they could last the course.'[20] Further parachutes were dropped during the night of the 16th in another attempt to deceive the British into believing enemy agents or troops had landed.

Equipment was being sent to army units undertaking the anti-invasion role, but these units were still weak. The intensified air war meant that Britain's industrial effort had to be directed towards the RAF rather than the Army or Navy. During the afternoon of 16 August the War Cabinet had agreed that industrial priority should continue to be accorded first to aircraft, then to instruments and equipment for these aircraft, followed by anti-aircraft weaponry. Only then were listed small arms and small arms ammunition, with bombs coming next. Tanks were well down the list – and in fact these essential weapons of land warfare would not be given top priority status until July 1941.

On the morning of 17 August Brauchitsch and Halder attended final landing exercises at a training establishment near Le Touquet. They watched the troops running ashore from the ten-man rubber boats which would be used for the last few yards of approach; other units made use of converted fishing smacks. The German army was rapidly completing its preparations. The Italian diplomat Dino Alfieri reported to Ciano on recent talks with the German Foreign Minister; Ciano noted in his diary that 'according to von Ribbentrop, every effort must be concentrated against Great Britain, because there, and there alone, is "the question of life and death".'[21] But Hitler, who had returned to Berlin at the start of the main air offensive, once more journeyed back to his Berghof villa on 17 August, and there he continued to receive conflicting reports from his Naval and Army chiefs over the feasibility of

Sea Lion; Goering, on the other hand, still maintained that the chances of the Luftwaffe obtaining air superiority were 'absolutely favourable'. The *Reichsmarschall* believed the climax approached, with the Luftwaffe soon being able to make use of its numerical advantage.[22]

Experienced airmen from obsolescent Battle squadrons of RAF Bomber Command started transferring to Fighter Command. After a short conversion course they would help fill fighter pilot ranks: in the period 8 August to midnight on 17 August, Fighter Command had suffered ninety-two pilots killed or missing.[23] But the Luftwaffe was also experiencing stern difficulties. The Ju 87, the famous Stuka which had created such terror during *Blitzkrieg* operations in Poland, Belgium and France, had been found to have serious drawbacks in the Battle of Britain. The aircraft was extremely slow when compared to Hurricanes and Spitfires, only able to reach 150 mph when diving owing to the dragging effect of the externally slung bombs. 'As the required altitude for the dive was 10,000–15,000 feet,' commented Galland, 'the Stukas attracted the Spitfires and Hurricanes as honey attracts flies. The English soon realised that the Stukas, once they peeled out of formation to dive singly on to their targets, were practically defenceless until they had reassembled.' This imposed an increasing burden on the escorting Messerschmitt pilots, and the losses of Ju 87s had steadily risen. 'We fighter pilots were blamed,' complained Galland. He and his colleagues had long argued against the dive-bombing technique as a strategic method – the Stukas were of best value as a tactical weapon in support of a ground army, especially tanks, and the Battle of Britain role was totally unsuitable. Yet the German Command had persisted with the concept, despite casualties. Now, however, the Stukas began to be withdrawn from operations against England; this meant a considerable weakening of Luftwaffe strength – dive-bombers represented almost a third of the overall bombers, numbering about 250 aircraft in Luftflotten 2 and 3 at the start of the Battle of Britain. On the other hand the withdrawal of the Stukas could lighten the load for German fighter escorts.[24]

Enemy operations on 17 August proved slight, despite good weather: Fighter Command reported that GAF activity seemed restricted to reconnaissance flights over south-east England.[25] British pilots welcomed the lull; some managed to slip up to London for a weekend leave. Churchill journeyed to Chequers and prepared a speech he would make the following Tuesday, and which would be one of his most famous. War Cabinet Ministers also left the capital for the weekend. Sir Alexander Cadogan, visiting Eton, wrote in his diary: 'Walked in the Playing Fields. Fell in with the Vice-Provost who invited us to tea... Very pleasant. W strolled round again after. *What* a delightful place. We saw one "student" on a bicycle with (a) a rifle, (b) a pair of cricket pads, and (c) a steel helmet. *How* that would puzzle Hitler, who, by the way, has ceased his air attacks today. Has he had enough?'[26]

Next day, Sunday 18 August, the Luftwaffe again struck at airfields in southern England. The main operations began at noon, with raiders crossing the coast between North Foreland and Dungeness and penetrating deep into Kent. Aircraft from Lieutenant-General Fröhlich's *Kampfgeschwader* 76 split into high and low level formations as they approached the sector stations of Kenley and Biggin Hill; Fighter Command aircraft had already been scrambled. No. 615 Squadron had rushed southward to protect the coastal airfield of Hawkinge and engaged the high-level enemy bombers en route, claiming twelve Luftwaffe aircraft destroyed. The rest swept on, numbering over forty machines. An interception was attempted by Spitfires from 64 Squadron, but many enemy aircraft managed to reach their target. Hurricane pilots of 111 Squadron had insufficient time to block the low-level assault and aircraft in the latter pressed on with their attack on Kenley, covered by trees and buildings from anti-aircraft gunners on the ground. About a hundred bombs dropped from the combined high and low level attacks; the Kenley operations room was temporarily put out of action, and the runway was too badly damaged for returning aircraft of 615 and 64 Squadrons, who flew instead to Croydon and Redhill. Croydon itself received some damage from a subsidiary strike. The assault on Kenley had lasted only a few minutes, but during that time ten aircraft had been destroyed or damaged on the ground, including four operational Hurricanes completely demolished; ten hangars had been shattered and numerous other buildings; nine service personnel had been killed. The Kenley damage was sufficient to reduce the number of squadrons which the station could accommodate from three to two for the rest of the Battle of Britain.[27] Simultaneously, the Luftwaffe bombers roared over Biggin Hill and this airfield also received considerable damage, although it remained fully operational. Soon afterwards two formations of Do 17s and Me 109s struck at Manston in shallow dives from about 5000 feet to as low as 400 feet, but the attack proved inaccurate. West Malling again received Luftwaffe attention, with thirty bomb craters spread over the runway after a sudden raid.[28]

During mid-afternoon further waves of German bombers crossed the

137

Channel, aiming towards the Portsmouth area with RAF establishments at Thorney Island, Gosport, Ford and Poling among the targets. The raid marked the last major effort by Stukas in the Battle of Britain, and the result confirmed the wisdom of pulling these aircraft from the struggle. Four Ju 87 *Gruppen* were involved. They reached their objectives and attacked with some success – the radar station at Poling was rendered inoperative for the rest of August – but before the Stukas could re-form for their return flight they were vigorously intercepted by Spitfires of 152 Squadron and Hurricanes of 43 Squadron. One Ju 87 *Gruppe* of twenty-eight aircraft suffered twelve destroyed and six others which barely managed to make the return to the French coast; the other *Gruppe* suffered almost as badly.[29]

The third main thrust approached the coast between Harwich and Dungeness at 5 pm, with the majority of the enemy aircraft flying up the Blackwater and Thames. Fighter Command intercepted successfully and the shattered German formations made for home. Bombs were jettisoned, and again some fell on the south-east London suburbs – houses on the outskirts of the capital had already been damaged during the raid on Croydon earlier in the day, even though Hitler had still to lift the restriction on bombing this area. 'I am convinced that the Germans were after military objectives,' declared Ed Murrow after a five-hour tour of the suburbs that day. His radio talk went on to describe the attitude of Londoners in the affected areas, and already these men and women were acquiring their reputation for stoic bravery. 'Those people were calm and courageous,' Murrow told his American listeners. 'About an hour after the "all-clear" had sounded people were sitting in deck-chairs on their lawns, reading their Sunday papers... There was no bravado, no loud voices, only a quiet acceptance of the situation. To me those people were incredibly brave and calm. They are the unknown heroes of this war.' Murrow added: 'Politicians have repeatedly called this a people's war. These people deserve well of their leaders.'[30]

Winston Churchill raised the subject of bomb-threatened Londoners in the War Cabinet meeting at noon next day: there had been several air raid warnings in Central London during the previous few days, although air fighting had yet to spread in from the suburbs, and he expressed continuing concern at the disruption to daily life by the sirens; he wanted to avoid 'unnecessary stoppages of work' and he asked Ministers to do their best in encouraging staffs to continue work, despite red warnings, until the last possible moment. Ministers at this War Cabinet session also received figures of casualties inflicted and suffered the previous day, and estimated enemy losses were even more optimistic than usual. The Vice-CoAS believed 126 Luftwaffe aircraft had been destroyed, plus twenty-six probables and forty-five damaged, including thirteen shot down by anti-aircraft fire.[31] Owing to the lull on Saturday 17 August, Fighter Command had been much improved by the time the main actions began at noon on the Sunday: the total of operational fighters stood at 706 compared with 631 twenty-four hours before. A further drop had resulted from casualties on Sunday afternoon, reducing the total to 689, but this still gave a greater number of operational aircraft than the total on the morning of Eagle Day, 13 August. During the twenty-four hour period beginning noon on Sunday, three pilots were killed, two reported missing and four injured.[32]

The number of German aircraft destroyed on 18 August was very much lower than the total given to the War Cabinet – about seventy-one rather than 126. But this was still far too high for Goering's liking, and his self-confidence now showed signs of deterioration. At noon on 19 August the Luftwaffe chief addressed a meeting of his senior officers, who had been urgently summoned to Karinhall. 'We have reached the decisive period of the air war against England,' declared Goering. 'The vital task is the defeat of the enemy air force. Our first aim is to destroy the enemy's fighters.' He expressed severe displeasure at the course of the battle so far – which by his original reckoning should already have been decided – and he insisted that losses were being suffered unnecessarily. Mistakes must be rectified immediately. 'We've got to preserve our fighting strength. Our formations must be safeguarded.' Better protection would have to be given to the bombers, and Goering again criticised the fighter escorts: fighter pilots had failed in their objective 'to weaken the enemy's fighter arm so that our bombers can proceed unhindered.' Changes would be made in personnel, with the more elderly *Geschwader* (Group) commanders being relieved and replaced by young men who had shown themselves able to kill the enemy. These replacements would set 'a shining example'. Goering still failed to recognise fighter pilot difficulties and merely blamed them for the present high casualty rate.[33] He insisted that bombers must always have priority. And, at this meeting, he extended the existing bombing policy in a way which had extremely dangerous implications for both Britain and Germany. Apparently acting on his own initiative, Goering ordered Luftflotte 3 to prepare for a night bombing attack on Liverpool, although he reserved to himself the right to order raids on that city and on London. Bombing of towns in England would meanwhile be increased, especially through night raids when the weather appeared suitable, even though such attacks would do nothing to help gain air superiority over south-east Britain: they might terrorise the population, but they could never win the Battle of Britain.

Galland journeyed back to his airfield from the Karinhall conference. 'Germany presented a picture of peaceful serenity. The war had hardly made any difference to the daily life at home. Those who were not yet called up earned good money... The I-could-not-care-less attitude at home and the general lack of interest in the war did not please me. I had come straight out of a battle for life and death, the brunt of which so far had been borne by the fighter force... For the moment the whole burden of the war rested on the few hundred German fighter pilots on the Channel coast.' The contrast between the uncaring life in Germany and the strain being imposed on the pilots 'had a deeply depressing effect on me'.[34] Other Luftwaffe pilots shared his feeling of being unappreciated.

'The gratitude of every home in our island,' declared Churchill to Members of Parliament next day, 'in our Empire and indeed throughout the world, except in the abodes of the guilty, goes out to the British airmen, who, undaunted by odds, unwearied in their constant challenge and mortal danger, are turning the tide of world war by their prowess and by their devotion.' The Prime Minister repeated the words he had uttered to Ismay five days before. 'Never in the field of human conflict was so much owed by so many to so few.'

'That must refer to mess bills,' one fighter pilot was alleged to have remarked, or, as Pilot Officer Michael Appleby of 609 Squadron commented: 'And for so little.'[35] Churchill's speech was not planned as an oratorical, morale-boosting performance, despite the fame which his words later acquired. 'It was a moderate and well-balanced speech,' commented one of the MPs, Harold Nicolson. 'He did not try to arouse enthusiasm but only to give guidance,'[36] Churchill nevertheless displayed his characteristic optimism. 'The enemy is of course far more numerous than we are. But our new production already largely exceeds his, and the American production is only just beginning to flow in. Our bomber and fighter strengths now, after all this fighting, are larger than they have ever been. We believe that we should be able to continue the air struggle indefinitely and as long as the enemy pleases, and the longer it continues the more rapidly will be our approach, first towards that parity, and then into that superiority in the air upon which in large measure the decision of the war depends.' Even while the Prime Minister spoke, MPs could hear the faint stuttering of aircraft machine-guns from high above the Houses of Parliament. People in the street outside could see 'tiny specks scintillating like diamonds in the brilliant sunshine'. A section of three Spitfires, led by Group Captain Victor Beamish, was chasing three Me 109s down the Thames in the Hammersmith direction.[37]

Already, by 9 am on that Tuesday, 20 August, Fighter Command operational strength had reached 718, an increase of twenty-nine in the last twenty-four hours, and the steady rise would continue. Time was being allowed for pilot replacements, with men rushed from training and from Bomber Command. Moreover, RAF commanders used the quiet period to attempt improvements in the defensive system. Like Goering, Park had been assessing recent performance; the 11 Group commander issued instructions on 19–20 August that wherever possible pilots must fight over the English countryside rather than out to sea, and if they had to cross the coastline they should try to remain within gliding distance of land. He also decided that the principal effort should be directed against enemy bombers, rather than their fighter escort: this would both help protect the airfields and would result in fewer Fighter Command losses. Park also appealed for reinforcements to be sent from 12 Group, if necessary, to help defend sector stations.[38]

The respite renewed speculation over German intentions. 'While there is no indication that an attempted invasion is imminent,' stated the Fighter Command Intelligence survey on 20 August, 'there is considerable evidence that a seaborne expedition has been for some time in preparation. It is possible that its despatch has already had to be postponed. A final decision will probably depend on the degree of success which the GAF can achieve against our air defences.'[39] On that Tuesday the first of 1130 barges required for the first invasion wave began to move from their collection points to ports between Ostend and Boulogne.[40] Officially, the date for the start of Sea Lion was still scheduled for 15 September, but disagreement continued to hamper planning: the Navy insisted that the Army's proposal for a four-division first wave was quite unacceptable. The matter was again referred to Hitler, probably on 21 August: next day Jodl's deputy, Colonel Warlimont, tried to sooth naval fears by saying that 'Sea Lion, according to the Fuehrer's wishes, will only be carried out if an especially favourable initial situation offers sure prospects of success.'[41]

On that day the Germans began operating a new weapon against the threatened south coast of England. Heavy artillery batteries on and around Cape Gris Nez began their bombardment of Dover, after having fired a number of ranging rounds during the preceding ten days; the enemy propaganda radio declared that this shelling indicated a German intention to land in the Dover area – the NBBS also warned of the destruction of London by 'aerial torpedoes carrying many tons of HE and guided by radio'.[42] Other items of German propaganda were analysed by the British Air Ministry weekly résumé issued the same day. 'Germany is describing her recent activities to have been only in the nature of armed reconnaissance flights and a preliminary to further action. This description is accompanied by threats of further mass air attacks to come.' The résumé added that during the week beginning noon 15 August, attacks had been directed against over fifty different British airfields.[43] The War Cabinet résumé issued to Ministers next morning, 23 August, went into greater detail. Eleven airfields had suffered considerable damage, but the survey declared that the air situation was 'not materially affected', although forty-one operational aircraft had been destroyed on the ground and hangars containing a further forty-seven twin-engined trainers were burnt out. Fighter Command had flown 4932 sorties, losing eighty-nine aircraft in the air. The résumé revealed the rise in bombing casualties: during the week 298 people had been killed by daylight raids, 4888 seriously injured, and thirty-three had died in night attacks. Of these, 173 died and 179 were seriously injured during the raids on Croydon, south-west London and Northfleet on 15 and 16 August.[44]

No civilian casualties had been suffered since 17 August, and Fighter Command losses of aircraft and men had subsided dramatically. Three pilots were killed on 19 August, but only one each day on 20, 21, 22 and 23 August. Fighter Command operational strength had risen to its highest level by the evening of 23 August – 740 aircraft. This compared with only 413 on 3 June after Dunkirk and 675 at the beginning of August. Britain stood in a far better situation than ever before, owing to the weather, Goering's delay, the magnificent fighter production rate and the skill of the pilots themselves.[45] Recent Luftwaffe activity had been confined to aircraft operating singly or in small formation, mainly attempting machine-gun attacks on wireless stations, factories and on one train. Manston received some damage on the evening of 22 August, with a hangar being damaged and two Blenheims destroyed on the ground.[46]

Many senior RAF officers, Dowding among them, continued to view the situation with understandable but nevertheless exaggerated pessimism. The tension and the anxiety obscured the facts. In order to arrive at a better consideration of the actual position, Churchill had already asked the Air Ministry on 14 August for a more definitive calculation of possible pilot losses; now, on 23 August, the Air Ministry obliged with a paper presented to the Defence Committee at 10 am. This showed how the postulated figure of 746 pilots lost per month had been reached, based on a possible increase in operations compared with those in June and July. Churchill refused to accept this terrifying figure, but the Air Secretary, Sir Archibald Sinclair, answered by saying that Fighter Command casualties had in fact been running at a higher rate than even the 746 estimate. Churchill remained unconvinced, and his attack on the Air Ministry paper revealed sarcasm – and common sense. 'If it were assumed that 600 out of the 746 casualties were in battle, and if the claim made by the Air Ministry to destroy German aircraft in a ratio 3 to 1 were accepted, then the German postulated wastage in battle would be 1800 a month. To this figure we should add the German accident casualties, which, if their force were double ours, would work out at about 280 per month giving a grand total of 2080 lost each month. The Germans would thus have to produce over 14,000 pilots in the next seven months to make good their wastage.' The Prime Minister enquired 'whether the possibility of such an output of pilots by the Germans had been investigated.' He added it was clearly out of the question that the Germans could make good such losses, and this indicated our own figures for wastage were much too high. Churchill considered that a figure of 'about 500 would more nearly represent our wastage through the winter months.' Training plans should accordingly be based on this figure.[47]

Fortunately, even the Prime Minister's more sober assessment would prove totally incorrect, and Sinclair's statement, that losses in the sixteen days prior to 23 August showed a higher wastage rate than 647 a month, is thrown into doubt by an examination of Fighter Command daily returns. These reveal that 139 pilots were killed, wounded and reported missing in battle during the sixteen days, an average of just over eight a day; this would give a monthly total of 248 if the rate had continued.[48] It would be highly unlikely that non-battle casualties, through accidents, could have brought this total anywhere near the Air Ministry's 746 for RAF losses as a whole.

Reduced fighting cut pilot casualties, yet led to restlessness among the young airmen tensed for action. 'We used to long for bad weather to come and give us some relief,' commented Crook. 'Now, when matters became quieter and we had no fighting, we all got very bored after a few days and longed to shoot down some more Huns. Human nature is never satisfied for long.'[49]

Boredom abruptly ended at 12.30 pm on Saturday 24 August. The weather began to clear during the morning and a number of minor threats caused several squadron sections to be scrambled. Then, soon after noon, radar stations detected enemy aircraft assembling at a number of points from Dunkirk to Boulogne. As in the past, the Luftwaffe intended to launch two widely separated blows, first a thrust into Kent, then another against the Sussex/Hampshire area. Fighter Command airfields would again provide the main target. From the start the enemy displayed new tactics, evolved during the lull: following Goering's instructions issued at the 19 August conference, the German bomber formations were smaller and with a closer escort of fighters; the latter were under orders to guard their charges at all times and not to chase after their British opposition. This system, although causing additional discouragement to aces such as Galland, threatened to nullify the orders which Park had given that British pilots must concentrate on bombers and not fighters: the two types of aircraft now flew too close together to be separated. Moreover, the greater number of smaller enemy formations severely disrupted the Fighter Command defensive network: radar plotting was difficult and RAF squadrons were liable to be sent rushing in one direction then another, opening the way for a sudden attack through the resulting gaps.

Bombers in the first attacking wave penetrated the defensive network in the Manston area while the majority of British fighters patrolling in this region were re-fueling and re-arming. The enemy reached Manston virtually unimpeded, with twenty Ju 88s sweeping in from the south. The airfield, which had already received smaller raids at 8 and 11.20 am, suffered extensive damage; workmen began repairing the runway even while the raid continued and hose-pipes were repeatedly punctured by machine-gun bullets. For almost two hours the numerous German excursions towards the English coast kept RAF squadrons airborne, with nearly a hundred sorties flown by 11 Group aircraft between 1 and 3 pm, almost all of which were fruitless: the Luftwaffe usually turned east or west when reaching the coast, patrolling up and down attempting to lure out British fighters. Soon after 3 pm German bombers suddenly struck inland again, fifty or more crossing the coast. Some roared towards Manston, where bombs added to the fires still flickering on the airfield; other succeeded in reaching Hornchurch, where about a hundred HE bombs were dropped from medium-high altitude, only seven of which were reported to have hit the airfield. Defiants of 264 Squadron, which had only arrived from Kirton-in-Lindsey forty-eight hours before, were caught on the Hornchurch runway but managed to climb aloft unscathed. A third enemy force attacked North Weald and again caused damage, although the airfield remained fully serviceable.[50]

Harassed Fighter Command pilots darted backwards and forwards across Kent trying to deal with threatened penetrations. Many of these airmen remained astonishingly cheerful. 'Took off 15.45 hours,' wrote Flying Officer B. J. Lane of 19 Squadron in his pilot's log. 'Ran into a bunch of Huns over [Thames] Estuary. Had a bang at Me 110 but had to break away as tracer was coming over my head from another behind me. He appeared to be hitting his fellow-countryman in front of me but I didn't wait to see if he shot him down. Had a crack at another and shot his engine right out of the wing. Lovely!'[51] On the ground the WAAF personnel were winning ready admiration from officers who had previously viewed with suspicion this incursion of 'petticoats into the RAF'. Group Captain Bouchier, CO at Hornchurch, wrote: 'In a flimsy building on the aerodrome, I saw my WAAF plotters with their earphones pressed to their heads to keep out the inferno of noise from the torrent of bombs that were bursting all round, steady and calm at their posts, plotting – not a murmur or movement from a single one; though the whole building was literally rocking and each one knew that she and the building might at any moment be airborne.'[52]

At about 3.45 pm enemy aircraft from Luftflotte 3 entered the battle further west. Accurate radar plotting of the enemy approach from Cherbourg and the Channel Islands was severely handicapped by the presence off the south coast of numerous other small aircraft groups. Defensive measures by squadrons from 11 and 10 Groups were therefore confused, and about a hundred enemy aircraft managed to reach Portsmouth. Moreover some British squadrons, such as 609, were deployed at insufficient height to deal with the medium-to-high altitude attacks now being launched – the Luftwaffe had abandoned the dive-bombing strikes against which the RAF low-level patrol was intended to operate.

'Very soon a terrific AA barrage sprang up ahead of us,' wrote Crook, flying with other 609 Squadron pilots, 'looking exactly like a large number of dirty cotton-wool puffs in the sky. It was a most impressive barrage; besides all the guns at Portsmouth, all the warships in the harbour and dockyard were firing hard. A moment later, through the barrage and well above us, we saw a large German formation wheeling above Portsmouth. We were too low to be able to do anything about it.' The raid marked the implementation of another policy revealed by Goering at his conference a few days before. Unlike earlier attacks, this time the bombs were aimed as much against civilian as military targets. 'I cannot imagine a more flagrant case of indiscriminate bombing,' stated Crook, flying his Hurricane above the city. 'The whole salvo fell right into the middle of Portsmouth, and I could see great spurts of flame and smoke springing up all over the place.'[53] The same applied to a raid on Ramsgate, made earlier in the day while Manston was being attacked. 'It was a murderous attack,' wrote the journalist Pratt Boorman, who visited the town immediately afterwards. 'Most of the damage was to workers' houses in a residential area. A large number suffered.'[54]

Raids on Portsmouth and Ramsgate appeared 'to be the first instances of deliberate day bombing of town and city property', declared the Fighter Command Intelligence summary issued after the day's fighting. One reason for the indiscriminate bombing resulted from the decision to withdraw the single-engined Ju 87 dive-bombers from the struggle: attacks would now be from a higher altitude and therefore would inevitably be less accurate. These alterations were also noted by Fighter Command Intelligence: 'A change in GAF tactics appears to have taken place ... (i) the size of the fighter escort was reduced, being more in the proportion of one fighter to one bomber. (ii) Only twin-engined bombers were employed. (iii) Bombers flew mainly in tight formation of 20–30, between 14–18,000 feet, and high level bombing was principally employed.'[55] The Germans revealed other unpleasant surprises before the fighting ended on 24 August. Daylight faded, yet enemy activity continued with night-time bombing on a far heavier scale than ever before. About 170 bombers struck at targets spreading from Northumberland southwards, including Cardiff, Swansea, Birmingham, Tyneside, the Hartlepools, Middlesbrough, Hull, Leeds and Rotherham. Moreover, bombers aiming for the oil tanks at Thameshaven and aircraft factories at Rochester and Kingston again struck London. Bombs fell in the suburbs of Islington, Tottenham, Millwall, Finsbury, Stepney, East Ham, Leyton, Coulsdon and Bethnal Green. In the latter district about a hundred houses were destroyed. Bombs also fell in the City of London, at London Wall and Fore Street.[56]

This attack on the capital was still unauthorised by Goering or by Hitler. A teleprinter message reached the Luftwaffe bomber group HQ early next morning, 25 August: 'It is to be reported forthwith which crews dropped bombs in the London prohibited zone. The Supreme Commander reserves to himself the personal punishment of the commanders concerned by remustering them to the infantry.'[57] But the damage had been done and in Britain the raids seemed deliberate. Added to the other bombs dropped in the London area during recent days, and to other bombing attacks on British cities, the RAF now planned their reprisal operation. In turn this would precipitate the last phase in the Battle of Britain.

◡

CHAPTER ELEVEN

The War Spreads

25–29 August

Clouds returned during the morning of Sunday 25 August, but feints and threats to the south coast were again keeping Fighter Command squadrons under pressure. Moreover, Saturday's fighting had shown considerable enemy success. Although many of the target airfields had continued to function without serious interruption, the squadron using Manston had been withdrawn during the afternoon and urgent repairs had still to be completed elsewhere. Fighter Command claimed forty-two enemy aircraft destroyed plus eighteen probable – a total of thirty-eight would have been correct – but twenty-two British aircraft had been lost. The number of serviceable aircraft in Fighter Command dropped from 740 at 9 am on 24 August to 727 on the morning of the 25th. Remarkably few pilot casualties were reported: only two dead and seven missing in the twenty-four hours beginning noon on 24 August.[1]

Fighter Command was holding its own, but the new Luftwaffe tactics caused concern: the concentration on airfields combined with multiple smaller-scale thrusts; the withdrawal of vulnerable dive-bombers; above all, the increase in night attacks against which the RAF had virtually no defence to offer. Only six specialised Blenheim night-fighter squadrons existed, and these were unable to locate and engage bombers flying at speed above 12,000 feet.

The weather began to improve during the afternoon of 25 August, and just before 5 pm it appeared that the enemy were about to launch another major attack against the south-west. A Luftwaffe force of an estimated 100 aircraft was detected by radar off St Malo and within a few minutes almost all available aircraft based between Exeter and Tangmere were ordered aloft. The radar contact severely underestimated the enemy strength: at about 5.30 pm some 180 bombers and fighters swept towards the Portland/Poole area aiming for Warmwell airfield and RAF establishments near Yeovil. British aircraft patrolling off the coast immediately intercepted, among them pilots of 609 Squadron. 'I happened to be almost last in the line,' wrote David Crook, 'and I shall never forget seeing the long line of Spitfires ahead, sweeping down and curling round at terrific speed to strike right into the middle of the German formation. It was superb!'[2] But the British aircraft, only comprising about two complete squadrons, were hopelessly outnumbered; the majority of raiders broke through, even though part of the enemy formation was broken and 609 Squadron alone claimed six or seven German aircraft destroyed. Another squadron intercepted just before Warmwell, but many bombers still reached their target. Hangars and other buildings were destroyed, and communications at the airfield were disrupted for eighteen hours; the runway remained serviceable.[3] At about 6 pm a Luftwaffe attempt in the Kent area, probably aiming at Eastchurch, was successfully blocked near Dover; forty-five minutes later more enemy aircraft were intercepted near Maidstone and these also turned back without inflicting significant damage. Despite Warmwell, Fighter Command could find reason for relief in this Sunday's performance. Forty-seven aircraft were claimed destroyed plus fifteen unconfirmed, and although the actual total was more likely about twenty enemy aircraft brought down, compared to a Fighter Command loss of sixteen, the latter had already been replaced by Sunday evening: the number of serviceable RAF fighters rose to 728. Two British pilots had been killed; none was reported missing.[4]

As dusk fell, British retaliatory steps were being taken in reply to the new German bombing policy of indiscriminate attacks on civilian targets. Bomber Command aircraft were being readied at airfields in the south of England; the target was Berlin, considered by Hitler and Goering as totally safe. 'The War Cabinet was much in the mood to hit back, to raise the stakes, and to defy the enemy,' wrote Churchill in his war memoirs. 'I was sure they were right, and believed nothing impressed or disturbed Hitler so much as his realisation of British wrath and will-power.'[5] In fact the War Cabinet was never consulted over the decision to bomb Berlin; no meetings were held during the weekend. The decision stemmed from the Air Ministry alone, although when finally informed British Ministers voiced whole-hearted approval, and by that time the Germans themselves had struck at cities, bombing Birmingham, Coventry and other targets during the night of 25 August.

Sirens wailed in Hitler's capital at 12.20 am. 'The concentration of anti-aircraft fire was the greatest I've ever witnessed,' wrote Shirer in his diary. 'It provided a magnificent, a terrible sight. And it was strangely ineffective. Not a plane was brought down.' He continued: 'The Berliners are stunned. They did not think it could happen. When this war began, Goering assured them it couldn't...The Berliners are a naïve and simple people. They believed him. Their disillusionment today therefore is all the greater.'[6] Next morning the Berlin newspapers appeared with banner headlines: 'Cowardly British Attack...British Air Pirates over Berlin'.

In London, *The Times* appeared on that Monday with exuberant accounts of the air battle over Britain and the losses being inflicted on the Luftwaffe. The newspaper also contained fashion hints for female readers, recommending a 'battle-dress siren suit in washable corduroy with skirt to match.' British citizens were being advised on more practical matters: how to lie down when bombs fell. 'The position officially recommended,' observed Ed Murrow, '[is] flat on the ground, face down, mouth slightly open, and hands covering ears.'[7] War Cabinet Ministers assembled at 10 Downing Street at 12.30 pm to hear of the raid on Berlin. Results seemed to be satisfactory, said Newall, although weather had prevented a number of the British aircraft from locating their targets: the latter, unlike German bombing objectives, were still officially designated as military rather than civilian; moreover, the CoAS pointed out that British pilots had instructions to bring their bombs back if the targets could not be located, unlike German bombers which merely dumped their loads. 'This point was worth bringing out from the point of view of public opinion in the United States.' Ministers also discussed the advisability of continuing to publish the monthly casualty figures suffered from air raids on Britain: the next month's figures were likely to be high and publication might damage morale. But the general opinion of the War Cabinet was to retain the monthly reviews. 'The figures of casualties were not high if expressed as a percentage of the normal death rate, or even of the peacetime road casualties.'[8]

Battle of Britain activity continued the pattern of previous days, weather permitting: a strike against airfields in Kent and the Thames Estuary, followed by a thrust in the Portsmouth–Portland area. The first main assault came at midday, directed at the Folkestone region, but few enemy bombers penetrated far inland. About 3 pm German aircraft swept over the Channel again on a wider front extending north of the Thames. Bombers apparently aiming for Hornchurch and North Weald were successfully intercepted over the Thames Estuary and further south a raid on Manston was also blocked. But enemy aircraft managed to slip through the Fighter Command network to strike at Debden: protective forces rushed to the area from 12 Group were scrambled too late, and 11 Group fighters attempting to intercept were unable to manœuvre through the bomber escort. Debden received heavy damage, although the airfield remained in service. During the late afternoon about a hundred aircraft from Luftflotte 3 thrust towards Portsmouth but suffered heavily from 11 Group squadrons and from anti-aircraft fire; several bombers dropped their loads in apparent panic, and the success seemed to justify the Fighter Command assessment issued after the day's fighting: 'Generally speaking, all these attacks were intercepted early and well, and the enemy do not appear to have been so successful in attaining their objectives.'[9] The Luftwaffe returned after dark despite low cloud which hindered navigation. Sixty fires were started in Birmingham and factories were damaged; Coventry was also attacked, and fifty bombers struck at Plymouth. Sirens wailed in towns throughout the Midlands and the south of England, disrupting sleep even if the enemy aircraft were far away. 'Every time I fly,' boasted one German navigator, 'a million people take to their shelters.'[10] But forty-one German aircraft were destroyed during 26 August, only four less than Fighter Command claimed at the time, and the number of operational British fighters remained level at 728.[11]

Despite Goering's propaganda, the RAF had clearly still to relinquish air superiority. Hitler issued instructions on 27 August which took fully into account the naval objections to the Army's Sea Lion proposal. 'Army operations must allow for the facts regarding available shipping space and security of the crossing and disembarkation.' This document laid down the final landing plans: all proposed invasion areas north of Dover were abandoned, but the invasion area was extended slightly eastwards towards Bognor, with four main targets to be selected within this stretch.[12] The clumsy progress of Sea Lion planning continued to form a marked contrast to Hitler's handling of preparations for the offensive against Poland and against France; the German Army and Navy continued to labour under Hitler's lack of drive and enthusiasm, and from their own disagreement; the Luftwaffe still suffered from Goering's inflated optimism and its sacrifice went on. But although late, the Sea Lion plans were in an advanced stage, with troop deployment completed and naval transports almost prepared.

The strain on Fighter Command had reached its peak. In each of the past three weeks the Command had flown well over 4000 sorties – in the seven days ending 22 August the total had been a record 4932;

this compared with a total of only 1447 during the week ending 4 July and less than 1000 at the end of June. In addition, the latest German tactic of flying a great number of smaller raids was imposing added stress upon both machines and men. 'We were dead,' remembered one pilot. 'We were too tired even to get drunk.'[13] Park introduced a new procedure on 27 August in an effort to make greater use of his resources: this 'Tally-Ho' system specified that formation-leaders should give the 'Tally-Ho' attack message over the radio as soon as they contacted the enemy, plus particulars of height, course, position and numbers, so enabling controllers to direct other squadrons in more certain fashion. But this in turn kindled controversy over whether interception was best accomplished by large formations, as advocated by Leigh-Mallory, or by a greater number of smaller groups, as argued by Dowding and by Park himself. Meanwhile, a drop in enemy activity prevented the Tally-Ho procedure from being employed effectively on its first day of operation. Pilots welcomed the slight rest, even though many stayed at full alert: the weather seemed insufficiently overcast to hinder Luftwaffe sorties, and raids were therefore constantly expected. Towards evening enemy fighter patrols increased over the Channel 'with the evident object of drawing and testing the strength of fighter defences', according to Fighter Command Intelligence.[14] More bombing raids were launched against the Midlands during the night.

The lessening of enemy daylight activity, probably caused by the reorganisation of Luftwaffe command structure ordered by Goering on 19 August, came to an end again early on 28 August. A few minutes before 9 am about twenty bombers approached Dover under close escort, with other fighters sweeping the surrounding area. Four British squadrons were unable to prevent the enemy reaching the Coastal Command airfield at Eastchurch and 264 Squadron suffered heavily, losing two Defiants and another four damaged. In this attack Fighter Command lost eight aircraft, including six pilots, while five German aircraft were destroyed in return – and the day had only just begun. After a tense four hours of waiting and false alarms, Fighter Command squadrons were scrambled again at 12.30 pm to meet another German thrust, this time directed at Rochford on the north side of the Thames Estuary. An estimated sixty Do 17 and 215 bombers, escorted by the same number of Me 109s, curved in from the sea and crossed the coast despite strong resistance from several squadrons. Eleven Hurricanes from 1 Squadron dived on the enemy above Rochford itself, destroying at least two with no British loss; about eighty HE bombs landed in the area, with some thirty hitting the airfield. Rochford, according to Fighter Command Intelligence, was 'reported still to be usable in all directions by single aircraft with great care'.[15]

Churchill was visiting Kent during the afternoon of the 28th. He toured the coastal area inspecting bomb damage, and the sight of the rubble and human misery had a severe effect on him. Sirens sounded while he was visiting Ramsgate, following a threat from a tip-and-run raid by two German aircraft, and the Prime Minister and his party were hustled into a public shelter. A large notice declared: 'No Smoking'; Churchill obediently stubbed out his newly-lit cigar. 'The first thing that we saw on coming to the surface again,' remembered Ismay, 'was a tea shop which had been wrecked by the blast of a bomb. Part of the roof had fallen in, and there was a shambles of broken crockery, chairs and tables. The aged proprietress, her livelihood gone, was sobbing her heart out.' Churchill turned to Ismay when they had boarded their train. 'Arrangements must be made for poor people like that,' he declared, and immediately began dictating a minute to the Chancellor of the Exchequer.[16] Churchill composed another minute after visiting Manston airfield, victim of repeated Luftwaffe attacks, and this time his sentiments were far less sympathetic. 'I was much concerned,' he informed the Air Secretary and CoAS, 'to find that although more than four clear days have passed since it [Manston] was last raided the greater part of the craters on the landing ground remained unfilled and the aerodrome was barely serviceable...' Every crater unfilled within twenty-four hours, he declared, should be the subject of a special report with explanations to higher authority.[17]

During that afternoon further operations in Churchill's tour area underlined the continuing strain being experienced at Kentish airfields. At 4 pm a force of an estimated 100 fighters, mainly Me 109s, embarked on a high-level sweep over the county at about 25,000 feet; British fighters climbing to intercept were placed in an extremely vulnerable position, with the enemy above them and with the RAF pilots unable to organise full attacking formation before contact. Two hours later another high-level sweep, this time by about fifty Me 109s, lured out further British fighters; casualty figures were probably equal – nine aircraft each. About thirty German aircraft were destroyed during the day, with Fighter Command claiming only twenty-seven confirmed and fourteen probables; the British lost about twenty aircraft, but the continuing flow of replacements meant that the total of Fighter Command operational aircraft only dropped from 723 to 720.[18]

Much depended on the continued energetic production of fighters, and the Luftwaffe night raids were clearly intended to disrupt these factories and other industrial plants. On the night of 28 August about 180 bombers struck at cities and other targets; in addition, about 160 bombers were directed towards Merseyside in the first large-scale raid on the Liverpool–Birkenhead area. Approximately ninety-five bombers reached their target in this region, dropping 103 tons HE and 190 incendiary canisters.[19] Once again RAF Bomber Command struck back at Berlin, inflicting the first fatal casualties: the official German count was ten killed and twenty-nine wounded. William Shirer noted: 'I think the populace of Berlin is more affected by the fact that the British planes have been able to penetrate to the centre of Berlin without trouble than they are by the first casualties. For the first time the war has been brought home to them. If the British keep this up, it will have a tremendous effect upon the morale of the people here.'[20]

The British CoAS reported to the War Cabinet at noon next day that the Berlin bombing had been 'most successful'. Churchill said he proposed sending a message of congratulations to Bomber Command, which would be published and which would mention 'the restraint exercised by our pilots in refraining from unloading their bombs if they were not certain of hitting military targets.' But Churchill also told his Ministers: 'In view of the indiscriminate bombing practised by the Germans we might have to consider in the near future making a temporary but marked departure from our policy.' The Prime Minister had also been following up his impressions gained during his visit to Ramsgate the previous afternoon; with his typical efficiency and ability to attend to a vast variety of matters simultaneously, he had examined the effect of the raids on the ordinary men and women. He told the War Cabinet that he had made enquiries 'into the consequence of air raids on poorer classes'. Local authorities were doing their best, but 'the trouble was the inadequacy of the present legislative provision for compensating those who had lost their household effects, or the stock in trade of their small businesses... His view was that considerably more would have to be done for persons of limited means.' Churchill had therefore asked the Chancellor of the Exchequer to examine the possibility of compensation, fed by a levy on all householders.[21]

Cadogan noted after this War Cabinet meeting on 29 August: 'Winston thinks German scheme is to hammer Kent promontory flat and then attempt invasion.'[22] But the Italian Foreign Minister, after talks with Hitler and Ribbentrop at Berghof on 28 and 29 August, reported to Mussolini that doubts now seemed to hang over this offensive. Ciano wrote in his diary: 'Hitler explains the failure of the attack on Great Britain as due to the bad weather. He says that he will need at least two weeks of clear weather to neutralise British naval superiority, but from all that he said it seems to me probable that there is now a definite postponement of the attack. Until when?'[23]

'It is still too early to state with assurance that the [German] High Command has been forced to revise its offensive policy,' declared the Air Ministry weekly situation report. 'It is significant, however, that night attacks have been intensified and the scale of attack by day reduced. Furthermore, the claim to air superiority is probably an attempt to justify the curtailment of heavy attacks by day which may have become necessary due to heavy losses.' The survey claimed 913 German aircraft destroyed during the period 8–28 August, plus 315 probables; on the other hand a survey of German pilot prisoners had shown that morale 'is still very high'.[24] Air activity remained minimal on 29 August until 3 pm, when an estimated 200 aircraft moved towards the south coast. The enemy force split into two main formations, one crossing the coast between Hythe and Ramsgate and the other between Hastings and Beach Head. The aim still seemed to be to tempt British fighters into the air, and apart from a small number of bombers which penetrated to Gatwick the bulk of the enemy formations dispersed soon afterwards. About fifty Me 109s flew over East Kent at 6.30 pm, but in general air engagements were restricted: Fighter Command only claimed nine enemy aircraft shot down for certain, plus ten probables. Six RAF pilots were reported missing and one killed; the number of operational British fighters dropped by three to 717.[25] The enemy's principal effort was again reserved for bombing attacks after dark, and for the second night in succession Merseyside received concentrated attention. About 137 enemy aircraft reached the Liverpool–Birkenhead region, dropping 130 tons HE and 313 incendiary canisters – substantially more than on 28 August.[26] Moreover, the raids on British industry seemed to be causing concern to Beaverbrook; Sir Alexander Cadogan noted in his diary late that day: 'Beaverbrook rather fussed – or affected to be – about our aircraft losses and damage to factories.'[27]

Next day, 30 August, saw a sudden upsurge in the daylight Battle of Britain. The Luftwaffe, after regaining breath over the previous forty-eight hours and vastly underestimating remaining RAF strength, now made a great bid for supremacy: young fighter pilots, already numb with weariness, would be called upon as never before.

155

~

CHAPTER TWELVE

End and Beginning

30 August–7 September

'I had information that was not generally known,' wrote Dowding later. 'There was the information about the build-up of the invasion forces across the Channel on the one hand, and on the other our own wretched chance of resisting if an attack was made.'[1] Dowding, unemotional and outwardly cold, believed only his pilots – 'my fighter boys' – could guard against a successful German landing on British beaches. He also believed that the airfields from which the pilot flew must be protected at all costs – and yet in defending these bases, Fighter Command losses must be kept as low as possible or air superiority would be threatened. This dilemma had faced Dowding since the start of the Battle of Britain, and now it would become more acute than at any other period in the conflict.

Friday 30 August opened with a bank of cloud stretching 7000 feet over Kent but weather reports indicated this blanket would soon clear. Luftwaffe forces were detected just before 9 am, with the enemy apparently assembling a large number of aircraft over Cape Gris Nez. Cloud still restricted visual plotting for the RAF, and Park had to scramble a larger number of squadrons at an earlier moment in order to prevent an enemy break-through using this cover. In fact the main Luftwaffe formations delayed their move across the Channel until shortly before 10.30 am, by which time many of 11 Group squadrons were having to come down to re-fuel. A last minute shuffle of squadrons took place, with Park ordering aircraft from Biggin Hill south over Surrey, leaving the protection of Biggin Hill itself to a reinforcement squadron which Park had requested from Leigh-Mallory's 12 Group further north.[2] Main enemy formations crossed the coast in strength, estimated at the time as about 300 aircraft: the main targets proved to be Biggin Hill and Lympne. The reinforcement squadron from 12 Group failed to prevent bombers aiming at Biggin Hill and the airfield suffered substantial damage, although many bombs fell wide. Lympne was also struck, to a lesser degree, and only six enemy aircraft were brought down; Fighter Command lost eight, including five pilots. Recriminations broke out almost immediately over the failure of 12 Group protection for Biggin Hill, although the airfield remained in operation. Sporadic smaller-scale raids continued over Kent and Surrey, with Fighter Command sorties rapidly mounting. But the worst had still to come.[3]

Hitler arrived in Berlin during the day to hold further discussions on Sea Lion and to consider a German policy to counter RAF raids on the capital. With the first, he told Jodl that he would decide about 10 September whether or not to launch the invasion in 1940. 'It can only be a question now of finishing off an enemy defeated by the air war. Failure of the operation must be excluded: a setback would be intolerable in view of the complete success of the war up to the present.' Turning to the insolent raids on Berlin, Hitler insisted upon reprisal through intensified bombing attacks on Britain. These, he declared, must 'exterminate their cities'. Hitler ordered Goering to issue a preliminary directive to this effect, while he himself planned a speech aimed at reassuring the morale of Berliners.[4] In London, a War Cabinet document completed on this Friday examined the morale of British air-raid sufferers. The paper resulted from a survey of censored mail sent by British civilians to America, and the conclusions seemed excellent. 'Civilian morale in this mail is outstandingly good. Complete confidence in ultimate victory, and a pleasurable anticipation of the excitements that must come first, are the key note in almost all letters. Complaints of nerve strain are so few as to be almost negligible... Recent intensification of air raids seems to have had a most exhilarating effect on people's spirits.' Morale seemed highest in places which had been most badly bombed. Praise of the fighting services was especially strong with regard to the RAF, and the survey quoted one letter as saying: 'If we hear an unfamiliar sound in the sky, we just leave it to the RAF. Aren't they grand.' Fear of invasion was almost nil.[5]

Luftwaffe aircraft came again at 3 pm, this time against Sussex with about fifty bombers and fighters. Park had to direct his squadrons in a westerly direction to guard this flank, without weakening his front. Sixty minutes later bombers suddenly struck along this front in addition to striking further east in the Thames Estuary. As with the morning attack about 300 enemy aircraft were estimated to have taken part in heavy raids which lasted over 120 minutes. Time after time the small Fighter Command forces flew to confront huge enemy formations. 'They looked just like a vast swarm of bees,' remembered one pilot. This anonymous section leader led his nine Hurricanes against an estimated 100 bombers and Me 110s just north of the Thames.[6]

Enemy bombers still managed to penetrate beyond Enfield to Luton, and a heavy attack on the airfield and surrounding area killed about fifty people and damaged the Vauxhall factory. Meanwhile, as the ten squadrons attempting to block the enemy in this area were returning to base, other enemy bombers roared through the gap in the Fighter Command screen and put the Coastal Command airfield at Detling out of action for fifteen hours. Bombs were also dropped at Lambeth. Numerous other engagements took place over Kent. Hop-pickers, many of them from London's East End, had journeyed to the Kentish farms as usual for their annual fortnight's employment. Now they watched the dog-fights above them – 'goofing' as they called it. One farmer wrote: 'I could guarantee to my friends that here they would see at least one German plane brought down on any fine day. My diary has an entry for Friday 30 August: "British pilot comes down by parachute. Germans riddle him with bullets as he comes down".'[7] German pilots fared better. A Luftwaffe airman, taken prisoner on Earl de la Warr's estate in Sussex, was escorted indoors by the butler who announced: 'There is an officer of the German armed forces waiting to see you in the drawing room, M'Lord.'[8]

During late afternoon the Luftwaffe achieved its most dramatic success of the day, with less than a dozen aircraft. This small formation flew along the coast to Sheppey, then suddenly swung inland towards Biggin Hill. The bombers appeared over the airfield while the mess of the morning's raid was still being cleared. 'The steady sound of patrolling aircraft overhead turned to the zoom and roar of dog-fights,' remembered WAAF officer Felicity Hanbury, later Dame Felicity Peake, head of the WAAF. 'Bombs fell across the aerodrome, getting louder and louder. The thundering was so loud I clutched my ears. I thought they would burst otherwise. Bombs were falling all round... One bomb fell a few feet away from the entrance to the shelter. Stones and earth flew in, and a hot blast of air pushed us sideways across the trench. Then another bomb dropped near, and again the shuddering and noise of engines, AA guns, bombs and machine-guns, made me feel as though I were falling to bits.'[9] About fifteen tons of bombs fell, all accurate. The sticks straddled workshops, hangars, stores and offices, ripping the runways and severing service mains. The airfield was reduced to a shambles and sixty-five people were killed or seriously injured. According to the official historian, Basil Collier, the setback was 'one of the worst that Fighter Command's ground organisation had yet suffered'.[10] This second attack of the day on Biggin Hill also intensified the feeling in 11 Group that insufficient reinforcements were being supplied from Leigh-Mallory's 12 Group, and relations suffered even greater strain. 'Things went from bad to worse,' wrote the ex-Battle of Britain pilot, Wing Commander Allen. 'The news leaked down that the two Group commanders were at logger-heads... The precious line of liaison... fell to pieces.'[11] Lack of smooth cooperation could not have occurred at a worse moment: indeed, the stress of this peak period was one of the main reasons for the damaged relationship. Fighter Command pilots flew 1054 sorties during daylight on this Friday – the previous record total during the Battle of Britain had been 936 on 24 August. Moreover, darkness brought further Luftwaffe operations, with 109 bombers again appearing over Liverpool and Birkenhead in addition to smaller raids elsewhere. Fighter Command claimed sixty-two enemy aircraft destroyed – about twenty-six more than the actual figure – but the RAF had lost twenty-five, and the total of Fighter Command operational aircraft dropped from 717 to 700 in the twenty-four hours ending 9 am 31 August.[12]

Saturday 31 August brought an even higher level of Luftwaffe activity. The Fighter Command Intelligence summary described this day as 'the biggest enemy effort over this country so far'. Continuous attacks were launched from 8 am to 2 pm and again from 5.30 to 7.30 pm, with an estimated 800 enemy aircraft taking part. Airfields were again the main targets – and battered Biggin Hill received further punishment.[13] Operations revealed another shift in Luftwaffe tactics: greater escort strength was being provided for the bombers. This was quickly noted by Fighter Command Intelligence, who observed that formations of fifty to a hundred Me 109s and Me 110s were accompanying the striking bombers. 'When both these types of fighters are escorting bombers, it is general for the Me 110 to be level with or just above the bombers at 15,000 feet, with the Me 109s at 20–25,000 feet.' British fighters were thus obliged to operate at a great height against the Me 109s or risk being attacked from above; but in order to climb against the upper escort, they either had to split their slender forces or risk the bombers below sneaking through to their targets – and, from about 31 August onwards, German fighters were frequently three times greater in number than the bombers they were protecting, flying a thick defensive screen.[14]

The first major raid on 31 August began about 8 am with 250 aircraft aiming north of the Thames. Hurricanes of 111 Squadron engaged bombers probably making for Duxford, and forced these to jettison their loads. But the Luftwaffe fighter escort proved too strong for Fighter Command attempts to block another raid, heading towards Debden, and this airfield received heavy damage. North Weald, between Debden and London, was also hit. Among the RAF aircraft engaged in this area were seven Hurricanes of 1 Squadron, which clashed with a mixed formation of over a hundred Do 17s and Ju 88s, escorted by a flock of Me 110s so large that the British pilots 'did not bother to try and count them'. The squadron historian continued: 'With nothing but their grim determination, the seven Hurricane pilots pulled their boost plugs, climbed into the protection of the morning sun and swung back into the heart of the German raid.' These pilots claimed at least two enemy aircraft destroyed and three severely damaged; one of the Hurricane airmen was forced to bale out.[15]

At about 10 am, while raids continued north of the Thames, about 120 aircraft struck south of the river into Kent. Eastchurch was bombed and Me 109s machine-gunned Detling. Then came a short respite; Park tried to reorganise his scattered squadrons, watched at his Uxbridge HQ by Churchill. Some shot down RAF pilots just had time to return to their base – one used a taxi – and for a while life in the villages of southern England returned almost to normal. 'We held our fête on Saturday,' declared a letter in the *New Statesman and Nation*, 'with stalls, side-shows, dancing on the lawn, and the acting of scenes from *Twelfth Night* under the old mulberry tree... The sun shone from a clear sky and there were some 250 of us sitting on the lawn. There were mothers with babies and there were about twenty or thirty children playing about and sometimes getting mixed up with the actors. And then just when the Clown was singing "Come away, come away, Death", the sirens began to wail. Not a soul moved; the play went on. I thought to myself that at least a mother or two would take her children off to shelter. But not a bit of it; they sat there and watched the children sprawling on the lawn as if Goering and his Luftwaffe were as unreal an innocuous as Malvolio.'[16]

Raids began again at 2 pm. This time simultaneous attacks were

160

launched by an estimated hundred aircraft at Croydon, with the enemy approaching via Pevensey, and on Hornchurch via Dover. Aircraft of 54 Squadron tried to take off from Hornchurch when the bombs began to fall: three of the Spitfires scuttled over the runway amidst the explosions but none managed to gain sufficient speed. The blast of an explosion flung Flight Lieutenant Al Deere's machine upwards and then on to its back, and the aircraft slewed along the runway for over a hundred yards, with propeller screaming, then spun like a huge top still upside down. Nearby the second Spitfire had collapsed in a heap, both wings broken off. Despite sprained ankles its pilot, Pilot Officer Edsell, crawled over to Deere's shattered Spitfire – and found him dazed but only slightly hurt. The third Spitfire pilot, Sergeant Davies, had disappeared. And then he walked back into the airfield uninjured: his aircraft had been catapulted into the adjacent field. Within a few hours all three pilots had climbed into replacement aircraft and had rejoined the battle.[17]

At about the same time Tom Gleave was flying in his Hurricane ten or so miles to the south. 'Right ahead of us were rows of Hun bombers,' he wrote later. Gleave and his companions immediately attacked, with Gleave inflicting raking bursts of fire on two Ju 88s in succession. Then he heard a sharp metallic click above the roar of his Hurricane engine. 'A sudden burst of heat struck my face, and I looked down into the cockpit. A long spurt of flame was issuing from the hollow starboard wing-root. The flames increased until the cockpit was like the centre of a blow-lamp nozzle. There was nothing left to do but bale out. The skin was already rising off my right wrist and hand, and my left hand was starting to blister.' Gleave managed to open the cockpit cover on his second attempt. 'There was a blinding flash, I seemed to be travelling through yards of flame; then I found myself turning over and over in the air.' Gleave managed to jerk his rip-cord; he felt himself tugged into a vertical position and moments later struck the ground. He struggled to his feet. 'My slacks had disappeared except for portions that had been covered by the parachute harness. The skin on my right leg, from the top of the thigh to just above the ankle, had lifted and draped my leg like outsize plus-fours. My left leg was in a similar condition except that the left thigh was only scorched... Above each ankle I had a bracelet of unburnt skin: my socks, which were always wrinkled, had refused to burn properly... Skin from my wrists and hands hung down like paper bags. The underside of my right arm and elbow were burnt and so was my face and neck... I came to the conclusion that the services

161

of a doctor were necessary.' Gleave became one of the first RAF patients of the famous plastic surgeon Archie McIndoe at East Grinstead.[18]

The Luftwaffe began its third main effort at 5.30 pm, with a formation of an estimated 300 aircraft penetrating Kent at Hastings then dividing into two sections: one headed north to attack Hornchurch again, with less success than the previous raid, and the other struck at Biggin Hill. Insufficient time had been allowed at this latter station for the dead to be buried from the previous day and the fires had only just been quenched. The bombs began to fall again; flames swept the operations and communications centres. WAAF personnel continued at their posts until the last moment; many were buried beneath the tangled girders. Yet only one person received fatal injuries, a boy bugler borrowed from a local volunteer organisation to help the signals staff. But so complete seemed the devastation that a courier sent over from Kenley reported back that 'the airfield was like a slaughter-house'. GP engineers and other technicians toiled to create an emergency communications centre while squads of workmen rushed out on to the pock-marked runways.

Some enemy aircraft meanwhile ranged as far north as London, and dog-fights spread over the southern suburbs watched by Londoners 20,000 feet below. 'I was in the garden,' remembered Donald Bruce at Woolwich, 'and heard the fighters diving and letting off bursts of machine-gun fire, in fact empty cartridge cases cascaded into the garden and when I picked some up they were still warm. Suddenly there was the noise of a plane diving at great speed and then a plane broke through the haze heading straight for the deck. Its wheels were down and at first sight I thought it was a Ju 87B, it turned very slowly, in a lazy sort of spin and as its silhouette appeared I recognised it as a Spit-fire... As it neared the ground the wheels flapped a little and then just before it reached the balloon barrage the engine seemed to blow up and disintegrate... It disappeared from my sight behind some houses and crashed on Woolwich Common.' The pilot's body was later identified as that of Flying Officer R. 'Bubble' Waterston, 603 Squadron.[19]

German aircraft at last departed, leaving many RAF airfields in apparent confusion. Yet the situation was far less critical than many thought at the time, and an analysis of the position on that evening indicates a further Luftwaffe failure. On that Friday and Saturday bombs had fallen on seven main airfields: Biggin Hill, Luton, Detling, Debden, Eastchurch, Croydon and Hornchurch. All were fully in use again within a few hours, except for Biggin Hill where efficiency was reduced by over two-thirds for about a week. This drop at Biggin Hill, added to damage already suffered at Manston and Lympne, represented the most serious punishment inflicted by the Luftwaffe on airfields in the south of England, despite the despatch of over 2700 enemy sorties in daylight hours on Saturday and Sunday. Although Biggin Hill was one of 11 Group's seven sector stations, and hence of added importance, twelve other airfields in this Group area alone were still functioning with reasonable normality. Conditions on these airfields were extremely miserable, increasing the strain on the pilots – but stress being suffered by Luftwaffe aircrew had also intensified. Raids on 30 and 31 August cost the Luftwaffe seventy-seven aircraft; the RAF lost sixty-five, but a higher percentage of pilots survived. The enemy would have to achieve far greater success if air supremacy was to be won. Even Fighter Command Intelligence adopted a realistic attitude in its summary of the 31 August fighting: 'If a deliberate attempt to immobilise an aerodrome by cratering is to be made, it is estimated that 900 250-lb bombs would be required to immobilise completely a landing ground of 1000 yards diameter.' Only about fifteen craters would result from up to 300 bombs dropped haphazardly.[20]

Nevertheless, as dusk fell the Fighter Command chief experienced acute anxiety. His pilots had flown 978 sorties during the day, and had lost thirty-nine aircraft. In the forty-eight-hour period from noon 30 August to noon 1 September a total of six pilots were reported killed and eleven missing. So, although Fighter Command claimed the incredibly high total of eighty-five German aircraft destroyed on the 31st – more accurately about forty-one – Dowding still believed that decreasing manpower might swing the battle against the RAF.[21] At the time it was feared that the current level of activity might continue for day after day. 'I naturally had to try and figure out what they were going to do next,' wrote Dowding, 'and I had that on my mind all the time. And with the inexplicable changes of tactics which they indulged in that was not at all easy.' Dowding was therefore always looking to the future and fearing the worst. As it was, RAF aircraft losses were still being replaced with brilliant efficiency. Despite losses from the Luftwaffe's weekend onslaught the total of operational machines actually rose between 9 am 31 August and 9 am 1 September, from 700 to 701. Replacements were often the far less valuable Defiants or Blenheims, yet the number of Hurricanes only dropped during these hectic twenty-four hours from 417 to 405 and Spitfires from 212 to 208.[22]

Moreover, the German High Command was in the process of altering

163

tactics once again. The decision would result in unprecedented misery to thousands of British civilians, but it would also mean deliverance for Dowding. During the afternoon of 31 August Goering issued a directive which followed the decision reached by Hitler the previous day: the Luftflotten were ordered to prepare for concentrated attacks on British cities; these would begin as soon as possible, and now London would be a primary target. The offensive against RAF airfields would inevitably lessen once this bombing campaign opened, and the chances of the Luftwaffe obtaining air supremacy would be reduced still further, but Hitler clearly believed that political considerations must now be rated higher than purely military factors. A crushing blow was to be struck 'at the political and economic centre of the British Empire and at the morale of London's civilian population', stated a Luftwaffe General Staff study.[23] Merseyside was again bombed after dark on 31 August, with 107 aircraft out of 145 reaching their targets: the Luftwaffe situation report considered opposition to have been 'very slight'.[24]

Despite the decision to begin the full Blitz, German preparations for the cross-Channel invasion continued. Plans had also been drawn up for the occupation of conquered Britain. A month earlier Goering had issued instructions to Reinhard Heydrich, head of the Reich Central Security Office which itself controlled the Gestapo, to formulate detailed methods for dealing with the defeated British. By now Heydrich had organised six *Einsatzkommando* units which would be based in London, Bristol, Birmingham, Liverpool, Manchester and either Edinburgh or Glasgow. Heydrich had provisionally chosen Dr Franz Six to head SS activities, with his headquarters in London. Among the primary tasks would be the arrest of all those named on the Special Search List – about 2300 people including Churchill and the Cabinet Ministers, other politicians, journalists, authors, academics, exiled foreigners and other notables who Heydrich considered especially dangerous to the occupying forces.

Other measures contemplated by Heydrich and his staff included the seizure by Army Commanders of 'agricultural products, food and fodder of all kinds, ores, crude metals... minerals and oils of all kinds; industrial oils and fats... rubber in any form...'[25]

First the invasion forces would have to make their successful lodgement. By now, at the opening of September, the German Army and Navy Staffs had managed to reach some semblance of agreement. Final Sea Lion plans specified that the initial landings would be concentrated against small areas in Kent and Sussex. Units of the 16th Army would cross from ports between Rotterdam and Calais, aiming at the area from Folkestone to New Romney and in the neighbourhood of Camber, Rye and Hastings. Further west units of the 9th Army would cross from Picardy and Normandy to extend the front to Worthing – later changed to Brighton. Paratroops would seize Brighton and the high ground north of Dover. Another German wave, from Army Group B, might move from Cherbourg to the Lyme Bay/Weymouth area prior to an advance on Bristol.

Subsequent to successful beach-heads being secured, the troops of General Busch's 16th Army would push inland to a line extending from Canterbury through Ashford to the vicinity of Hawkhurst. General Strauss' 9th Army would advance towards a line from Hadlow Down, ten miles west of Hawkhurst, to the high ground west of Lewes. After consolidation a further advance by both armies would aim at a line from the Thames Estuary veering south-west through the Guildford region towards Portsmouth. Mobile formations would then push forward west of London to sever communications with the south-west. London would be taken, and selected German units would capture crossings over the Thames ready for the advance in the direction of Watford–Swindon.

Other German forces were being prepared for invasion, ostensibly to strike between Edinburgh and Newcastle, from the Wash to Harwich, and against southern Ireland. Only a handful of the most senior German officers knew that these preparations were in fact part of a vast deception plan to confuse British defences – and especially Royal Naval anti-invasion plans. The possibility of a German invasion attempt against targets other than on the south coast had been among the reasons put forward by the C-in-C Royal Naval Home Fleet for remaining at Scapa Flow. Admiral Forbes had continued to insist upon this base throughout July and August. At the beginning of September seven capital ships were at Scapa, plus the aircraft-carrier *Ark Royal*. Also based at this northern anchorage were twelve cruisers and seventeen destroyers. Only two capital ships were kept elsewhere – the *Resolution* and *Revenge* at Portland.

Naval defences, at least for the initial assault, rested mainly on destroyers distributed on a wide basis – nine in the Humber, nine at Portland, eight at Rosyth, nine at Dover, twelve at Portsmouth and thirty-two at Plymouth. These warships were extremely active, most of them putting to sea each night and by day primed to reach any threatened point within three hours of receiving an alarm. The Naval Staff now insisted, with justification, that a surprise crossing by the enemy would be 'a most hazardous undertaking'.

Should such an enemy attempt nevertheless succeed, the British Field Army was in a far better condition to repel German invasion forces than it had been three months before. Despite the urgent demands made on industrial capacity by the needs of the air war, non-stop production from arms factories had managed to bring about an impressive improvement in weaponry and equipment.

Twenty-seven infantry divisions had now been collected into the Home Forces of which half had had collective training. Four were fully-equipped, eight rather less so, and with the rest still deficient. Transport remained a primary problem, but firepower had been urgently increased: 425 25-pounders had been added to the artillery and the number of two-pounder anti-tank guns had risen from 120 on 4 June to just under 500. Despite the low priority accorded to tanks, the armoured units possessed about 240 medium and 108 cruiser tanks armed with two-pounders in addition to the less valuable light tanks, of which there were about 514.[26]

In all, Britain had passed well beyond her most vulnerable stage. Moreover, the latter period of the German build-up allowed a greater number of enemy targets against which RAF Bomber Command could strike. This especially applied to Sea Lion transports. The movement of barges to the embarkation ports, begun on 20 August, had quickened in the last days of the month, and on 1 September the transfer of larger shipping also started. In London, evidence began to accumulate of the presence of the barges and other shipping in ports opposite Dover, revealed by RAF photographs: on 31 August eighteen barges had been detected at Ostend and this total would rise to seventy within forty-eight hours. Luftwaffe activity on 1 September dropped from that of the previous day, without lessening the strain on Fighter Command: airfields were again the target. About 120 bombers and fighters thrust into Kent at 11 am splitting into two main formations; one was intercepted and broken up over the Thames Estuary, but the other attacked the Medway Towns and Biggin Hill. At 1 pm, after an upsurge of flights by Luftwaffe reconnaissance aircraft, raiders again reached for Biggin Hill; others were turned back from Kenley. Hawkinge, Lympne and Detling were attacked between 3.30 and 5 pm, mainly by Me 109s, and the Dover balloon barrage was hit. The temporary communications centre at Biggin Hill was destroyed through the raids, and only one of the original three squadrons at the airfield was able to continue

The three chiefs of the fighting forces arriving at 10 Downing Street: left to right: Sir Edmund Ironside (Army), Sir Cyril Newall (RAF) and Sir Dudley Pound (Navy)

Churchill visiting the bombed areas of London

August 1940: night fighter pilots waiting in the Orders Room at a Fighter
Command Station

15 September 1943, the Anniversary of the Battle of Britain at an RAF
station: left to right: Sir Trafford Leigh-Mallory, Air Chief Marshal Lord
Dowding and General Pile

A Merlin engine is
made: a former
textile finisher
operates a No. 7
Ward combination
lathe, producing
sealing rings for the
cylinders. If an error
of ·001″ were made
the completed engine
would seize up

Londoners taking
refuge in an air-raid
shelter

The Parliamentary Home Guard

operations. Forward airfields near the coast, notably Hawkinge, also suffered from enemy shells fired from the cross-Channel batteries: this bombardment had intensified during recent days, and on 1 September the New British Broadcasting Service boasted that Dover was 'already practically German territory'.

Fourteen German aircraft were shot down by Fighter Command on 1 September against the RAF loss of fifteen: for the first time since Eagle Day more RAF aircraft had been destroyed than the enemy, even though the Luftwaffe daytime sorties dropped to 640 on 1 September compared with 1450 on 31 August. Moreover, the total of Fighter Command operational aircraft fell from 701 at 9 am on 1 September to 690 at 9 am the next day.[27] Five pilots were reported killed and ten seriously injured. 'One of the worst features of the battle from my point of view,' wrote Dowding, 'was the continuous anxiety for the lives of my fighter boys and the wish that it might be possible to ameliorate their lot.'[28] Signs of the incredible strain being imposed on Fighter Command were beginning to show: accidents, and deaths through faulty judgement brought about by exhaustion, were increasing.

And yet the situation could still seem worse than it actually was; many of the Fighter Command pilots felt far more optimistic than their chief, and despite the strain some squadrons even felt their own positions had improved. No. 1 Squadron was typical of those that believed the run of bad luck had ended: another, 609, was also reaping the rewards of greater experience. 'At the end of the month we were able to add up our score,' wrote David Crook of 609 Squadron. 'This was forty-seven enemy aircraft definitely destroyed or damaged, and our only loss was one pilot killed. This result is astonishing when compared with that of the previous month, July, when in a very few engagements only we lost four pilots and shot down about five Huns – almost equal numbers. We had learnt our lessons.'[29] Crook also noted other factors. First, the days were shortening with dusk falling soon after 7 pm, hence reducing daylight operational hours and lessening the strain. Secondly, 'enemy bombers showed a much greater tendency to jettison their bombs and turn back when attacked, and this was a great contrast to the earlier showing, when attacks were usually pressed home with the utmost determination.'[30] To British pilots such as Crook, this dwindling determination indicated sagging enemy morale, and a post-war study of Luftwaffe records proves this assessment correct. An examination of the strain on British pilots can be a valuable means of judging performance only if it is linked with a similar examination 'over the hill'.

'We ran daily into the British defences,' wrote Galland, 'breaking through now and then, with considerable loss to ourselves, without substantially approaching our final goal.' This Luftwaffe commander added: 'Failure to achieve any noticeable success, constantly changing orders betraying lack of purpose, and obvious misjudgment of the situation by the Command, and unjustified accusations, had a most demoralising effect on us fighter pilots.'[31] 'Utter exhaustion from the English operations had set in,' wrote Lieutenant Hellmuth Ostermann. 'For the first time one heard pilots talk of the prospect of a posting to a quieter sector.' Luftwaffe fighter units were now flying up to five sorties a day across the Channel; always they knew that if they were forced to bale out in the operational area, they would be captured; always they flew at the limit of fuel range, and this threat of having insufficient fuel for the return flight added a heavy extra burden of strain. 'There were only a few of us,' commented First-Lieutenant von Han, 'who had not yet had to ditch in the Channel with a shot-up aircraft or stationary airscrew.'[32]

The part played by British production workers in the aircraft factories during this critical period cannot be overstressed: the flow of replacement aircraft continued to be a primary factor in the RAF's ability to survive. Beaverbrook continually exhorted his factory managers to demand even greater efforts from their workers, and the latter responded in magnificent fashion. With a mixture of publicity stunts, bullying and a deliberate cultivation of the 'Dunkirk spirit', the Minister of Aircraft Production apparently achieved the impossible. Sometimes his exhortations bordered on farce, leading to a host of well-told stories. One of these related to a visit made by Beaverbrook to an aircraft factory, where he was informed that a new type of aircraft would be ready in two months, all being well. Beaverbrook replied that the machine must be completed within two days.

'The whole factory was organised into getting the plane ready in two days. The whole production schedule was disorganised, the assembly lines stripped, everything concentrated on to the plane. By a stupendous effort of organisation the plane was ready in two days, flown to the aerodrome, and handed over to the RAF. The job Beaverbrook asked for had been done, though the production of the factory would be interfered with for weeks after. That night, within forty-eight hours of Beaverbrook's visit, the plane went over to bomb Berlin. When the bomb aimer pulled the stick, out fell two members of the night shift.'[33]

Among Beaverbrook's most important methods was to create a feel-

168

ing among workers that they, almost as much as the pilots, were in the front line of the fighting. Production formed part of the battle. Soon the reality of this attitude would be underlined in stark fashion by the horrors of the Blitz. Meanwhile the efforts of the workers reaped dividends, fully revealed by a report sent to Churchill by Beaverbrook on 2 September.

'It will be seen that the RAF has drawn from the Aircraft Ministry nearly a thousand operational machines since your Government was formed, for the purpose of strengthening units. In addition all casualties had to be replaced.' The report ended: 'Nobody knows the trouble I've seen.' Churchill minuted in the margin: 'I do.'[34]

Churchill enjoyed the ability to see through the tangle of daily events; his statements to the War Cabinet and COS constantly revealed his broad vision, and, being the person he was, his assessments were usually optimistic even when the news seemed black. At noon on Monday 2 September he gave such a statement to his War Cabinet Ministers which, with the benefit of hindsight, can now be seen as a far more accurate verdict than Dowding's understandably anxious reports. The Prime Minsiter reviewed the figures of the air fighting during August, then declared: 'We had every right to be satisfied with those results.' The official minutes continue: 'He [Churchill] was tempted to ask why the enemy should continue attacks on this heavy scale – which included some days as many as 700 aircraft – if it did not represent something like their maximum effort. This might not, of course, be the explanation, but our own air force was stronger than ever and there was every reason to be optimistic about the 1940 air Battle of Britain.' This opinion was private, given in the seclusion of 10 Downing Street and not therefore intended as morale-boosting propaganda. Indeed, at this meeting Churchill said he planned to make a statement to Parliament when the House reassembled on Thursday, which would give a 'guarded' account of the air battle progress, 'indicating that the results were generally satisfactory'. Churchill described his visit to Park's HQ on 31 August; he had found it 'very instructive to watch the officers of Fighter Command deploying their forces and building out at the threatened point', and he urged other members of the War Cabinet to make similar visits.

The meeting then turned to the other pressing subject: the possibility of invasion. Discussion was prompted by the question of whether more forces should be sent to the Middle East despite the consequent lessening of strength in the UK. With this, Churchill expressed some caution. He regarded fog, which was more likely in the autumn, as a great ally to an invader especially as sea mists were usually accompanied by a calm sea. The First Sea Lord believed that 'the indications pointing to invasion had never been more positive than they were at the present time', but the weather would deteriorate after about 21 September, and during the winter the Germans would be unable to use the barges and small craft now accumulating across the Channel. The question of Middle East reinforcements was deferred.[35]

Airfields were again attacked on 2 September. A raid at 8 am, probably aiming for Eastchurch, was broken up by fighter action and AA fire, although eleven bombs were dropped on Gravesend airfield and others landed in Chatham, Dartford and Tilbury. At 12.30 pm another attack was launched against the same area, with bombs dropping in Maidstone. A double raid on the Biggin Hill–Hornchurch area was mainly blocked at about 4 pm; one enemy formation reached Eastchurch and bombs fell on the eastern edge of the airfield, but no damage to buildings or aircraft was reported to Fighter Command HQ. Although nine pilots were reported missing and one killed, the total of Fighter Command operational aircraft rose from 690 to 707. Fighter Command Intelligence also reported some signs of a Luftwaffe change of tactics, although it was too early to hazard a meaning for this latest shift. A summary issued on 2 September declared: 'There are indications that one *Fliegerkorps* was for some reason or other taking a complete rest', and next morning the daily summary noted that Luftwaffe longrange bomber units in Belgium and France were being reinforced.[36]

Tuesday 3 September marked the first anniversary of Britain's entry into the war. 'A year ago tonight the weather was warm and muggy,' reported Ed Murrow in his early morning broadcast to America. 'It's the same tonight. Twelve months ago tonight we had a violent thunderstorm ... I saw white-faced people running for air-raid shelters. If there should be a similar storm tonight, there would be no panic: nerves are much steadier ... Then the theatres and movies were closed. Now they're open and doing good business.' Murrow added: 'Invasion is now one of the most favourite topics of conversation. These Londoners know what they're fighting for now – not Poland or Norway – not even for France, but for Britain.'[37]

'*Prime Minister to Home Secretary*,' declared a minute from 10 Downing Street. 'In spite of the shortage of materials, a great effort should be made to help people to drain their Anderson shelters ... Bricks on edge placed loosely together without mortar, covered with a piece of linoleum, would be quite good, but there must be a drain and a sump.'[38]

Goering was in deep discussion with his Luftflotten commanders: he had travelled to the Hague during this Tuesday morning to work out details of the intensified bombing campaign against Britain, especially against London. The *Reichsmarschall* discovered an acute divergence of opinion between Kesselring and Sperrle over the military wisdom of such a policy and over the amount of damage so far inflicted on Fighter Command. Sperrle believed the offensive against fighter bases should continue, and evidently disagreed with the Luftwaffe war diary entry for this day which declared: 'British fighter defence severely crippled.' Kesselring, on the other hand, considered that the attacks on the Fighter Command stations were virtually useless: if these airfields were too badly damaged the RAF squadrons could merely withdraw to bases north of London, most of which would be beyond German fighter range. Indeed, Kesselring seemed astonished that this move had not already been made, and he presumed that the reasons for not doing so stemmed from the psychological need to 'hold the front line', and 'set an example to the people'. He declared: 'We have no chance of destroying the English fighters on the ground. We must force their last reserves of Spitfires and Hurricanes into combat in the air.' This could be achieved by striking at London, psychologically the most important target of all.[39] Goering agreed. Moreover, the decision could not be based on purely military consideration: Hitler had decreed the attack for political motives. Also on 3 September a time-table was issued from the Fuehrer's HQ which provided the programme for the final offensive against Britain: a definite date was fixed for Sea Lion, allowing time for final preparations and for Goering's onslaught. 'The earliest date for the sailing of the invasion fleet has been fixed as 20 September, and that of the landing for 21 September. Orders for the launching of the attack will be given D-minus-10 Day, presumably therefore on 11 September.'[40]

Two main Luftwaffe attacks were launched during the day. The first, between 10 and 11.30 am, comprised a large formation which approached round North Foreland and then divided, part flying into Essex with North Weald as the objective and the other section turning south over Maidstone, Manston and Hawkinge. The latter airfield was dive-bombed by Me 109s which dropped six HE and some delayed action bombs; three aircraft appeared over Manston. Biggin Hill was attacked at 10.45 am, and once again most buildings suffered varying degrees of damage although the airfield remained usable for one squadron. The heaviest strike was made on North Weald by up to thirty

Do 215 or Do 17s flying in a wedge-shaped formation above 15,000 feet, escorted by an estimated fifty Me 110s. Some hangars and old administrative buildings were damaged, and the new operations room sustained a direct hit on the roof – without any damage resulting inside. According to Fighter Command Intelligence: 'All aerodromes remained serviceable with care at the end of the day.' The second major attack took place between 2 and 4 pm, with aircraft crossing the coast at Dungeness and making towards south London. Bombs fell at Barnes and West Malling, causing only negligible damage. Debden was struck soon after 2 pm. 'There was a solid ring of craters around us,' wrote a WAAF officer. 'We afterwards counted fifty within fifty yards of our two trenches, and an enormous one just outside the entrance to our shelter.'[41] This sector station also remained fully operational. About sixteen enemy aircraft were destroyed during the day; Fighter Command lost the same number, but the operational aircraft total stood at 704 by 9 am, 4 September, only three less than early the previous day. One pilot was reported killed; nine were missing.[42]

The British COS met on 4 September to consider the main courses of action now open to the enemy, and their assessment would soon prove accurate. The COS listed the possibilities: invasion; attacks on shipping, ports and industry combined with blows designed to shake British morale; an offensive against Gibraltar and north-west Africa; an attack on Egypt through Libya; an advance south-east through the Balkans. The COS agreed that invasion would be 'an immensely formidable undertaking' for the enemy, and was becoming increasingly so every day. 'The result of failure on German prestige in Europe and on German morale at home would be so grave that it is probable that Germany would not attempt such a gamble in the immediate future, unless she felt that no other course would offer her results in time.' The most likely course of enemy action was considered to be the second possibility, described by the COS as 'naval and air attack on shipping and ports with a view to cutting off supplies from the UK and breaking the blockade of Europe, combined with air attack on industry and morale, and an intensification of the propaganda campaign.' The COS added: 'At the same time she [Germany] will not lose sight of the possibility of invading the UK, and will complete all preparations so as to be able to strike when she considers conditions are suitable.'[43] The COS declared that British forces available for home defence amounted to the equivalent of twenty-eight divisions and ten unallotted brigades: this only represented an increase of one complete division since early

172

June, but troops for the defence of the island were infinitely better supplied and the construction of defensive positions had been virtually completed. Since mid-June the number of light tanks had risen from 178 to 514, two-pounder anti-tank guns from 176 to 498, and an additional 425 25-pounder field guns had been deployed. The mobile brigade groups comprised troops of excellent quality, although about half the divisions had only a minimum of collective training.[44] Brooke, commander of the Home Forces, still urgently needed more equipment, but forces were far better deployed with the emphasis now on south coast defence than the east. And as Montgomery wrote: 'Slowly but gradually a sense of urgency was instilled into the Army in England, and officers and men began to understand what it was all about and to see the need... We gradually got everyone on their toes.'[45]

As the British COS completed their perceptive assessment of future German policy, the Luftwaffe continued to strike against RAF airfields, attacking Eastchurch, Lympne, Brooklands, Shoreham, Rochester airport and Rochford. All were reported serviceable although some damage was inflicted to industrial premises in the neighbourhood. The Luftwaffe lost twenty-five aircraft to the RAF's seventeen; Fighter Command operational aircraft rose to 719.[46]

Unscheduled, Hitler suddenly appeared before a gathering of nurses and social workers at Berlin's *Sportpalast* during this Wednesday afternoon. His speech was aimed at boosting morale. British bombs on Germany would be answered by hundreds more dropped on Britain, he boasted. 'When they declare that they will increase their attacks on our cities,' shouted the Fuehrer, 'then we will raze their cities to the ground!' He paused to wait for the hysterical cheers to subside, then flung his fists in the air and declared: 'We will stop the handiwork of these air pirates, so help us God... The hour will come, when one of us will break, and it will not be the National Social Germany.' His audience chanted: 'Never! Never!' Hitler cried: 'England will collapse one way or another. I know no other end than this.' His voice dropped slightly. 'I shall of course prepare everything skilfully, carefully, and thoroughly. In England they're filled with curiosity and keep asking: "Why doesn't he come?" His voice grew steadily louder. 'Be calm. Be calm. He's coming! He's coming!'

'He must be nervous,' commented Ciano, listening to a broadcast of the speech later.[47] At 11.45 pm British bombers again appeared over Berlin. They droned above the city for about 120 minutes; and William Shirer jotted in his diary: 'The fact that the searchlights rarely pick up a plane has given rise to whispers among the people of Berlin that the British planes are coated with an invisible paint.'[48]

But German bombers also flew over London that night, dropping flares over the docks and southern suburbs as part of navigational preparations for the imminent Blitz. Next day, 5 September, Hitler insisted upon an early start of 'harassing attacks on the inhabitants and air defences of large British cities, including London, by day and by night.' Goering believed such an offensive alone would be sufficient to bring Britain down: it was reported at the OKW Operations Branch staff conference that 'the *Reichsmarschall* is not interested in the preparations for Operation Sea Lion as he does not believe the operation will ever take place.'[49] In London the weekly Air Ministry résumé provided the latest assessment of morale among Luftwaffe pilots, obtained from prisoner interviews. The latest pilots to be shot down seemed less confident in Germany's future. 'Belief in an early victory is not as strong as hitherto and the confidence of a certain number of prisoners has been shaken.'[50]

The Prime Minister concerned himself with the morale of Britishers. He told the House of Commons that an insurance scheme would be introduced against war damage by shell or bomb. 'I think it would be a very solid mark of confidence which after some experience we are justified in feeling about the way in which we are going to come through the war.' Churchill also found encouragement in the relatively poor results of enemy bombing so far: 'Out of some 12 million houses in this country only some 8000 had been hit, of which very few had been totally destroyed. This was a far smaller percentage than that estimated before the war.'

Churchill's figures would very soon have to be drastically revised. Meanwhile the enemy still attempted to pound Fighter Command airfields. About 170 aircraft came over the Channel at about 9.40 am that day, 5 September, mainly aiming for the Croydon–Guildford area: Biggin Hill was bombed again but without significant damage. Shortly after 3 pm an estimated 150-plus aircraft crossed between Deal and Dover, flying in three formations, one of which turned back after about two minutes. The other two penetrated to Canterbury. The larger formation of more than a hundred aircraft then headed for Biggin Hill but turned back when intercepted and flew out via Maidstone and Rochester. The smaller enemy formation was joined by another flying direct from France, and together they attacked Thameshaven while a fifth formation bombed Detling. Although causing the loss of twenty RAF aircraft

174

– three less than the German casualties – the raids failed to inflict serious damage to ground targets, and often the bombers seemed unwilling to press home their attacks.[51] The enemy flew nearly 700 sorties, but it almost seemed as if these were attempted for their nuisance value or as a cover for other activities. Staff officers studied a multitude of photographs, rumours and reports from agents and POW interviews in their effort to discern a possible pattern.

To GHQ Home Forces the evidence pointed to invasion. A memorandum was despatched from Brooke's headquarters to Army commanders. 'There are indications that Hitler may intend in the near future to carry out a direct attack against Great Britain ... The objective will probably be London, and the attack will be carried out ruthlessly with every means available.' Landings would be most likely attempted somewhere between Southwold and Shoreham. GHQ Home Forces based their conclusion on a number of factors: the intensification of U-boat action in the North-West Approaches; the withdrawal of Ju 87s from the air battle, perhaps to conserve these dive-bombers for invasion operations; reports of long-range bomber reinforcements moving from Norway to Belgium; enemy mine-laying off Texel; the detection of small craft moving into Dutch waters; the activity of German coastal guns. 'Conditions are most favourable for invasion about 12 or 13 September,' declared the memorandum, 'but the possibility of a change in the present fair period might decide the Germans to act at any time after 6 September.'[52]

Luftwaffe bombers struck at London on the night of 5 September, in addition to numerous targets elsewhere. Sixty-eight bombers from specially selected squadrons delivered the first planned raid on London's docks, dropping sixty tons of bombs. The last formation reported five large fires and four smaller.[53] Liverpool also suffered again. Casualties throughout the country were steadily mounting: early next morning figures were issued to War Cabinet Ministers revealing that in the week ending 6 am 4 September a total of 469 people were killed and 906 severely injured.[54]

Sirens sounded again in London at 8.45 am the next day, but few people bothered to take notice. 'I shall take no more count of these,' wrote Cadogan in his diary, 'as they are daily and constant, and interfere less and less with our routine.' His diary entry continued: 'Lovely and blazing hot day... Lot of air battles, in which we seem to be doing well.'[55] These battles began at about 8.30 am with some 250 enemy aircraft striking inland between Romney and Ramsgate and spreading out fanwise towards Hornchurch, Chatham, Kenley, Tunbridge Wells, Brighton and Hailsham. Fierce interceptions caused most of these enemy sections to break formation and wheel for home, but Fighter Command squadrons were fully stretched again shortly after 12.45 pm when four enemy formations approached along the Thames Estuary. Strikes were made towards Maidstone, Biggin Hill and Hornchurch. The House of Commons adjourned for thirty-seven minutes during an air-raid warning, but Churchill again criticised the waste of time caused by people taking shelter. 'There is no use having these banshee howlings of the siren two or three times a day,' he told MPs, 'simply because hostile aircraft are flying to or from some target.' The Prime Minister warned: 'We must prepare for heavier fighting in this month of September. The need of the enemy to obtain a decision is very great. The whole nation will take its example from our airmen and will be proud to share part of the dangers with them.'

Pilots were active again at about 5.30 pm, intercepting another raid of about 150 aircraft over the Thames Estuary. Enemy dive-bombers struck Thameshaven, causing extensive damage. Airfield targets were, however, attacked in inefficient fashion, despite about 720 Luftwaffe sorties during the day against which Fighter Command replied with 987: thirty-five enemy aircraft were destroyed, while Fighter Command lost twenty-three. After the battles that day Fighter Command operational strength stood at 694 aircraft – two more than at 9 am.[56] So, despite concentrated attacks on airfields since at least 30 August, Fighter Command was still operating in superb fashion.

Activity suddenly dwindled on the morning of Saturday 7 September. Earlier in the day about seventy-five Me 109s entered East Kent and twelve of them bombed Hawkinge from about 15,000 feet: about fourteen craters were made in the perimeter of the landing area but the station remained operational.[57] Then the raids ceased. Apart from routine patrols and interceptions of reconnaissance aircraft, the Fighter Command pilots were able to return to their airfields. And there they waited.

Across the Channel about 625 enemy bombers and over 648 single- and twin-engined fighters were being prepared at airfields inland from Cape Gris Nez. Earlier in the day operational orders had been issued by the GOC 1 Air Corps. These began: 'In the evening of 7.9 Luftflotte 2 will conduct major strike against Target Loge.' The word 'Loge' was the code-name for London. The initial attack would begin at 4 pm, with the main assault forty minutes later. 'Purpose of Initial Attack is to force

176

English fighters into the air so that they will have reached end of endurance at time of Main Attack.'[58] Just before 4 pm Goering stood with Kesselring on the French coast; he told news correspondents: 'I have taken over personal command of the Luftwaffe in its war against England.' Goering turned at the sound of approaching aircraft; they swarmed above him heading north; at about 4.10 pm the first flecks of these raiders appeared on British radar screens.

CHAPTER THIRTEEN

The Third Stage: Blitz

7–14 September

Kesselring's first wave of about 150 aircraft represented only the advance guard, intended to carve a way through the Fighter Command defences. This initial attack crossed the coast at about 4.30 pm and found defenders unprepared for a heavy assault on London. Churchill was journeying back from Chequers, where he had spent the previous night and the morning discussing dangers of imminent invasion with Dill and Brooke; Dowding was in conference at Bentley Prior with Park, with the two men considering better means of protecting sector stations. The raiders flew above the RAF airfields at heights up to 20,000 feet. They droned towards the Thames, with the sound of their engines preceding them. 'The massively awesome reverberations of a large formation of bombers approaching its target' was the most impressive feature of this first raid, according to one Londoner.[1] Ed Murrow, visiting Kentish villages on the Downs south of London, saw the aircraft approach. 'An air-raid siren, called "Weeping Willie" by the men who tend it, began its uneven screaming. Down on the coast the white puffballs of anti-aircraft fire began to appear against the steel-blue sky ... Hurricanes and Spitfires were already in the air, climbing for altitude above the nearby aerodrome.'[2]

Among these aircraft were eleven Hurricanes of 1 Squadron, led by Hilly Brown. Scrambled at 4.25 pm, they sighted the enemy formation above the Thames Estuary and immediately attacked. Sergeant Clowes destroyed one of the Me 110 escorts, while Flight Lieutenant Holderness, who had just joined the squadron, shot down a Do 17. But despite intervention by these and other aircraft and despite heavy fire put up by the Thames and Medway guns, the vast majority of bombers continued west towards Woolwich. The first bombs began to fall around the Royal Arsenal in the Woolwich area soon after 5 pm. Nineteen-year-old Donald Bruce, a temporary clerk in C.58 Gun Carriage shop at the Arsenal, filed into the long, narrow shelter with other workers and sat on the slatted wooden seat running the length of this concrete room. 'I was at the far end away from the door and when we heard the first bombs dropping they were close enough to be disconcerting and for the first time in an air raid I began to feel afraid. My feelings weren't strengthened when one man near the door rushed out in panic bellowing and shouting. More bombs were dropping nearer and some of the men near the door rushed out to drag him back in and they had to sit on him to hold him down... We heard the whistle of the bombs and the shelter rocked and jumped as though it were floating on water... My hands were gripping to the slats of the seats, with the knuckles all white.'[3]

Bombs were also falling on Thameshaven and West Ham, and for the most part the Luftwaffe force remained in excellent formation. Barbara Nixon, an air raid warden, described 'the miniature silver planes circling round and round the target area in such perfect formation that they looked like a children's toy model of flying boats or chair-of-planes at a fair.'[4] Not until the enemy turned for home did they begin to suffer heavier casualties, inflicted by aircraft from seven Fighter Command squadrons and anti-aircraft fire. Already, the main wave of bombers was moving out into the Channel.

In Whitehall the attack on London was seen as final evidence of a German invasion attempt. Soon after arriving at his Twickenham headquarters Brooke received an urgent summons to attend a COS meeting. This began at 5.20 pm; at that moment the second bombing wave had just crossed the south coast and the red warning light flicked on in the COS conference room about five minutes after their discussions opened. The chairman, Admiral Sir Dudley Pound, repeated the factors which seemed to indicate an invasion attempt. The COS were informed that local Royal Naval commands were already in a position to go into action without further warning; the RAF had come to a state of anti-invasion readiness which envisaged a landing within three days, and on the previous night Brooke had also issued instructions to Home Forces that 'Attack probable within the next three days'. The latter order, designed as a preliminary Invasion Alert, meant that Home Forces were at eight-hour notice. But no provision had been made for any stage of readiness intermediate between eight hours and 'immediate action'.

179

The next alert notice could only be the final 'Cromwell' code-word ordering troops to take up battle stations including Home Guard units. Receipt of 'Cromwell' would almost inevitably create the impression that invasion had actually begun. Nevertheless the COS agreed that 'the possibility of invasion had become imminent and that the defence forces should stand by at immediate notice.' The meeting then took note that this 'immediate action' – involving the drastic code-word Cromwell – would be ordered for troops in Eastern and Southern Commands.[5] Brooke rushed back to his HQ to supervise final arrangements prior to the issue of this critical order.

By now London was suffering from the concentrated attack of up to 300 enemy bombers and fighters. Formations approached in parallel lines about two to three miles apart, with the Dornier and Heinkel bombers escorted by Me 110s flying close above them and other fighters 4000 feet higher. The aircraft thundered over central London, banked, and flew back over the East End and Tilbury. At least four RAF squadrons engaged the enemy before this force reached London, and another was involved in a running fight over the capital, but for the moment the Luftwaffe retained cohesion. High explosive and incendiary bombs plunged into the dockland area and on to the crowded houses in the streets around. Unlike the Luftwaffe performance in many recent raids, the enemy pressed for the target with utmost determination. Fighter Command Intelligence reported: 'The enemy generally made marked endeavours to maintain formation in spite of losses by fighter attack and intense AA fire, which is even reported by pilots to have burst among some of their formations without breaking them up.'

Bombs fell on the East and West London docks, Surrey docks, oil stores at Thameshaven and in Woolwich, Tottenham, West Ham, Barking, Newington and as far away as Chelmsford and Tonbridge.[6] A higher proportion of bombs were the infamous UXBs or unexploded bombs, which would continue to claim casualties long afterwards. But potentially the most dangerous were the incendiaries – these would light the way for subsequent attacks. By 6 pm a vast white cloud of smoke covered the dock area, tinged black at the edge and with flames licking the base. 'The whole eastern suburb of London seemed to be burning,' commented a Polish Hurricane pilot. 'It was a very sorrowful sight, reminding me of a flight a year ago over Poland, near Lublin; it was the same spectacle.'[7]

For perhaps seventy-five minutes the skies were relatively clear of aircraft again. Sirens sounded the end of the raid. 'We went to a nearby

180

pub for dinner,' commented Ed Murrow, still at a Kentish village near London. 'Children were already organising a hunt for bits of shrapnel. Under some bushes beside the road there was a baker's cart. Two boys, still sobbing, were trying to get a quivering bay mare back between the shafts. The lady who ran the pub told us that these raids were bad for the chickens, the dogs, and the horses.'[8]

At 8.07 pm a short signal clicked over the teleprinter wires from Brooke's Home Forces HQ: 'HoFor London to C-in-C S and E Commands. CROMWELL ALL INFORMED.'[9] Brooke then went to dinner with Paget, his Chief of Staff. The signal, intended for troops in Southern and Eastern Commands, was repeated to all other commands for information only. But the receipt of the message throughout the country caused immediate confusion and considerable chaos. Most headquarters were sparsely manned this Saturday evening; officers were often unsure of the precise meaning of Cromwell; many under- or over-reacted.

Meanwhile, at 8.20 pm the German bombers had returned to feed London's fires. This time the aircraft from Kesselring's Luftflotte 2 were joined by those from Sperrle's Luftflotte 3 further west, and as dusk began to fall the enemy operated practically free from Fighter Command intervention. Single-seater fighters were notoriously ineffective for night engagement except when visibility was exceptionally good, and Park took the responsibility of preserving his Hurricane and Spitfire squadrons against the possibility of renewed daylight raids the following morning. This only left the two squadrons equipped with night-fighter Blenheims guarding the London area; one of these was based at Hornchurch where smoke from nearby fires proved so thick that the aircraft were unable to take off. London's defences consisted of the one remaining Blenheim squadron and of limited guns, balloons and searchlights. Raids continued for seven hours, involving about 250 enemy aircraft. Some 330 tons HE and 440 incendiary canisters were dropped, about nine-tenths of which landed within a ten-mile radius of Charing Cross. Ed Murrow described the sight from his Kentish vantage point: 'The fires up-river had turned the moon blood red. The smoke had drifted down till it formed a canopy over the Thames; the guns were working all around us, the bursts looking like fireflies... Huge pear-shaped bursts of flame would rise up into the smoke and disappear... the searchlights bored into that black roof, but couldn't penetrate it. They looked like long pillars supporting the black canopy... The shrapnel clicked as it hit the concrete road nearby, and still the German bombers came...'[10]

'After Lambeth it was nearly the light of day,' wrote A. P. Herbert, sailing down-river as part of the Royal Navy's Thames Auxiliary Patrol. 'The Temple and its lawns were brilliant and beautiful... The Pool, below London Bridge, was a lake of fire... Half a mile or so of the Surrey shore was burning... The fires swept in a high wall across the river.'[11] By 12.30 pm the bombs had caused nine fires rating as 'conflagrations' needing a hundred water pumps each. When the enemy left at 4.30 am on Sunday morning, 8 September, nineteen additional fires were burning rating thirty pumps or more, forty needed ten pumps and almost 1000 lesser blazes were scattered over London. Three main-line railway stations had been put out of action.[12]

Reports of the raid added to the confusion caused elsewhere in Britain by the 'Cromwell' alert. Church-bells were rung in many places as invasion alarms, road-blocks were closed, some telephone exchanges were taken over by the military; several bridges were demolished in Eastern Command and mines were laid in roads – causing the death of three Guards officers in Lincolnshire. In other districts the warning was virtually ignored because recipients were insufficiently aware of its meaning. 'I failed to recognise it for what it was,' admitted a Home Guard soldier in Somerset. 'No one was really expecting to hear such a call despite all the warnings so did not turn up on LDV parade until next morning... Neither did I hear the church bells ringing.'[13] To help clear the confusion a further signal left GHQ at 10.45 am addressed to Northern, Scottish, Western and Aldershot Commands, stressing that 'Cromwell' had been for their information only and not for action.'[14]

Dawn had broken soon after 6 am. The sky remained dark with smoke over London that Sunday, which had already been designated a National Day of Prayer. Much of London's dockland seemed completely devastated. Men, women and children emerged from their holes into the grey morning light, among them Donald Bruce after his night in the Woolwich shelter. 'I looked along the river as far as the eye could see and it was all flame and smoke and I thought to myself: "My God. What next?"'[15] Brooke believed a German invasion attempt still to be imminent. 'Everything pointing to Kent and East Anglia as the two main threatened points,' he wrote in his diary. 'All reports still point to the probability of an invasion starting between the 8th and 10th.' He added: 'I wish I had more completely trained formations under my orders. But for the present there is nothing to be done but to trust to God and pray for His help and guidance.'[16]

Dowding believed this heavenly help had already been sent. He considered the bombing of London to be 'a supernatural intervention at that particular time.'[17] Park agreed: 'I said "Thank God", because I realised that the methodical Germans had at last switched their attacks from my vital aerodromes on to cities.'[18] The beginning of the Blitz marked the end of the Battle of Britain's second stage. The first, from early July, had involved the attacks on convoys and coastal objectives including radar stations; the second, from Eagle Day onwards, had seen the concentrated attacks on airfields. Now, from 7 September until mid-November, London would be attacked nightly by an average of 160 Luftwaffe bombers with the only respite coming through foul weather on 3 November. Casualties on the night of 7 September were officially reckoned to be 306 killed in London and 1337 injured; although these figures were far lower than first thought, they provided a fearsome portent of future misery.[19] Yet suffering would not be in vain. The switch to the cities meant an end to all remaining frail chances of the Luftwaffe obtaining air supremacy over Southern England.

As the strain on Fighter Command airfields was reduced, so the stress upon Luftwaffe pilots increased. Bombing operations were beset by difficulties, especially those attempted in daylight. Assembly took place over some landmark on the French coast at a predetermined altitude and zero hour; strict timing and navigational accuracy were required for a coordinated effort, without the Germans being able to enjoy the advantages of radar guidance. 'Even our intercom did not work most of the time,' commented Galland. 'It happened more than once that the bombers arrived late. As a result the fighters joined another bomber formation which had already met its fighter escort and this flew doubly protected; while the belated formation had either to turn back or make an unescorted raid usually resulting in heavy losses.' Problems multiplied as the formations neared the British coast. Galland continued: 'All formations had to take the shortest route to London, because the escorting fighters had a reserve of only ten minutes' combat time. Large-scale decoy manoeuvres or circumnavigation of the British AA zone were therefore impossible.'[20] Once over the coast the bombers had to spend more time in British air space than on previous missions, and were thus vulnerable to attack on a greater number of occasions. The fighters became progressively less able also to give protection as the operation proceeded: by the time the raiders turned back from London the red warning lights in many of the Me 109s and Me 110s were already indicating a dangerously low fuel supply.

Perhaps most seriously, the Luftwaffe fighter pilots were even more tied to their bombers. Free-ranging excursions against Fighter Command were virtually impossible, and the British pilots could concentrate against the target offered. Dowding has been criticised for not having moved more squadrons up from the west at an earlier stage: during the most intense activity against airfields in Kent these squadrons had been relatively inactive. But such criticism takes an unfair advantage of hindsight: at the time Dowding and Park could never be certain that the Germans were not tempting such a transfer in order to leave Sussex, Hampshire and Wiltshire more vulnerable. But now a definite new phase had opened. And although a Spitfire Squadron based in Wiltshire had to fly a distance to London comparative to that of an Me 109 from behind Calais, Fighter Command could work with greater impact and could prepare for the climax of the battle. This would arrive in just eight days' time: 15 September, known thereafter as Battle of Britain Day.

Churchill toured the East End during that Sunday afternoon. Everywhere, he saw red-eyed, filthy men and women attempting to clear the debris of the previous night's attack. He suddenly put his hat on the end of his stick, twirled it high in the air, and bellowed: 'Are we downhearted?' The East Enders replied with a chorus of 'No!' and 'Never!' Beneath his showman's bravado the Prime Minister believed, like Brooke, that the country might be invaded at any moment and that the bombing might merely be a softening-up operation. 'Cromwell' remained in force and would do so for twelve days, although arrangements were already being devised to introduce intermediate stages into the alert sequence.

Across the Channel the Luftwaffe General Staff described aircraft losses from fighting the previous day, 7 September, as 'extraordinarily small'.[21] In fact forty-one Luftwaffe machines were shot down during the twenty-four-hour period, compared with twenty-eight RAF. Encouraged by the supposed results of the first Blitz raid on London, the Germans prepared to strike again. Meanwhile other attacks were limited to a raid on Dover at noon on that Sunday and another at 1 pm which was broken up over Kent. Then, at 7.45 pm, the first wave of about forty bombers crossed the coast at Beachy Head and headed north, spreading eastwards towards Maidstone. The Mayor and Corporation of Maidstone were attending the Parish Church service on this Day of Prayer. 'The siren wailed as the sermon was concluding,' wrote one worshipper. 'No one stirred. The people remained in their pews and listened to the drone of enemy 'planes as they passed by.'[22] The enemy bombers roared on towards London. Numerous Fighter

184

Command aircraft rose to intercept, including Hurricanes of 74 Squadron whose leader, Caesar Hull, was found later in the evening dead in the wreckage of his aircraft in a Kent poppy field. Around him lay the remains of two Dorniers which he had shot down.[23] The enemy bombers reached London soon after dusk and again concentrated on the East End. 'I counted over sixty bombs fall in the vicinity of one hour,' wrote Brooke in his diary, and he listed some of the damage: 'Two in St James's Park, one in Buckingham Palace, Madame Tussauds destroyed, South Kensington Natural History Museum, many power stations, stations, hospitals...'[24] The aircraft, eventually totalling about 171, killed 286 people and injured 1400.[25]

'While considerable damage had been done,' reported the CoAS to the War Cabinet next day, 'the intense bombing had had comparatively little effect on undertakings engaged on war production.' This meeting, held at 12.30 pm, decided to stimulate voluntary evacuation from towns between New Romney and Newhaven 'in view of the advanced state of the enemy's preparations for invasion.' Brooke would have preferred a compulsory evacuation scheme, but there seemed to be insufficient time available for the implementation of such a drastic measure.[26] During this Monday an acute invasion scare arose far away from the area considered most threatened – a false alarm set church bells ringing in five Scottish towns.

'What is happening in London under German bombing?' queried the Italian Foreign Minister in his diary. 'From here it is difficult to judge. The blow must be hard.' But Ciano added: 'Decisive? I don't believe it.'[27] In Berlin the German Army commander signed a directive dealing with the future of British men following a successful invasion. 'The able-bodied male population between the ages of seventeen and forty-five will, unless the local situation calls for an exceptional ruling, be interned and despatched to the Continent.'[28] On the same day the *New York Times* reported from Hitler's capital: 'Authoritative German quarters assert that "as yet, in spite of tremendous numbers involved in the present battles, only part of the forces of the Reich's air army has been sent into action. The attack will be carried further, systematically, and the possibilities of increasing its force are obvious."' At 4.20 pm the growing number of German patrols in the Channel area seemed to indicate a renewed mass assault. Park scrambled one squadron to patrol over Canterbury and within the next thirty minutes eight more squadrons were in the air above Kent, Essex and Surrey. At 4.40 the first wave of enemy aircraft came in between North Foreland and

185

Dungeness, comprising up to thirty aircraft; six more formations of about the same size followed at five-minute intervals. These enemy strikes showed signs of Luftwaffe failure to assemble efficiently: two of the waves consisted only of bombers, one of bombers with escort, and the remaining three were fighters only. None of the aircraft penetrated as far as London and most jettisoned their bombs in the Canterbury area. Targets were chosen at random, including a train moving from Ramsgate to Charing Cross which was bombed from behind, in front and on both sides as it passed through Kent yet still managed to reach London.[29]

But at 5.30 pm the Luftwaffe launched its main attack of the day, with about 150 bombers and fighters crossing at Hastings and making direct for the capital. Although shaken by interception from two forward squadrons, the raiders reached south-west London. Another squadron from 11 Group and a wing from 12 Group dived on the enemy and the bombers dropped their loads as soon as possible: indiscriminate damage spread over a wide area, including Epsom, Kingston, Richmond, Malden, Surbiton, Norbiton, Purley, Barnes, Wandsworth, Lambeth and Chelsea.[30] Frances Faviell was walking to report to duty at Chelsea Town Hall when the sirens went. 'Almost at once there were terrific noises of planes overhead, explosions, and activity in the sky. The first great thud came as I reached the turning of Flood Street... Up in the sky, very low indeed, a raider was being chased by a Spitfire and as it was chased it was unloading its bombs at regular intervals above the King's Road.' One dropped on a doctor's house in Bramerton Street, and the doctor's twelve-year-old daughter was only rescued from the rubble later in the week. 'This little girl, whose heroism became a byword in Chelsea, had been buried for four days and four nights and had been conscious most of the time. She was given tea through a rubber tube and biscuits, and she asked for her rosary before undergoing the terrible ordeal of being pulled inch by inch through the long tunnel.' Her father, mother and only brother were found dead.[31]

About 367 other people died in this raid – sixty-one more than during the night of 7 September. About 1400 were seriously injured. But although the Luftwaffe dropped about a hundred tons of bombs, less than half the raiding force had managed to reach the city and twenty-eight enemy aircraft were destroyed, primarily because the raid took place in daylight and because defences were well-prepared. Yet Fighter Command continued to suffer. Nineteen RAF aircraft were shot down, and the struggle to keep up the level of operational machines was becoming increasingly difficult: this total had dropped to 659 by 9 am the previous day – the lowest since 14 August – and although it rose to 697 by the next morning, the total sank to 676 during the day.[32] Dowding's troubles were by no means over. Yet he still had the advantage in this war of attrition: the Luftwaffe were no longer concentrating on military targets, and were experiencing mounting casualties with these daylight bombing attacks on London without effective damage to Britain's war effort.

'Still no invasion today,' wrote Brooke next day. 'I wonder whether he will do anything during the next few days?'[33] By now the German invasion preparations presented a far better target than had been the case the previous month. During the night of 9/10 September a total of 108 aircraft from Bomber Command raided enemy targets, with barges and shipping being the primary objectives. During September these invasion fleets in French and Belgian harbours would absorb about three-quarters of the total Bomber Command effort, resulting in over 1000 tons of bombs dropped. Already, in the first week of September, considerable damage had been caused even though the German Naval Staff believed that shipping and warships had been collected in sufficient numbers for Sea Lion to take place. The naval war diary for 10 September declared: 'According to the state of preparations today, the execution of the operation by 21.9.40 as previously arranged, is thus ensured.' But the diary also stated: 'The Fuehrer thinks the major attack on London may be decisive, and a systematic and prolonged bombardment of London may result in the enemy's adoption of an attitude which will render Sea Lion superfluous.'[34] This indication of Hitler's thoughts reveals the continued confusion in his mind: although the Blitz might be decisive, it would only be achieved after a prolonged period. Apart from raising the question as to whether the Luftwaffe itself could stand the strain of this lengthy offensive, it must have been clear to Hitler that the Blitz would not obtain the conditions necessary for Sea Lion – and the Blitz decision would anyway come too late for the invasion attempt to be launched in 1940. Once again, it appears that Hitler sanctioned the Blitz policy simply because he could see no alternative, despite the unprofitability of this assault in military terms. As Admiral Raeder also noted on the 10th: 'There is no sign of the defeat of the enemy's Air Force over southern England and in the Channel area.'[35]

Cloudy weather during the day enabled Fighter Command to recover strength. Enemy activity was confined to reconnaissance above cloud and isolated bombing attacks; no British pilots were reported killed and only one missing, and the operational aircraft total rose to 691 machines.[36] But in London considerable anxiety was being felt about the ability of citizens to withstand the nightly raids. By far the worst sufferers were the inhabitants of the East End, where almost 200,000 people were packed into houses at an average of twelve per dwelling, and where the incendiaries combined with the gigantic, gleaming, U-shaped bend in the Thames to attract bombers like moths. 'Everybody is worried about the feeling in the East End,' wrote Harold Nicolson in his diary. 'There is much bitterness.' There, among the crammed jerry-built houses, local administration creaked and verged on collapse. Sir John Anderson, Minister of Home Security, admitted to the War Cabinet meeting at 12.30 pm that 'a difficult situation was arising with regard to persons in the East End of London who had been rendered homeless. This matter had not, perhaps, been very well handled by all the local authorities, but arrangements had now been made for the matter to be taken over by the LCC.' A special organisation was being set up in Whitehall to arrange the transfer of homeless East Enders to accommodation further west.[37] One of the main causes of disquiet was the apparent lack of defence against night bombers: in addition to the absence of night-fighter aircraft, the situation was aggravated by the severe shortage of anti-aircraft guns covering the inner London area. Only ninety-two were deployed in the capital's inner artillery zone, and orders had been given that these should remain virtually silent. 'It was thought better to leave the air free for our night-fighters,' wrote Churchill, even though these aircraft were totally insufficient. At the beginning of the Blitz the impression was therefore very easily gained that no defence was being made against the night enemy. Now, on 10 September, permission was given for the AA guns to fire and for extra artillery to be drawn from the Midlands and South and East coast ports: this would increase the total of guns to 192 by the following day.[38]

Other urgent attempts were being made to organise Londoners to deal with this unexpected assault. Measures taken were often amateur and sometimes crude. 'People were being asked to form volunteer street fire parties to help fight fire bombs,' remembered Mr G. A. Le Good, who lived in Deptford. 'I contacted our Post Warden but he said he had not been able to get people interested, so I called at all eighty houses still occupied in the street, asking the men to come to a meeting... Knowledge of this got around the other seven streets... The result was, that each formed a fire party, and I undertook the training, I was selected as street leader. The council could only supply us with stirrup pumps, so we started a collection. We bought two extending ladders, axes, ropes etc, collected dustbins from bombed houses to use as water containers, these could be carried upstairs. One man had been a sick bay PO in the Navy, he trained six women in first aid...'[39]

About 148 enemy bombers managed to reach London after darkness that night, approaching from five directions ranging from Bournemouth to the Thames Estuary. High explosive tonnage dropped was lower than on previous nights, about 176, but more incendiary canisters fell – about 318. RAF bombers struck back against Hitler's capital. 'Last night the severest bombing yet,' noted Shirer next day. In London, the CoAS reported to the War Cabinet that the raid on Berlin had been successful; incorrectly, he claimed that Potsdam Station had been hit. Churchill, thinking aloud at this 12.30 pm meeting, considered 'it was by no means impossible that the Germans would in the end decide not to launch an attack on this country, because they were unable to obtain the domination over our fighter force.'[40] Brooke was also beginning to have doubts. 'Evidence of impending invasion has been accumulating all day... It is still possible that it may be a bluff to hide some other stroke.' This diary entry continued: 'The next day or two are bound to be very critical.'[41]

Coastal Command photographic aircraft continued to report the movement of barges and other shipping westwards down the French coast. Churchill, despite his note of optimism at the War Cabinet meeting, told his Ministers at this session: 'A powerful armada is thus being deployed.' Discussion at the meeting turned to the possibility of increased Royal Naval action against the enemy shipping; Churchill reported: 'The argument of the naval authorities was that if we were to send our ships to attack these concentrations of barges and merchant vessels along the French coast, we might well throw away forces which would be invaluable to us if these barges and merchant ships attempted to cross the Channel.' Instead, beach defences between North Foreland and Dungeness would be strengthened still further, and Bomber Command would continue to strike against the invasion fleets – although bombing raids were still restricted by the shortage of fighter escort.

'The crux of the whole war has arrived,' declared the Prime Minister in a broadcast on 11 September. 'We must regard the next week or so as a very important period in our history... It ranks with the days when the Spanish Armada was approaching the Channel, and Drake was finishing his game of bowls; or when Nelson stood between us and Napoleon's Grand Army at Boulogne...'

Sea Lion was scheduled to begin on 20 September, with at least ten days' notice required to set final moves in motion. This notice was now due, but Hitler made it known that the final decision would not be announced until 14 September: results of the air war were insufficiently apparent.[42] Goering acted as if in desperation, ordering the first Luftwaffe wave to attack during that afternoon, despite the daylight which gave Fighter Command so much advantage. The first of about 250 aircraft penetrated Kent at about 4 pm. This comprised four formations: the first turned back early, and the next two jettisoned their bombs in the Orpington, Bromley and Bexley areas after vigorous interceptions. The remaining formation managed to reach Woolwich, Deptford and Lewisham but suffered heavy casualties.[43]

'Party over London,' scribbled Flying Officer Lane of 19 Squadron in his log. 'Sighted big bunch of Huns south of river and got in lovely head-on attack into leading He 11s. Broke them up and picked up a small bunch of six with two Me 110s as escort. Found myself entirely alone with these lads so proceeded to have a bit of sport. Got one of Me 110s on fire whereupon the other left his charge and ran for home! Played with the He 111s for a bit and finally got one in both engines. Never had so much fun before!'[44] Also in this engagement were pilots of 74 Squadron led by the fighter ace Sailor Malan. His official report was subdued, as usual, describing in calm and technical terms how he mauled a Ju 88 at 20,000 feet. 'I delivered one head-on attack and blew large pieces from his port engine. I turned and delivered beam attack at 100 yards as enemy fighter dived down on me. I continued down... The enemy fighter, which appeared to be a He 113, followed me down to 10,000 feet, where I did a steep left-hand turn, blacking myself out, and shook him off. As my ammunition was expended I returned to Duxford.' Flying Officer Szcesny destroyed two enemy fighters within about two minutes. 'I fired at one from 200 yards, closing in to 100 yards, and the 109 dived steeply, apparently out of control. I then sighted one Me 111 and closed to attack from astern, giving five one-second bursts from 300–150 yards range. The 109 dived and crashed to the ground in flames. I then returned home.'[45]

Park, supported by Leigh-Mallory's squadrons from further north, had still to agree with the latter's 'Big Wing' concept, but nevertheless issued instructions that his fighter squadrons should operate in pairs of the same type wherever possible. The result, with the Luftwaffe offering a more concentrated target, was proving highly effective. Yet the problem of the night raids remained. About 180 aircraft reached the capital after dark on the 11th, dropping about 217 tons HE and 148 incendiaries chiefly in the city and dock area, and with damage also inflicted as far north as Islington and Paddington. About 235 people were reported killed and 1000 seriously injured. But this time Londoners heard the sound of their own guns. 'The full barrage of our anti-aircraft heavy guns opened up,' wrote Frances Faviell. 'The noise was appalling – but the effect on the morale of us Londoners was miraculous!' Ed Murrow announced in his broadcast later that night: 'Tonight the sound of gunfire has been more constant than the bestial grunt of bombs... There's a battery not far from where I live. They're working in their shirt sleeves, laughing and cursing as they slam the shells into their guns... Walking down the street a few minutes ago, shrapnel stuttered and stammered on the roof-tops, and from underground came the sound of singing, and the song was My Blue Heaven.'[46]

'The morale effect on our people had been excellent,' declared Sir John Anderson in the War Cabinet discussion of the AA fire next day, 12 September. Sir Archibald Sinclair, Air Secretary, told Ministers that about a hundred rounds per gun had been fired and 'as a result of the barrage one third of the raiders had turned back'. Enemy aircraft had also been forced to a higher level: bombers penetrating the defences earlier in the night had flown at about 180 mph at heights up to 16,000 feet, but after the guns opened they had flown at about 240 mph at about 27,000 feet.[47] Sinclair's report was in fact over-optimistic; AA fire at that stage was relatively ineffective, and as Churchill wrote: 'This roaring cannonade did not do much harm to the enemy, but gave enormous satisfaction to the population.'[48] Satisfaction was also being obtained from results in the air war generally: the War Cabinet weekly résumé issued on 12 September stated that 114 enemy bombers and 153 fighters had been destroyed for certain in the last seven days, giving a total of 299 against a Fighter Command loss of 114 aircraft shot down. At least sixty-nine of the RAF pilots were safe.[49] On the other hand, figures for the fighting on the previous day indicate the continuing pressure on Fighter Command, despite the opportunities now being offered: post-war records show that twenty-nine Fighter Command aircraft were lost on 11 September compared with twenty-five Luftwaffe, although once again a good proportion of the British losses had been made up by the next morning: operational strength stood at 679 aircraft, a reduction of twelve since 9 am on the 11th.[50] One pilot was reported killed and five missing.

'Morale of the GAF is still high,' stated an Air Ministry summary of POW interviews. 'This is especially so among the fighter pilots, the high morale among heavy bomber crews being not quite so outstanding. A report by a medical officer says, however, that many prisoners show signs of nervous exhaustion.'[51] Cloud spread over much of England on the 12th. Sporadic bombing attacks were made from this cloud cover on targets as far apart as Hornchurch, Colerne, Harrogate and London and the bad weather made interception difficult; twelve engagements nevertheless took place resulting in two enemy aircraft shot down. No British aircraft were lost. Churchill spent much of the day touring defensive positions in Kent with Dill and Brooke. 'PM wanted to watch airfight but there was none to see,' wrote Brooke.[52]

'The rumour is that the big invasion hop against England is planned for the night of 15 September,' commented Shirer in his diary, 'when there will be a full moon and the proper tide in the Channel.'[53] Also on the 12th a telegram arrived at the Foreign Ministry in Berlin from the chargé in Washington, Hans Thomsen, which referred to reports of 'immense difficulties of life in London' and quoted a *New York Times* correspondent who had queried 'how long the nerves of a people can withstand this kind of bombardment.'[54]

Only about forty-three bombers operated over London during the late afternoon and night of the 12th; about fifty-four tons HE dropped on the capital, plus sixty-one incendiaries. But a further forty people died, and the strain remained intense. Horror, sordidness and humanity's unpleasant aspects all lurked behind the shining 'London can take it' spirit which later became famous. Too much contrast seemed to be evident between the rich in the West End and the poor in the East. 'In the fashionable residential districts,' declared Ed Murrow, 'I could read the TO LET signs on the front of big houses in the light of the bright moon. Those houses have big basements underneath – good shelters, but they're not being used. Many people think they should be.'[55] Frances Faviell described conditions for those further East. 'There were often unpleasant incidents in the shelters, and men who were drunk would interfere with the habitual shelterers who wanted to sleep. Fights would break out.' She visited the famous shelter at Piccadilly underground station. 'There was a narrow piece of platform for the passengers marked with white lines. The stench was frightful, urine and excrement mixed with strong carbolic, sweat, and dirty, unwashed humanity.'[56]

London's Blitz situation, especially in the East End, was considered by the War Cabinet at 11 am on 13 September. 'The sewage situation was unsatisfactory,' reported the Minister of Health. 'A vital part of the sewage pumping machinery had been damaged and the main sewers broken in several places.' Although he claimed there had been a 're-markable' improvement in the morale of Londoners, this had impeded the evacuation of homeless: people preferred to stay. Another disquiet-ing feature was emerging: 'The population of certain parts of London were showing reluctance to make use of their Anderson shelters and of the street shelters. They preferred to congregate in other underground accommodation – for example under churches, schools and public buildings... This overcrowding might well give rise to a health prob-lem.'[57] One of the main reasons for this reluctance to use shelters was the distrust felt by many in these structures: when they were hit, the results were appalling. They had never been designed for complete pro-tection, but the terrible casualties caused by a direct hit nevertheless decreased public confidence in their value.

During the War Cabinet meeting an incident occurred which helped in some degree to boost morale: a lone German raider emphasised that all Londoners, rich and poor, were having to suffer. Ministers in 10 Downing Street heard the roar of a bomber overhead; minutes later a message was brought into the Cabinet room stating that Buckingham Palace had been dive-bombed. The King and Queen were only 800 yards from the nearest of the six explosions. Queen Elizabeth said after-wards: 'I'm glad we've been bombed. It makes me feel I can look the East End in the face.' Meanwhile the War Cabinet sent a message to the King containing congratulations on the 'providential escape from the barbarous attack'. The event would be given maximum publicity.[58]

Cloud again restricted daylight air activity on the 13th, apart from single raids such as that on Buckingham Palace. Fighter Command operational strength rose again to 693 aircraft.[59] But meteorological experts predicted that the weather might soon break, and the threat of invasion remained. 'Spent morning in the office,' wrote Brooke, 'studying increasing evidence of impending invasion.'[60] The War Cabinet situation report declared: 'Conditions indicating the imminence of invasion have increased. Considerable activity of shipping has been reported from a number of ports in the Baltic... A large number of barges, having been assembled in the canals of Holland and Belgium, has in the last three days moved southwards and westwards towards Ostend, Dunkirk, Calais and Boulogne. These movements, considered in conjunction with the increased scale of air attack on Lon-don, appear to indicate that attempt at invasion is likely.'[61]

193

In Berlin, Hitler conferred with his service chiefs over a frugal lunch at the Chancellery. 'The food was emphatically simple,' wrote Speer. 'A soup, no appetiser, meat with vegetables and potatoes, a sweet. For beverage we had a choice between mineral water, ordinary Berlin bottled beer, or a cheap wine. Hitler was served his vegetarian food.' Goering, a notorious gourmet, seldom came to these meals. 'The food is too rotten for my taste,' he declared.[62] But he appeared that day and proceeded to boast over the success of his raids against Britain; Hitler listened in almost total silence. His options were open: to continue the air war, to undertake Sea Lion even though air supremacy had not in fact been obtained, or to do nothing. The latter was unacceptable if only from the point of view of his own prestige. Hitler continued to prevaricate; Jodl received the impression that the Fuehrer had 'apparently decided to abandon Sea Lion' but planning would continue – the removal of invasion threats would 'make the German air attacks easier to bear'.[63]

Once again the bombers left for the British capital, where air raid sirens began to wail soon after 8 pm. About 105 enemy aircraft dropped their loads over wide areas, including the Horse Guards, the House of Lords, War Office – and the East End. Brooke, listening to the explosions as he wrote his diary at his Club, commented: 'Everything looks like an invasion starting tomorrow from the Thames to Plymouth. I wonder whether we shall be hard at it by this time tomorrow evening?'[64] Bomb casualties were relatively few: thirty-one dead and 224 injured, but damage seemed progressively worse. 'Another shelter received a direct hit in our area,' wrote Frances Faviell. 'This was the large shelter of Manor Buildings, an LCC block of flats in Flood Street. The water main had been severed and the poor sufferers were soaking wet... They were all filthy and had a lot of cuts and bruises and were all suffering from shock.' Miss Faviell added: 'Shelters were rapidly getting a bad name and some of the casualties said that it was obvious that they could be seen from the air!'[65] Donald Bruce, the young clerk at Woolwich Arsenal, saw further evidence of this lack of protection. 'Not so far from [shed] C.58 we came to one of those square brick type shelters with a heavy concrete roof. The blast had collapsed the walls and the roof had fallen on the occupants, no one had escaped. Among the rubble there was a cheap high-heeled shoe and a man's oily cloth cap. It was tawdry in a way but terribly pathetic.'[66]

The German Naval Staff war diary stated on 14 September: 'From a series of reports, sent by the Military Attaché in Washington, on the

194

morale of the population and the situation in London, it emerges that the will to fight of the London population is considerably affected by the lack of sleep. This physical weakness is regarded as the worst danger to morale. As regards damage, he reports that twenty-four large docks were totally burnt out and four gasometers were destroyed... Of ten good airfields round London, seven are almost completely unusable.'[67] RAF squadrons scrambled from these 'unusable' airfields during the early afternoon and successfully blocked an attempt by 150 enemy bombers to reach London: the majority of the raiders turned back.

A summit conference began in Berlin at 3 pm. The Fuehrer received a short message from Raeder just before discussions opened, which declared: 'The present air situation does not provide conditions for carrying out the operation [Sea Lion], as the risk is still too great.' Then the assembled officers listened to Hitler's general view of the situation. This continued to display the contradictory thoughts which had marred Hitler's decision-making since June, and his words lacked conviction. Twenty-four hours before, Hitler had seemed prepared to cancel Sea Lion completely; now, while agreeing with Raeder that the necessary conditions had not been realised, he declared: 'A successful landing followed by an occupation would end the war in a short time. England would starve... A long war is not desirable.' He believed 'the quickest solution would be a landing in England.' Necessary conditions had been achieved by the Navy, and only those of the Luftwaffe needed to be met. 'The operations of the Luftwaffe are above all praise. Four or five days of decent weather would bring the decisive results... We have a good chance of bringing England to her knees.' Yet he added: 'The enemy recovers again and again... Enemy fighters have not yet been completely eliminated.'

Gradually, Hitler's decision emerged from the tangle of his comments. The landing would be postponed, not cancelled. Meanwhile the Luftwaffe would continue its offensive. 'Successful landing means victory, but for this we must obtain complete air supremacy. Bad weather has so far prevented our attaining complete air superiority... Decision therefore: the operation will not be announced yet.' Hitler added: 'The air attacks up to now have had tremendous effect, though perhaps chiefly on the nerves. Even if victory in the air is only achieved in ten to twelve days the English may yet be seized by mass hysteria.' The Fuehrer therefore believed that the British people could perhaps be inflicted with sufficient punishment to make them sue for peace, yet his words indicated that he still considered this less likely than even the frail possibility of obtaining military victory in the air: the Luftwaffe would intensify operations, but the first priority would be the assault on military targets – 'attacks on military objectives are always the most important'. He refused to listen to contradictory words from Jeschonnek, Luftwaffe Chief of Staff, who declared: 'Material successes [of the bombing] exceed our expectations but there has been no mass panic up to now', and who urged greater attacks on residential areas to destroy British morale. Within two hours a directive emerged from the Chancellery. 'The Fuehrer had decided: The start of Operation Sea Lion is again postponed. A new order follows 17 September. All preparations are to be continued. The air attacks against London are to be continued and the target area expanded against military and other vital installations.'[68]

Brooke arrived at his GHQ Home Forces at 5 pm after visiting troops in the field and he immediately studied latest reports. 'Ominous quiet!' he wrote. 'German shipping moves greatly reduced and air action too. Have Germans completed their preparations for invasion? Are they giving their air force a last brush and wash up? Will he start tomorrow...?'[69] Sixty minutes later another wave of German bombers, estimated at 200 aircraft, crossed the Kent coastline and reached for London. Helped by cloud cover, many managed to penetrate the Fighter Command screen and bombs began to fall on the capital at 6.35 pm. One struck the Church of the Holy Redeemer in Chelsea, falling at an angle through the stained glass window, penetrating the floor and bursting among women and children sheltering in the crypt. 'People were literally blown to pieces and the mess was appalling,' wrote Miss Faviell. She helped with piecing the bodies together for burial. 'The stench was the worst thing about it... If one was too lavish in making one body almost whole then another one would have sad gaps.'[70]

Hitler's directive of 14 September in effect gave Goering until the 17th to batter the RAF sufficiently to allow invasion. And, as the dawn clouds cleared on Sunday 15 September, the Luftwaffe prepared to launch its supreme attempt: Battle of Britain Day began.

CHAPTER FOURTEEN

ᥱᶈ

Battle of Britain Day

By 5.30 am light night cloud had evaporated and the sun rose clear. 'It was one of those days of autumn when the countryside is at its love-liest,' remembered Park. Readers of the *Sunday Chronicle* were assured that 'if and when invasion comes, there will be no secrecy. The news will be given by the BBC and the newspapers.' Flying Officer Dundas, Yellow Section leader in 609 Squadron, woke one of his pilots, the US volunteer 'Red' Tobin, and when the latter demanded to know the reason for the early call, Dundas replied: 'I'm not quite sure old boy. They say there's an invasion on or something.'[1] A pilot in another squadron commented: 'To us it was just another day. We weren't inter-ested in Hitler's entry into London. Most of us were wondering whether we should have time to finish breakfast before the first Blitz started.'[2] No German aircraft appeared until mid-morning, apart from reconnais-sance flights; RAF patrols reported an empty, cloudless sky. Churchill noted the fine weather and guessed the enemy might soon be active; he called for his car and was driven from Chequers to Park's 11 Group headquarters, where he walked down to the bomb-proof Operations Room fifty feet below ground. Park said to him: 'I don't know whether anything will happen today. At present all is quiet.'

Fifteen minutes later, at 11 am, raid-plotters began to bustle about the 11 Group map tables. Reports were being received from radar stations: 40-plus enemy aircraft assembling in the Dieppe area, then a force of 20-plus, then another of 40-plus. But not until 11.30 am did these formations begin to move northwards: the Luftwaffe was launch-ing its assault without the usual feints and subsidiary attacks designed to lure Fighter Command aircraft prematurely into the air, and Park

197

had been given thirty minutes in which to organise his squadrons. These were fully prepared, with topped tanks and full magazines. By 11.30 seventeen British squadrons had been deployed, including one from 10 Group and five from 12 Group. The latter moved south in a single Big Wing formation, long urged by Leigh-Mallory, comprising three Hurricane and two Spitfire squadrons under the tactical command of the Big Wing advocate Douglas Bader.

The first of the estimated 200 enemy aircraft crossed the coast at Dover before noon. The Luftwaffe formation adopted a zig-zag course, turning south and south-west towards Maidstone, then spreading back for London. Bomber groups, mainly Do 17s and Do 215s, were smaller than usual – up to twenty aircraft in each – and fighter escort seemed sparse. The first pair of 11 Group Spitfire squadrons intercepted only a few miles from the coast, soon joined by the single squadron from Dover and a pair patrolling Maidstone. Within minutes the dog-fights seemed to be filling the sky above Kent. 'The hills around Canterbury in September were a wonderful vantage ground from which to see and assess the manœuvres,' wrote one eye-witness. But he added: 'There were so many descending parachutes and falling planes that as time went on...few people left their work to see what was happening.'[3]

Among those pilots twisting and diving in the struggle above Kent was Dundas of 609 Squadron. He led his Yellow Section into the attack south of Croydon. 'I turned in and attacked a bomber in the centre of the formation from below and the beam, and saw one of its motors stop. On breaking away I was attacked by a 109 from above and astern. After evading this I made a second attack on the Dorniers, this time from almost vertically below. I was then attacked by three Me 109s which peeled off from 2000 feet above but gave themselves away by opening fire at excessive range. They did not stay to fight.'[4] Churchill, in his seat at Park's HQ, experienced the mounting tension as increasing numbers of Fighter Command aircraft were committed to the battle. 'Presently the red bulbs showed that the majority of our squadrons were engaged. A subdued hum arose from the floor.'[5]

Still the enemy bombers pressed on. The main formations had now reached the Thames. 'Ran into the whole Luftwaffe,' wrote Flying Officer Lane of 19 Squadron in his log book. 'Wave after wave of bombers covered by several hundred fighters. Waded into escort as per arrangement and picked out a 109. Had a hell of a dog-fight.'[6] 'The bombers were approaching London from the south-east,' wrote John Sample, hurrying towards the enemy with his 504 Squadron. 'We opened our throttles and started to climb up towards them...I recognised the river immediately below me through a hole in the clouds. I saw the bends in the river, and the bridges, and idly wondered where I was. I didn't recognise it immediately, and then I saw Kennington Oval, and I thought to myself: 'That's where they play cricket.'"[7]

Bombs were whistling down from Beckenham to Westminster: houses were hit at Camberwell, Lewisham, Battersea, Lambeth; a bomb landed in the grounds of Buckingham Palace but failed to explode. Keith Ogilvie and Sergeant Holmes, respectively of 609 and 504 Squadrons, were both chasing a Dornier. Their bullets shredded the bomber's wings; the tail unit burst from the fuselage, and the ruined aircraft plunged downwards. Its disintegration was 'a most amazing and terrifying sight,' reported Ogilvie. 'I could see fire in the Dornier's cockpit. As I went beneath it I saw two men jump and their parachutes open.' These two Germans drifted down on the Oval: the main section of their aircraft had already crashed in Victoria Station forecourt and the tail unit 'just outside a Pimlico public house,' according to the 609 Squadron diary, 'to the great comfort and joy of the patrons.' Sergeant Holmes's Hurricane went into an uncontrollable spin immediately after the engagement and he had to bale out: he landed on a Chelsea roof-top.[8]

By now the Big Wing from 12 Group was engaging the enemy. 'This time, for a change, we outnumbered the Hun,' declared Bader over the radio later, 'and believe me, no more than eight got home from that party. At one time you could see planes going down on fire all over the place, and the sky seemed full of parachutes. It was sudden death that morning, for our fighters shot them to blazes.'[9] But the Big Wing meant that even more Fighter Command squadrons were committed. Four further squadrons engaged the enemy as the bombers began to bank back over Kent and Sussex, and other aircraft were having to return to base to re-fuel and re-arm. Churchill watched the 'At Readiness' lights go out at 11 Group's headquarters display board, and spoke to Park for the first time since battle began. 'What other reserves have we?' 'None,' replied Park.[10]

Even though Park referred only to reserves which could be made immediately available, his Group was nevertheless extremely hard-pressed; a second Luftwaffe offensive at this moment would have placed him in a more critical position than at any other time in the Battle of Britain. But as the ragged enemy formations retreated back across the Channel the activity subsided, for a precious ninety minutes. Fighter Command rushed to recover. Meanwhile the calm voice of Frank

Phillips announced the BBC's 1 pm news. 'The first air raid on the London area today began just over an hour ago... At least fifty aircraft are said to have been engaged in a battle area over the outskirts of the city.' The weather had begun to deteriorate slightly, with thin veils of cloud gathering over Kent and Sussex at about 4000 feet.

Radar contacts were reported at about 1.20 pm. This time the enemy gave shorter warning. Park nevertheless managed to scramble six pairs of squadrons while the enemy were still over the Channel, and another thirteen plus one half squadron were airborne by the time the enemy reached the coast. Luftwaffe formations were larger than in the morning, with up to forty bombers in a group: one wave comprised three such formations approaching in line astern with Me 110s between each.[11] The main body came inland between Dungeness and Dover at about 2.15 pm; Fighter Command interceptors were fully engaged by the time the bombers reached Canterbury, with most of the Spitfires and Hurricanes driving straight at the enemy aircraft. 'Machine-gun fire crackled on every side,' reported Hörst Zander, a radio operator in one of the Do 17s, 'and twice there was a hell of a thump quite close to us. Two British fighters must have collided with two of our Dorniers. The aircraft went spinning down in flames, and below us several parachutes opened. We looked at each other and gave the thumbs-up. This time we had come out of the mêlée unscathed.' The bombers closed the gaps in their ranks and pushed on, although further west another enemy formation jettisoned loads near Edenbridge and turned for home.

Again the battle seethed towards London. Despite repeated RAF strikes the enemy seemed too numerous to be prevented from reaching the capital; and some of the Luftwaffe aircraft seemed to take too long to die. 'I attacked him four times altogether,' wrote John Sample, once more in the air with his 504 Squadron. 'I fired at him from the left, swung over the right, turned in towards another hollow in the cloud, where I expected him to reappear, and fired at him again. After my fourth attack he dived down headlong into a clump of trees in front of a house.'[12] The enemy reached Dartford at 2.40 pm, to be intercepted by a further five pairs of squadrons from 11 Group and Bader's Big Wing from 12 Group. 'One unfortunate German rear-gunner baled out of the Dornier 17 I attacked,' commented Bader, 'but his parachute caught on the tail. There he was, swinging helplessly, with the aircraft swooping and diving and staggering all over the sky... That bomber went crashing into the Thames Estuary, with the swinging gunner still there.'[13]

The fighting raged above London for twenty-five minutes. The bombers made no attempt at accuracy, but released their bombs as soon as they could; areas on both banks of the river received substantial damage, especially at West Ham and Erith. Stretches of railway were shattered; at East Ham a gas-holder and a telephone exchange were wrecked, and hundreds of people were again rendered homeless. Rescue workers, still toiling in the rubble of the morning raid, continued their desperate attempts to bring out trapped victims. Frances Faviell described one incident which reflected both the horror of the Blitz and the heroism which would enable Londoners to overcome this threat to morale. Stripped of her dress to avoid its folds catching the debris and bringing more down, Miss Faviell was dangled head first down a hole to administer to a trapped man. 'The sound coming from the hole was unnerving me – it was like an animal in a trap.' A doctor lowered her into the opening; she gripped a torch between her teeth. 'The torch showed me that the debris lay over both arms and that the chest of the man trapped there was crushed into a bloody mess – great beams lay across the lower part of his body – and his face was so injured that it was difficult to distinguish the mouth from the rest of it – it all seemed one great gaping red mess... The stench of blood and mess down there caught the pit of my stomach and I was afraid of vomiting and dropping the precious torch...'[14]

By 3.15 pm the German formations 20,000 feet above had been ripped apart. 'Our Gruppe had become split up,' commented Hörst Zander. 'Every crew sought its own safety in a powered gliding race down over the sea and for home.' Many of the bombers had become separated from their escorts and the Fighter Command pilots engaged in countless duels with the Messerschmitts: contrary to Goering's boasts, the Spitfires and Hurricanes appeared as effective as ever. Individual aircraft from the Luftwaffe raids were chased back over the coast. Zander's Dornier was among those that barely survived: a blinding flash was followed by black smoke gushing through the fuselage, and an icy gale whistled back from the shattered perspex. 'The cabin was full of blood. Our pilot was hit. In the inter-com I heard him say feebly: "Heinz Laube, you have to fly us home!"... Our observer took over the shot-up machine. Twenty minutes later, the aircraft bucking like a horse, he managed to land us safely.'[15] The Luftwaffe continued to claim Fighter Command victims, even at this moment of RAF triumph. Adolf Galland, rapidly approaching forty 'kills', turned upon a Hurricane west of Dungeness. 'I had damaged her badly and she was on fire. She ought to have been a dead loss. Yet she did not crash but glided down in gentle curves. My flight companions and I attacked her three times – without a final result. I flew close alongside the flying wreck, by now thoroughly riddled, with smoke belching from her. From a distance of a few yards I saw the dead pilot sitting in his shattered cockpit, while his aircraft spiralled slowly to the ground as though piloted by a ghostly hand.'[16]

The day's battle ended with a final attack by a small force in the Southampton area, this time intercepted by a total of five squadrons. The bombers missed their target but damaged nearby property. During the late evening the air raid sirens again began to wail in London, and an unfortunate incident occurred which revealed the strain of the Blitz on East Enders: as the alert sounded about a hundred East Enders rushed into the Savoy Hotel and insisted upon occupying the luxurious shelter in the underground banqueting hall. The demonstration soon ended – in apparent good spirits – with the sounding of the all-clear. But tension remained high that night. The day's activity might still indicate the beginning of the German invasion. A signal had reached GHQ Home Forces at 4.57 pm, sent by the Nore Naval Command. 'German W/T traffic suggest a movement of naval units, possibly destroyers or larger, from Bight to Southward possibly into Channel. This movement may commence tonight or at an early date. It is also consistent with an operation in the Southern North Sea or Channel.'[17] 'Everything remains keyed up for an early invasion,' wrote Brooke in his diary that night, 'and the air war goes on unabated. This coming week must remain the critical one.'[18] Montgomery sent a signal to Auchinleck during the day, concerning the difficulty of differentiating German from British troops should the invaders wear British uniform. 'I am told that no German can say "North Sea" properly.'[19]

'Much of the talk, as you would expect, is about invasion,' said Ed Murrow in his nightly broadcast. 'On that score there is considerable confidence. Everyone is convinced that it will be beaten back if it comes. There are some who fear that it will not come.'[20] On that Sunday evening, with the streets of London still reeking of explosives, with tired RAF mechanics patching bullet-holes in aircraft wings and preparing the Spitfires and Hurricanes for another day's battle, no one could possibly have suspected that the climax had been reached and conquered. The Battle of Britain had been won.

War Cabinet Ministers were informed at noon on the 16th that 186 enemy aircraft had been shot down the day before, plus forty-six probables and seventy-two damaged. British losses were twenty-five aircraft, with thirteen pilots killed or still missing. 'The fighting of the previous day had been most successful. The enemy adopted bolder tactics; these had served only to increase his losses. The figures of enemy bombers destroyed were very striking.'[21] As usual, the totals were over-optimistic: the Luftwaffe probably lost about sixty aircraft. But the implication of the result was still the same; nor was it lost on the German High Command. Evidence had already indicated that air supremacy could not be won within a short time and now it became clear that air supremacy was virtually impossible to achieve. The RAF could be defeated only through daylight attacks, yet these would be too costly for the Luftwaffe, and night raids could never obtain the requisite conditions for Sea Lion. The Blitz terrors would continue, with the death total eventually reaching about 51,500, but the morale of Londoners would stand the strain.

British industry had already begun to disperse in order to make smaller targets, and despite the heavy damage still suffered production continued at a high rate. Aircraft flowed to the squadrons, and soon the output of artillery, small-arms and tanks would steadily increase to enable Britain to take the offensive. Industrial workers displayed new courage under the onslaught of the Blitz, a continuation of the Dunkirk spirit which had sustained them throughout the summer. Only 941,000 man-days were lost to industry through strikes in 1940, 400,000 less than 1939. Unfortunately, industrial disputes still simmered beneath the surface and would break out again when pressure eased: the total of days lost through strikes rose to 1,077,000 in 1941.[22]

Meanwhile British bombers would continue to strike at German targets during this autumn of 1940, underlining Britain's defiance. An attack on 16 September surprised a large invasion training exercise causing heavy casualties, and when the wounded arrived in Berlin the story immediately spread that an invasion had actually been attempted and had been repulsed. By mid-September almost a tenth of the transports and barges for Sea Lion had been lost or damaged through British action, including 214 barges and 21 transports. This total would have been insufficient to stop the embarkation of a determined invasion force, but the attacks – combined with others by Bomber Command – constituted a significant blow to German morale. During the first four months of its offensive against German targets, Bomber Command flew about 8000 sorties for a loss of 163 aircraft – a loss rate of about 2 per cent – and the continuation of the raids emphasised the hollowness of Goering's previous boasts.[23]

Hitler issued another directive on Tuesday 17 September; this time he postponed Sea Lion 'until further notice'. The German Naval War Diary entry declared: 'The enemy Air Force is by no means defeated. On the contrary, it shows increasing activity. The weather situation as a whole does not permit us to expect a period of calm... The Fuehrer therefore decides to postpone Sea Lion indefinitely.' The threat of invasion would continue, but Hitler's mind turned to the other alternative – Russia; his directive of 17 September amounted to an admittance that invasion of Britain was impossible. It is highly probable that the Fuehrer had known this in his own mind for many weeks.

With hindsight, it emerges that Fighter Command was further from defeat in September 1940 than it had been in May. Hitler's only chance of a successful invasion was in the immediate aftermath of Dunkirk; if the Fuehrer had been a better forward thinker, preparing for the invasion even while the campaign in France took place, he could have struck Britain at her weakest moment. The scale and difficulties of the cross-Channel operation were such that the plans, if left until after the defeat of France, would have taken too long to complete. In the event, British preparations kept pace and the RAF remained far from relinquishing air superiority. An examination of Fighter Command's daily operational strength reveals that replacements continued to arrive and that even at the height of the battle the aircraft total remained higher than on 13 August, Eagle Day. The opening of the Blitz on 7 September did not lessen the number of Fighter Command engagements and casualties remained high, yet production more than succeeded in matching the losses. Even on the morning of 16 September, after the heavy fighting on Battle of Britain day, Fighter Command still had an operational strength of 659 aircraft, and by 20 September the total had risen to 711.

Moreover, the airfields to the south of London were still mainly in service on 7 September. Even if a greater number had been put out of action, cover could still have been provided by more squadrons operating from the north Thames area. Indeed, a shift further north would have brought definite military advantages; Kesselring, in conference with Goering on 3 September, had puzzled as to why the RAF had not already taken this obvious step. Bases north of London were at the limits of Luftwaffe fighter range, and whereas RAF pilots scrambling from the Kentish airfields were often forced to engage while still climbing, those further north had already obtained superior altitudes.

Nor were pilot losses as threatening as usually thought. A study of official documents once again reveals a situation very different from the popular version. Pilots suffered greater casualties during the fighting over France during May and early June than in the Battle of Britain: 318 were killed or reported missing in June, plus forty-three wounded, giving a total of 361, and even in July a total of 278 were killed, missing or seriously wounded. The Defence Committee was informed on 14 August that the replacement rate being allowed for at training establishments was 746 a month to cover losses in the intensified air operations. In fact, during the most active period of the Battle of Britain, 7 August–15 September, 260 Fighter Command pilots were killed and reported missing, according to the daily returns, plus 128 wounded. This gave a total of 388: thus, during these five weeks only seven more casualties were recorded than in the four-and-a-half weeks of June.[24] Despite the early losses, Fighter Command manpower strength had risen to only seventy-four short of its 1400 establishment on 7 August; replacements continued and the establishment remained satisfactory. No reports indicate a serious drop in efficiency by individual squadrons; the replacements, often from the quieter area covered by 13 Group, fitted in with relative ease, and the arrivals in the latter period of the battle were no more inexperienced than Fighter Command pilots as a whole had been in the early phase. During June and July the Fighter Command operations revealed serious deficiencies in tactics, which were soon corrected: the wisdom gained from these mistakes must surely have outweighed the inexperience of newcomers in the later weeks of conflict.

A more critical situation than actually occurred is often presented, mainly because insufficient account has been taken of replacements of both machines and men. Arguing that the Luftwaffe probably gained air superiority over 11 Group at about the end of August, Wing Commander Allen wrote: 'During the fortnight 24 August–7 September, 466 Spitfires and Hurricanes were destroyed or seriously damaged. To put it in the simplest terms, Park lost approximately twice his front-line strength of aircraft and 231 pilots were killed or badly wounded within a fortnight... This represented a condition of German air superiority in the skies over the 11 Group area.'[25] In fact during that fortnight the total of operational Spitfires in the whole of Fighter Command only dropped from 238 to 223 and Hurricanes from 408 to 398; according to the daily returns to the Air Ministry, a total of 177 pilots were reported killed, missing or wounded for the whole of Fighter Command during this same fortnight – not 231 killed and wounded for 11 Group alone.

Over-gloomy estimates given in the heat of the battle, when the situation seemed worse than it actually was, can easily be understood. Yet even Park provided one of the most realistic and honest assessments in a report completed on 12 September, three days before the climax when the future seemed so uncertain. The 11 Group commander considered each phase of the battle in turn: from 8 July–18 August, with the increased attacks on shipping, ports and coastal airfields; 19 August–5 September, covering the attacks on inland airfields, aircraft factories and industrial targets; and the third phase beginning 6 September. Of the first phase, Park commented: 'Results were satisfactory, the proportion of enemy shot down to our own losses being about four to one, slightly below the average when fighting over France. As much of this fighting took place over the sea, casualties were higher than they would have been if the fighting had been over land. The results of air combat were good because the enemy fighters were frequently too high to protect their bombers. Moreover, the Ju 87 proved an easy prey... It would appear that our fighter defences proved too good for the enemy.'

Despite increased activity, flying hours were kept much the same during the second stage through the abolition of close convoy escort work. But Park admitted that the attacks on airfields caused considerable strain: 'The heavy fighting much depleted many squadrons, and a number were withdrawn... for rest and training of new pilots, their places being taken by fresh squadrons from Northern Groups which had been comparatively inactive. It was again very noticeable that the heaviest casualties were experienced in the newly-arrived squadrons, in spite of their being strong in number.' Later in the report Park added: 'The enemy's bombing attacks by day did extensive damage to five of our forward aerodromes, and also to six of our seven Sector Stations. The damage to forward aerodromes was so severe that Manston and Lympne were on several occasions for days quite unfit for operating fighters.' Dowding, normally pessimistic, criticised this conclusion when he studied the report on 22 September: 'I must point out... That thirteen aerodromes in the Group underwent a total of over forty attacks in three weeks, but Manston and Lympne were the only two that were unfit for day flying for more than a few hours...' Regarding the third phase, Park said increased protective measures were being introduced at airfields, and better armour being fitted in Hurricanes. An improved system of pilot replacements was being started. The new phase had not so far resulted in an increase in the volume of Fighter Command flying. Park finished by declaring: 'Confidence is felt in our ability to hold the enemy by day and to prevent his obtaining superiority in the air over our territory, unless he greatly increases the scale or intensity of his attacks.'[26]

Hitler had two ways in which he could have attempted the defeat of Britain by military conquest in 1940: either a previously prepared all-out attack directed against the south coast after the fall of France, undertaken without regard to cost; or a long and intense air campaign. The latter would have resulted in crippling losses for the Luftwaffe, perhaps three times as many aircraft destroyed and pilots killed as suffered by the RAF. The strain on the Luftwaffe would have been as great as that on the RAF; daily flying hours would have been steadily reduced as winter approached and the periods of bad weather lengthened. Hitler, always lacking in conviction regarding the decisiveness of the air offensive, would have had to face a terrible Luftwaffe toll before the RAF could be eliminated. The most serious reduction in RAF operational fighters occurred on 31 August, with the total of 717 dropping to 700. If this had continued it would still have taken over twenty-two days of fighting at the same high level before Fighter Command strength could have fallen to the operational total existing in July. Yet the Luftwaffe lost about forty-one aircraft on 31 August – another twenty-two days of such casualties would have resulted in 900 aircraft destroyed: equivalent to over half the serviceable strength of Luftflotte 2 and 3 when battle began.

Having missed the first opportunity in June, the subsequent policy involving the Battle of Britain originated not from military necessity or military preference but, like the fumbling Sea Lion project, simply stemmed from frustration. Hitler could think of nothing else to do: the war had been won, he believed, but the vanquished refused to accept Germany's victory. Goering had no real chance of success in the limited weeks of summer 1940, however differently he might have directed the Battle of Britain campaign. His many mistakes were irrelevant to the outcome. If he had continued his attacks on the convoys, or the airfields, without switching to another phase, the result would have been little different by autumn. Given the RAF casualty replacement achievement, the growing skill of the fighter pilots, and their advantage of shorter operational range, Fighter Command would still have survived. As it was, in early September Fighter Command had more machines and more men than three months before, and even without defensive measures by the Royal Navy was in a far better position to prevent invasion. The Battle of Britain never came near to being lost by Fighter

Command; the post-war belief that the 'few', battling for Britain's very survival, came to within days of defeat, is totally false.

This assessment adds to, rather than reduces, Fighter Command achievements during the summer of 1940. The RAF fulfilled its task in superb fashion. The heroism and endurance of the pilots, mechanics and all who fought in the Battle of Britain stand untarnished whatever the hindsight verdict might be regarding the basic hopelessness of the Luftwaffe offensive. Nothing could detract from the courage of the 'few', but their success must be placed in proper perspective.

'The Battle of Britain in September 1940 was a great victory,' declared the *New York Times* a few weeks before America entered the war. 'It was a victory, first, for the British people ... for the sergeant pilots, tramway conductors, women serving beer in pubs and women in uniform running ambulances, for common, ordinary people ... who didn't know how they would take it but did take it.' And Winston Churchill's own attitude was summed up in his words: 'This was a time when it was equally good to live or die.'[27]

Appendix 1

Daily totals of Fighter Command operational aircraft, pilot casualties and aircraft losses during the main phase of the Battle of Britain, 5 August–20 September

On 3 June 1940, Fighter Command operational strength had stood at 79 Blenheims, 162 Spitfires, 163 Hurricanes and 9 Defiants, giving a total of 413; on 30 June the respective figures were 74, 247, 255, 26, a total of 602; on 1 August they were 63, 329, 348, 25, a total of 675.

Notes
i) Aircraft strengths are those recorded at 9 am on the day concerned; pilot casualties are those suffered in the twenty-four hours ending at noon on the day specified.
ii) Losses are for those covering the twenty-four hours. The six days 19–23 August inclusive are not tabled individually, since activity was minor.
iii) All losses refer to those in action, thus excluding accidents.
iv) *Sources:* Aircraft strengths and pilot casualties: Air Ministry file AIR 22/ 33 at the PRO, London. Fighter Command and German Air Force aircraft losses: Collier, *The Defence of the United Kingdom*, Appendix X, XII, XIV, XXIV.

AUG.:

	5	6	7	8	9	10	11	12	13	14	15	16	17	18	19	20
Aircraft operational																
Blenheims	63	67	66	66	64	60	60	60	71	59	61	64	50	50	49	53
Spitfires	257	257	256	257	228	245	247	248	226	219	233	216	208	228	219	240
Hurricanes	373	370	368	370	370	382	373	363	353	342	351	345	345	396	388	396
Defiants	26	23	24	20	23	22	24	24	26	25	25	24	28	27	27	22
Gladiators	–	–	–	–	2	8	2	4	2	2	2	4	1	5	6	7
TOTAL	719	717	714	713	687	717	706	699	678	647	672	653	631	706	689	718
Pilots																
Killed	–	–	–	1	2	1	–	2	–	1	–	2	4	3	1	3
Missing	–	1	–	–	13	3	3	21	12	3	4	8	11	2	2	5
Wounded	–	1	1	1	1	–	–	3	3	4	2	3	6	4	3	7
TOTAL	0	1	1	2	16	4	3	26	15	8	6	13	21	9	6	15
FC A/c loss	1	1	–	20	4	–	32	22	13	8	34	21	–	27	11	11
GAF A/c loss	6	1	2	31	5	–	38	31	45	19	75	45	3	71	32	32

AUG./SEPT.:

	21	22	23	24	25	26	27	28	29	30	31	1	2	3	4	5
Aircraft operational																
Blenheims	58	58	55	63	54	56	55	55	53	52	54	57	60	53	50	49
Spitfires	239	219	236	238	233	240	228	225	230	234	212	208	204	221	218	214
Hurricanes	400	412	410	408	416	408	420	413	412	410	417	405	398	400	407	422
Defiants	25	26	26	23	18	18	18	23	18	14	13	24	21	25	21	25
Gladiators	7	6	6	8	6	6	7	7	7	7	4	7	7	8	8	9
TOTAL	729	721	733	740	727	728	728	723	720	717	700	701	690	707	704	719

210

Pilots casualties and aircraft strengths, September (days 6–21).

Pilots

	6	7	8	9	10	11	12	13	14	15	16	17	18	19	20	21
Killed	1	–	–	–	2	2	4	–	1	1	5	5	5	1	2	5
Missing	–	–	1	1	7	–	12	1	2	6	5	2	5	9	1	4
Wounded	1	1	1	2	3	3	3	3	4	1	3	10	4	11	6	2
TOTAL	2	1	2	3	12	5	19	4	7	8	13	17	14	21	9	11
FC A/c loss	11	11	11	22	16	31	1	20	9	26	39	15	31	16	17	20
GAF A/c loss	32	32	32	38	20	41	9	30	17	36	41	14	35	16	25	23

SEPT.:

Aircraft operational

	6	7	8	9	10	11	12	13	14	15	16	17	18	19	20
Blenheims	52	44	50	55	47	61	50	51	52	47	60	49	51	51	55
Spitfires	200	223	197	220	225	214	208	208	215	192	216	222	212	211	237
Hurricanes	410	398	381	392	375	387	392	393	403	389	356	362	362	364	391
Defiants	21	20	23	22	21	21	21	18	16	24	19	23	25	21	21
Gladiators	9	9	8	8	8	8	8	8	7	8	8	5	5	7	7
TOTAL	692	694	659	697	676	691	679	678	693	660	659	661	655	654	711

Pilots

	6	7	8	9	10	11	12	13	14	15	16	17	18	19	20
Killed	5	3	1	5	–	1	–	1	–	1	5	–	3	1	1
Missing	7	6	5	7	1	5	3	3	3	4	7	2	2	3	–
Wounded	3	8	5	5	1	3	2	5	1	2	2	2	1	1	1
TOTAL	15	17	11	17	2	9	5	9	4	7	14	4	6	5	3
FC A/c loss	23	28	2	19	1	29	–	1	14	26	1	5	12	3	1
GAF A/c loss	35	41	15	28	4	25	4	4	14	60	9	8	19	7	5

Appendix 2

Contemporary figures for bombing casualties 18 July–15 September

	Killed	Injured
Week ending noon 25 July'	33	206
Week ending noon 1 August	15	54
Week ending noon 8 August	8	84
Week ending noon 15 August: Day	75	410
Night	42	218
Week ending noon 22 August: Day	298	488
Night	33	91
Week ending noon 29 August: Day	167	313
Night	129	222
Week ending 6 am 5 September	469	906
Week ending 6 am 11 September	1211	5547

(including 966 killed and 4149 seriously injured in London)

Week ending noon 19 September	988	4051

(including 711 killed and 1042 seriously injured in London)

Breakdown of bombing casualties 6 am 7 September–6 am 14 September

	London		Elsewhere	
Period 6 am to 6 am	*Killed*	*Injured*	*Killed*	*Injured*
7/8 September	306	1337	6	9
8/9 September	286	1400	2	4
9/10 September	370	1400	15	38
10/11 September	18	280	8	60
11/12 September	235	1000	68	173
12/13 September	40	58	28	73
13/14 September	31	224	6	47
	1286	5699	133	404

Sources

Note. War Cabinet, War Office and Air Ministry papers used in this book are to be found in the Public Record Office, London, and the numbers given in the source lists relate to the basic file numbers. The following are among the files consulted:

CAB 65: War Cabinet Minutes
CAB 66: War Cabinet Memoranda
CAB 69: War Cabinet Defence Committee
CAB 79: Chiefs of Staff Committee
CAB 80: Chiefs of Staff Committee, Memoranda
CAB 81: Chiefs of Staff Committees and Sub-Committees
CAB 82: Deputy Chiefs of Staff Committee
CAB 93: War Cabinet Home Defence Committee
AIR 4:   Pilot Log Books
AIR 16: Fighter Command papers
AIR 22: Periodical returns, summaries and bulletins
AIR 24: Command Operations Record Books
AIR 25: Group Operations Record Books
AIR 27: Squadron Operations Record Books
WO 106: Directorate of Military Operations
WO 199: Military Headquarters Papers, Home Forces

Further details of papers available are given in *The Second World War: A Guide to Documents in the Public Record Office*, published by HMSO for the PRO. This, while giving the general subject in each class file, does not attempt to provide additional information on the multitude of topics covered by these general subjects.

Full details of all the books mentioned below are to be found in the Bibliography; unless otherwise stated the reference to 'Collier' relates to Basil Collier's *The Defence of the United Kingdom* and not to the same author's *The Battle of Britain*. DGFP stands for *Documents on German Foreign Policy*.

Notes

ONE: DELIVERANCE
1. AIR 4
2. Hay 63
3. Boorman 9, 10
4. Faviell 51
5. Bryant 155
6. Horrocks 91
7. Montgomery 68
8. Collier 83–5; CAB 79; CAB 65
9. WO 199
10. Collier 124–5
11. CAB 65
12. Churchill 122, 125; Collier 127
13. AIR 4
14. Montgomery 68
15. Murrow 136–7
16. Wheatley 53–4
17. ibid. 5–10
18. ibid. 19–21
19. Speer 169
20. Shirer, *Berlin Diary*, 309
21. Boorman 8
22. Mrs A. M. Peacock in
    correspondence with author
23. Fleming 68
24. CAB 81
25. Mrs A. M. Peacock to author
26. Churchill 131
27. Kennedy 52
28. Macksey 178
29. WO 199

30. WO 199
31. CAB 65
32. Churchill 144
33. ibid. 217
34. Wheatley 22
35. CAB 66
36. CAB 79
37. CAB 65
38. CAB 66
39. AIR 22
40. CAB 65
41. CAB 66
42. Collier 135
43. CAB 66

TWO: THE FALL OF FRANCE
1. Fleming 91
2. Mrs A. M. Peacock to author
3. Gaulle de, 62–3
4. Faviell 53–4
5. Kennedy 52–3
6. Wheatley 22
7. Ciano, *Diary*, 264
8. Ismay 191
9. CAB 69
10. Bishop 27
11. CAB 65
12. Bryant 162
13. Collier 133
14. Faviell 9–10
15. CAB 65

16. Cadogan 297
17. CAB 79
18. CAB 79
19. CAB 65
20. Fleming 96
21. Shirer, *Berlin Diary*, 316
22. Wheatley 16, 23
23. Shirer, *Rise and Fall*, 898
24. CAB 65
25. CAB 65

THREE: CONFUSION ACROSS THE
CHANNEL
1. Ismay 146–7
2. CAB 65
3. CAB 79
4. WO 199
5. WO 199
6. Faviell 70–71
7. Calder 111
8. Ciano, *Diary*, 266, 267; Ciano,
Diplomatic Papers, 373
9. CAB 69
10. Price 12–13
11. Wheatley 27–8
12. ibid. 26
13. Shirer, *Rise and Fall*, 895
14. Horrocks 94
15. Kennedy 58
16. CAB 65
17. Halder, *Diary*, 22 June
18. Wheatley 18
19. Eden 119
20. WO 199
21. Fleming 216; CAB 66
22. Churchill 120
23. CAB 66
24. CAB 79
25. CAB 79
26. Collier 142
27. CAB 79
28. CAB 66
29. Bryant 189
30. Churchill 151
31. ibid. 148
32. CAB 66
33. CAB 66

34. AIR 16
35. Speer 171–2
36. CAB 66
37. CAB 66
38. Bryant 190
39. Cadogan 308
40. Ciano, *Diary*, 272
41. ibid. 273
42. Wheatley 31–2
43. Bekker 148
44. CAB 65
45. Montgomery 69–70
46. WO 199
47. WO 199
48. AIR 22
49. Wright 165
50. Collier 135
51. AIR 16
52. WO 199
53. Shirer, *Rise and Fall*, 901

FOUR: FINAL DAYS
1. CAB 79
2. AIR 16
3. CAB 65
4. Collier 139–40, 224
5. CAB 69
6. Churchill 211
7. Ciano, *Diary*, 274
8. CAB 66
9. AIR 22
10. Churchill 211
11. ibid. 235
12. ibid. 566
13. Wright 136–7
14. AIR 16
15. Macmillan 94
16. Fleming 85
17. WO 199
18. Ciano, *Diary*, 277
19. Ciano, *Diplomatic Papers*, 378
20. Collier 164
21. Jones 224
22. Crook 28–30
23. Wheatley 65
24. Henry 100
25. CAB 65

FIVE: THE FIRST PHASE
1. Jones 226–7
2. Collier 165
3. Jones 227–8
4. Bekker 130–33; Bishop 17–18; Collier 165–6
5. AIR 22
6. Fleming 101
7. Collier 138; Fleming 168
8. FCNA 60–66
9. Wheatley 59
10. CAB 66
11. AIR 22
12. Cadogan 312
13. Collier 166–7
14. Crook 34
15. AIR 27
16. Ziegler 106–7
17. Crook 36
18. AIR 16
19. Galland 29
20. ibid. 29
21. AIR 16
22. Wheatley 35
23. DGFP, X, 209–11; Halder, *Diary*, 13 July
24. Wright 142
25. WO 199
26. Faviell 75
27. Murrow 146
28. Wheatley 41
29. Trevor-Roper 74–8
30. AIR 16
31. Boorman 118
32. Bekker 141
33. AIR 22; Collier 450
34. Bishop 49
35. Wheatley 39, 113
36. CAB 80
37. Bryant 194–5; Churchill 233–4
38. CAB 66
39. Wheatley 41
40. Shirer, *Berlin Diary*, 353
41. Bekker 142; Allen 143; Bishop 96
42. CAB 66
43. Macleod 387
44. Bryant 196

SIX: IN THE NAME OF REASON
1. Shirer, *Diary*, 354–6; Shirer, *Rise and Fall*, 904; Ciano, *Diary*, 277
2. Bekker 148
3. Shirer, *Rise and Fall*, 905
4. Ciano, *Diary*, 277
5. Ciano, *Diplomatic Papers*, 381; Ciano, *Diary*, 278
6. CAB 65
7. Ciano, *Diary*, 278
8. Wheatley 60–61; Butler 536
9. Bekker 150; Wheatley 60
10. Mr G. Jarret in correspondence with author
11. Wheatley 43; Butler 536
12. DGFP, X, 287
13. AIR 16
14. Crook 39
15. AIR 27
16. Galland 26
17. ibid. 27
18. Wheatley 43–4
19. Fleming 249
20. Bryant 200; CAB 79
21. CAB 69
22. CAB 66
23. Crook 35–6
24. Bishop 93–4
25. Jones 215
26. ibid. 235; AIR 27
27. Wheatley 45–6
28. Halder, *Diary*, 29 July
29. AIR 16
30. CAB 65
31. Boorman 12
32. AIR 22
33. Collier 451; Wheatley 58
34. Cadogan 318
35. AIR 27
36. Crook 37–8
37. Nicolson 101

SEVEN: A PROGRAMME PREPARED
1. Halder, *Diary*, 31 July; Wheatley 47–50; Shirer, *Rise and Fall*, 915, 954
2. Wheatley 79–80
3. ibid. 45

4. Galland 19
5. Allen 129; Bishop 36; Churchill 287; AIR 27
6. Collier, *Battle of Britain*, appendix 19
7. Galland 20–21
8. Bekker 150–51; Collier 183
9. Churchill 232
10. WO 199
11. Murrow 150–152
12. AIR 22
13. CAB 66
14. Wheatley 65–6
15. AIR 22; CAB 65
16. Speer 178
17. Shirer, *Rise and Fall*, 918; Halder, *Diary*, 7 August
18. CAB 66
19. AIR 22

EIGHT: THE SECOND PHASE
1. CAB 66
2. AIR 22
3. Crook 40; Bishop 110–11
4. AIR 4
5. Crook 41
6. Collier 183
7. Crook 42
8. CAB 65
9. AIR 22
10. Wheatley 63
11. ibid. 66–7
12. Jones 238–9; AIR 27
13. Jones 241; AIR 27
14. Crook 42–3; Collier 183
15. Galland 50–51
16. Bekker 144
17. Jones 238, 242; AIR 27
18. Bishop 118; AIR 27
19. CAB 65
20. AIR 22
21. Crook 43
22. AIR 22
23. AIR 22
24. CAB 65
25. Bekker 146
26. Beauman 126
27. Crook 44–5

28. Mrs A. M. Peacock to author
29. Boorman 113–14
30. AIR 16; Bekker 146–7
31. Bishop 119
32. Gibbs 120
33. Faviell 92
34. Crook 46
35. Bekker 146–7
36. Price 13–14
37. CAB 65
38. AIR 16
39. AIR 22
40. AIR 22
41. Collier 170–71; AIR 22

NINE: DAYS OF THE EAGLE
1. Bekker 151
2. Mrs A. M. Peacock to author
3. Collier 185
4. Collier 185–6; Bekker 151
5. AIR 22
6. Bishop 128–9
7. AIR 4
8. Bryant 152
9. Crook 78
10. Bishop 133
11. Bekker 153
12. Bryant 153
13. CAB 65
14. Wheatley 68–9
15. ibid. 69
16. Crook 47–8; AIR 4; Ziegler 122; AIR 27
17. Mr A. E. Schaefer in correspondence with author
18. Crook 48; Bekker 154; AIR 4
19. Bekker 153–4
20. Collier 188
21. Jones 245–6
22. Boorman 17
23. Fleming 116, 117
24. CAB 65
25. Bekker 155
26. AIR 22
27. Crook 49; AIR 4
28. CAB 69
29. CAB 65
30. AIR 16

31. Crook 50–51; AIR 4
32. CAB 65; AIR 22
33. Fleming 252
34. Wheatley 70–71
35. WO 199
36. CAB 65
37. Bekker 156
38. Bekker 158–9; Collier 193–5;
    Bishop 145; AIR 16; AIR 27
39. AIR 16; Bekker 160; Shaw 154
40. Bekker 160
41. Ismay 179
42. Crook 51–2; AIR 4
43. Bishop 146
44. Ismay 179–80
45. Ministry of Information 30
46. Faviell 82
47. Boorman 19
48. Bekker 163
49. Ismay 180

TEN: THE FEW
1. Cadogan 321
2. AIR 22
3. Bekker 163
4. AIR 22
5. AIR 16
6. CAB 66
7. Galland 34
8. Shaw 154–5; AIR 27
9. Galland 39
10. Murrow 133–4
11. AIR 16
12. Boorman 149, 154
13. Shaw 155–6
14. AIR 4
15. AIR 27
16. AIR 22
17. Bishop 149, 154
18. AIR 16
19. AIR 16
20. Bryant 212
21. Ciano, Diary, 284
22. Wheatley 59
23. AIR 22
24. Galland 31
25. AIR 16
26. Cadogan 321–2

27. AIR 16; Bishop 170–71
28. AIR 16
29. Bekker 165; Collier 199
30. Murrow 159–61
31. CAB 65
32. AIR 22
33. Bekker 165; Wheatley 73;
    Galland 36–7
34. Galland 36
35. Ziegler 129; AIR 27
36. Nicolson 106
37. Jones 249–50
38. Collier 203–4
39. AIR 16
40. Wheatley 100, 102
41. ibid. 71
42. Fleming 120–21
43. AIR 22
44. CAB 66
45. AIR 22
46. AIR 16
47. CAB 69
48. AIR 22
49. Crook 55
50. Collier 206–7; AIR 16
51. AIR 4
52. Beauman 128
53. Crook 57
54. Boorman 26
55. AIR 16; AIR 25
56. Collier 207–8; AIR 25
57. Bekker 172

ELEVEN: THE WAR SPREADS
1. AIR 22; AIR 25
2. Crook 60
3. Collier 209; AIR 25
4. AIR 22
5. Churchill 302
6. Shirer, Diary, 380–81
7. Murrow 162
8. CAB 65
9. AIR 16
10. Calder 152
11. AIR 22; AIR 25
12. Wheatley 71; Halder, Diary, 26
    August
13. Jullian 135

14. AIR 16
15. AIR 16
16. Ismay 186–7
17. Churchill 587
18. AIR 22; AIR 24
19. Collier 461; AIR 24
20. Shirer, *Berlin Diary*, 384
21. CAB 65
22. Cadogan 324
23. Ciano, *Diary*, 286
24. AIR 22; AIR 24; AIR 25
25. AIR 22
26. Collier 461
27. Cadogan 324

TWELVE: END AND BEGINNING
1. Wright 180
2. Collier 214; AIR 24
3. AIR 16; Collier 214
4. Wheatley 76–7
5. CAB 66
6. Ministry of Information 46
7. Boorman 29
8. Bishop 180
9. Beauman 129
10. Collier 214
11. Allen 97
12. AIR 22; AIR 25
13. AIR 16
14. Bekker 166
15. Shaw 159
16. *New Statesman*, 31 August
17 Bekker 167
18. Gleave 220
19. Mr D. Bruce in correspondence
   with author
20. AIR 16
21. Wright 180
22. AIR 22
23. Wheatley 78
24. Collier 461; Wheatley 74
25. Shirer 936–7
26. Collier 178, 219
27. AIR 22
28. Wright 181
29. Crook 61
30. ibid. 66
31. Galland 34

32. Bekker 169
33. Calder 257–8
34. Young 158
35. CAB 65
36. AIR 16; AIR 22
37. Murrow 166–7
38. Churchill 313
39. Bekker 172
40. Shirer, *Rise and Fall*, 920
41. Beauman 140
42. AIR 16; AIR 22
43. CAB 66
44. Collier 219; AIR 24
45. Montgomery 74
46. AIR 16; AIR 22
47. Ciano, *Diary*, 288
48. Shirer, *Diary*, 389
49. Wheatley 77
50. AIR 22
51. AIR 16
52. WO 199
53. Bekker 172
54. CAB 66
55. Cadogan 325
56. AIR 22
57. AIR 16
58. Bekker 368–9

THIRTEEN: THE THIRD STAGE:
BLITZ
1. Mr D. Bruce to author
2. Murrow 171
3. Mr D. Bruce to author
4. Nixon 13
5. Butler 288; Collier 223; Bryant
   212; CAB 79
6. AIR 16
7. Calder 155
8. Murrow 172
9. WO 199
10. Murrow 173
11. Herbert 163–5
12. Calder 157; O'Brien 100
13. Mr G. Jarrett to author
14. WO 199
15. Mr D. Bruce to author
16. Bryant 214
17. Wright 184

18. Clark 142
19. CAB 66
20. Galland 42
21. Wheatley 77
22. Boorman 41
23. Jones 231
24. Bryant 215
25. CAB 66
26. CAB 65
27. Ciano, *Diary*, 289
28. Shirer, *Rise and Fall*, 936
29. Boorman 40; AIR 16
30. Collier 241; AIR 24
31. Faviell 109
32. AIR 22
33. Bryant 215
34. Wheatley 106
35. ibid. 79
36. AIR 16; AIR 22; AIR 24
37. CAB 65
38. Collier 252
39. Mr G. A. Le Good to author
40. CAB 65
41. Bryant 215
42. Wheatley 77
43. AIR 16
44. AIR 4
45. Jones 256–8; AIR 27
46. Faviell 111; Murrow 183–4
47. CAB 65
48. Churchill 303
49. CAB 66
50. AIR 22
51. AIR 22; AIR 24
52. Bryant 215
53. Shirer, *Diary*, 395
54. Wheatley 81
55. Murrow 188
56. Faviell 126, 140
57. CAB 65
58. CAB 65
59. AIR 22
60. Bryant 216

61. CAB 66
62. Speer 117–19
63. Shirer, *Rise and Fall*, 922; Fleming 290; Wheatley 80–81
64. Bryant 216
65. Faviell 112
66. Mr D. Bruce to author
67. Wheatley 80–81
68. Shirer, *Rise and Fall*, 923–4; Wheatley 83–4
69. Bryant 216
70. Faviell 114–15

FOURTEEN: BATTLE OF BRITAIN DAY
1. Ziegler 143
2. AIR 24
3. Boorman 58
4. Ziegler 143
5. Churchill 295
6. AIR 4
7. Bishop 201–2
8. Ziegler 144
9. Ministry of Information 47
10. Churchill 296
11. AIR 16
12. Bishop 203
13. Ministry of Information 48
14. Faviell 142
15. Bekker 175
16. Galland 44
17. WO 199
18. Bryant 266
19. WO 199
20. Murrow 193–5
21. CAB 65
22. Calder 259
23. Shirer 925; Collier 227; Price 14
24. AIR 22
25. Allen 163
26. AIR 16
27. Churchill 246

Select Bibliography

AIR MINISTRY, *The Battle of Britain*, London HMSO, 1941

ALLEN, WING-COMMANDER H. R., *Who Won the Battle of Britain*, London, 1974

BEAUMAN, KATHERINE BENTLE, *Partners in Blue: The Story of Women's Service with the RAF*, London, 1971

BEKKER, CAJUS, *The Luftwaffe War Diaries* (translated and edited by Frank Ziegler), London, 1967

BISHOP, EDWARD, *The Battle of Britain*, London, 1960

BOORMAN, PRATT, H. R., *Hell's Corner 1940*, Maidstone, 1943

BRICKHILL, PAUL, *Reach for the Sky*, London, 1954

BRYANT, ARTHUR, *The Turn of the Tide, 1939–1943*, Study based on the Diaries and Autobiographical Notes of FM The Viscount Alanbrooke, London, 1957

CHURCHILL, SIR WINSTON, *Their Finest Hour*, London, 1949

CIANO, COUNT, *Diary* (edited by Malcolm Muggeridge), London, 1947

CIANO, COUNT, *Diplomatic Papers* (edited by Malcolm Muggeridge), London, 1948

CLARK, RONALD, *Battle for Britain*, London, 1965

COLLIER, BASIL, *The Battle of Britain*, London, 1962

COLLIER, BASIL, *The Defence of the United Kingdom*, UK official history, Military Series, London HMSO, 1957

CROOK, D. M., *Spitfire Pilot*, London, 1942

DEERE, ALAN C., *Nine Lives*, London, 1947

DGFP, *Documents on German Foreign Policy*, vol. X, London, 1957

DILKS, DAVID (ed.), *The Diaries of Sir Alexander Cadogan, 1938–1945*, London, 1971

DOWDING, AIR CHIEF MARSHAL, *Official Despatch*, London Gazette, September, 1946

EDEN, ANTHONY, LORD AVON, *The Reckoning*, London, 1965

FARRER, DAVID, *The Sky's the Limit*, London, 1943

FAVIELL, FRANCES, *A Chelsea Concerto*, London, 1959

FCNA, *Fuehrer Conference on Naval Affairs*, London, 1948

FLEMING, PETER, *Invasion 1940*, London, 1957

221

GALLAND, ADOLF, *The First and the Last*, London, 1955
GAULLE, GENERAL CHARLES DE, *The Call to Honour*, New York, 1955
GIBBS, AIR MARSHAL SIR GERALD, *Survivor's Story*, London, 1956
GLEAVE, T. P., *I had a Row with a German*, London, 1948
GRAVES, CHARLES, *The Home Guard of Britain*, London, 1943
HALDER, FRANZ, *Hitler als Feldherr*, Munich, 1949
HAY, IAN, *The Battle of Flanders*, London, 1941
HENRY, ROBERT, *The Siege of London*, London, 1946
HERBERT, A. P., *The Thames*, London, 1966
HILLARY, RICHARD, *The Last Enemy*, London, 1942
HORROCKS, SIR BRIAN, *A Full Life*, London, 1960
ISMAY, LORD HASTINGS, *Memoirs*, London, 1960
JONES, IRA, *Tiger Squadron*, London, 1954
JULLIAN, MARCEL, *The Battle of Britain*, London, 1967
KENNEDY, SIR JOHN, *The Business of War*, London, 1967
LEE, ASHER, *The German Air Force*, London, 1945
MACKSEY, KENNETH, *Armoured Crusader: Major-General Sir Percy Hobart*, London, 1967
MACLEOD, R. and KELLY, D., *The Ironside Diaries*, London, 1962
MACMILLAN, HAROLD, *The Blast of War*, London, 1967
MINISTRY OF INFORMATION, *We Speak from the Air: Broadcasts by the RAF*, London, 1947
MONTGOMERY, FM the VISCOUNT, *Memoirs*, London, 1958
MURROW, EDWARD, *This is London*, London, 1941
NICOLSON, HAROLD, *Diaries and Letters*, vol. II, *1939–1945*, London, 1967
O'BRIEN, T. H., *Civil Defence*, London, 1955
PRICE, ALFRED, *Battle over the Reich*, London, 1973
RICHARDS, DENIS, *History of the RAF, 1939–1945*, vol. 1, *The Fight at Odds, 1939–41*, London, 1974
SHAW, MICHAEL, *Twice Vertical: The History of No. 1 Squadron RAF*, London, 1971
SHIRER, WILLIAM L., *Berlin Diary 1939–1941*, London, 1960
SHIRER, WILLIAM L., *The Rise and Fall of the Third Reich*, London, 1960
SPEER, ALBERT, *Inside the Third Reich*, London, 1970
TAYLOR, TELFORD, *The Breaking Wave*, London, 1967
THOMPSON, LAWRENCE, *1940*, London, 1965
TREVOR-ROPER, HUGH (ed.), *Hitler's War Directives*, London, 1964
WHEATLEY, RONALD, *Operation Sea Lion*, Oxford, 1958
WRIGHT, ROBERT, *Dowding and the Battle of Britain*, London, 1969
WYKEHAM, AIR MARSHAL SIR PETER, *Fighter Command*, New York, 1965
YOUNG, KENNETH, *Churchill and Beaverbrook*, London, 1966
ZIEGLER, FRANK, *The Story of 609 Squadron*, London, 1971

Maps

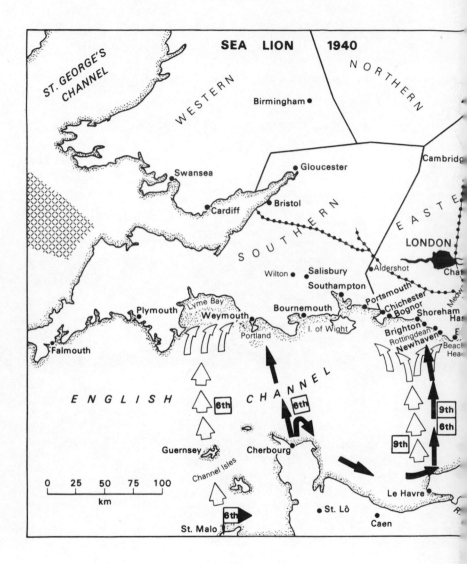

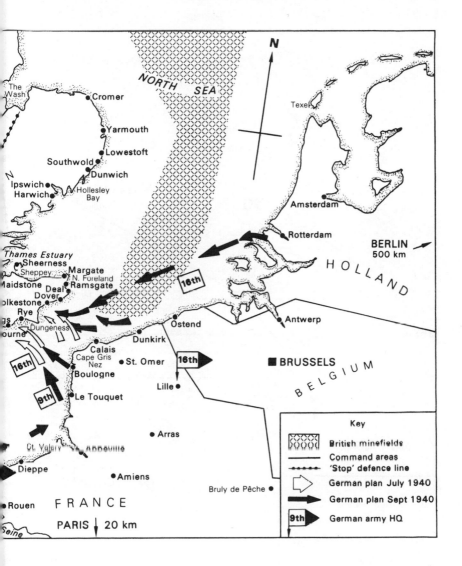

Key

▨ British minefields
— Command areas
•••• 'Stop' defence line
⬜ German plan July 1940
⬛ German plan Sept 1940
🔟 German army HQ

NORTH SEA

N

The Wash
Cromer
Yarmouth
Lowestoft
Southwold
Dunwich
Ipswich
Harwich
Hollesley Bay
Thames Estuary
Sheerness
Sheppey
Margate
N. Foreland
Ramsgate
Maidstone
Deal
Dover
Folkestone
Rye
Dungeness
ourne
Calais
Cape Gris Nez
Boulogne
Le Touquet
St. Valery
Abbeville
Dieppe
Rouen

FRANCE

PARIS ⬇ 20 km

St. Omer
Lille
Arras
Amiens
Bruly de Pêche

Ostend
Dunkirk
Antwerp
BRUSSELS
BELGIUM

16th
16th
9th

Texel

Amsterdam
Rotterdam

HOLLAND

BERLIN
500 km →

Seine

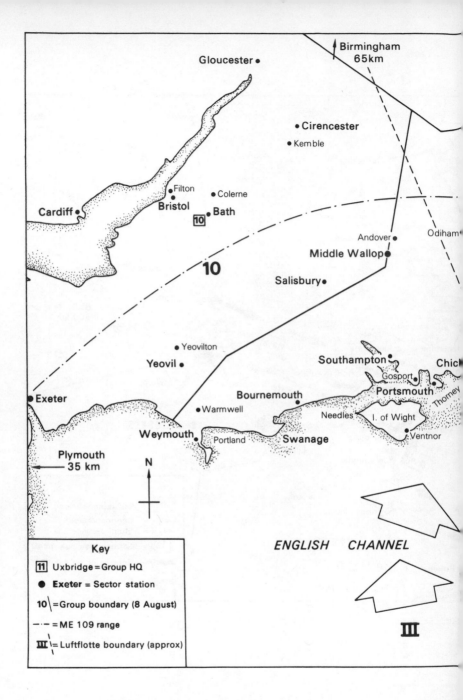

Gloucester •

• Cirencester
  • Kemble

Birmingham
65km

Cardiff •

• Filton
Bristol •
[10] • Bath
• Colerne

Odiham

Andover •
Middle Wallop •

10

Salisbury •

• Yeovilton

Yeovil •

Southampton
Gosport •
Portsmouth
Thorney
Chic

Exeter •

Bournemouth
• Warmwell

Needles   I. of Wight

Ventnor

Weymouth
Portland
Swanage

Plymouth
← 35 km

N

ENGLISH   CHANNEL

Key

[11] Uxbridge = Group HQ

● **Exeter** = Sector station

10 \ = Group boundary (8 August)

—·— = ME 109 range

Ⅲ \ = Luftflotte boundary (approx)

Ⅲ

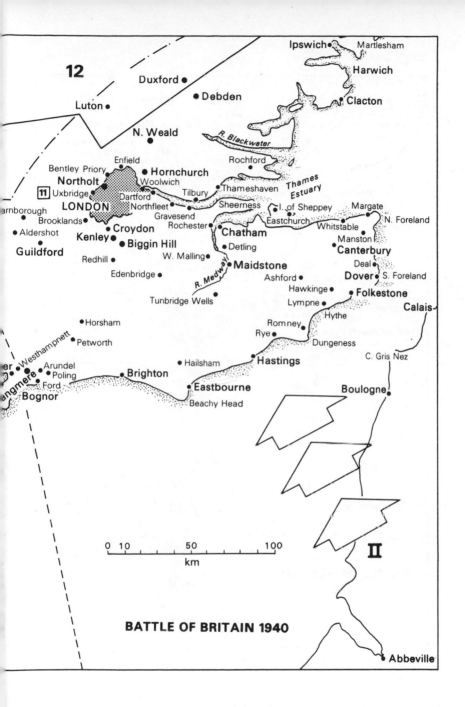

BATTLE OF BRITAIN 1940

12

Ipswich • Martlesham
Harwich
Duxford •
• Debden • Clacton
Luton •

N. Weald
R. Blackwater

Enfield
Bentley Priory • Hornchurch
Northolt Woolwich
11 Uxbridge Tilbury Thameshaven Thames Estuary
arnborough LONDON Northfleet Sheerness I. of Sheppey Margate
Brooklands Gravesend Eastchurch N. Foreland
Aldershot Croydon Rochester Whitstable
Kenley Chatham Manston
Guildford Biggin Hill Detling Canterbury
Redhill W. Malling Deal
Edenbridge Maidstone Dover S. Foreland
R. Medway Ashford Hawkinge Folkestone
Tunbridge Wells Lympne Calais
Hythe
Horsham Romney
Petworth Rye Dungeness
Westhampnett Hailsham C. Gris Nez
Arundel Hastings
er Poling Brighton Boulogne
Ford Eastbourne
angmere Bognor Beachy Head

II

0 10 50 100
km

Abbeville

227

Farne Isles 60 km

13 S. Shields
Newcastle
Sunderland
Usworth
Seaham

Hartlepool

Middlesbrough
Darlington
Catterick

13

Dishforth
Linton
Harrogate York
Leeds Church Fenton

NORTH SEA

Flamborough Head

Driffield
Hornsea
Leconfield

Hull

Kirton
in Lindsey

Spurn Head

Sheffield

Lincoln
Digby

12 Nottingham

12

The
Wash

Colly Weston Stamford
Wittering

Coltishall
Norwich

Yarmouth

**BATTLE OF BRITAIN
1940**

Lowestoft

Cambridge

Orfordness

Martlesham
Ipswich

0 10   50   100
km

Key

12 Nottingham = Group H.Q.

● Digby = Sector station

13 Group boundary
(8 August)

—·—· Me 109 range

Ⅴ = Luftflotte

228

Index

231

233